Beyond English

Literatures as World Literature

Can the literature of a specific country, author, or genre be used to approach the elusive concept of "world literature"? **Literatures as World Literature** takes a novel approach to world literature by analyzing specific constellations—according to language, nation, form, or theme—of literary texts and authors in their own world-literary dimensions.

World literature is obviously so vast that any view of it cannot help but be partial; the question then becomes how to reduce the complex task of understanding and describing world literature. Most treatments of world literature so far either have been theoretical and thus abstract or else have made broad use of exemplary texts from a variety of languages and epochs. The majority of critical work, the filling in of what has been traced, lies ahead of us. **Literatures as World Literature** fills in the devilish details by allowing scholars to move outward from their own areas of specialization, fostering scholarly writing that approaches more closely the polyphonic, multiperspectival nature of world literature.

Series Editor:
Thomas O. Beebee

Editorial Board:
Eduardo Coutinho, Federal University of Rio de Janeiro, Brazil
Hsinya Huang, National Sun-yat Sen University, Taiwan
Meg Samuelson, University of Cape Town, South Africa
Ken Seigneurie, Simon Fraser University, Canada
Mads Rosendahl Thomsen, Aarhus University, Denmark

Volumes in the Series
German Literature as World Literature, edited by Thomas O. Beebee
Roberto Bolaño as World Literature, edited by Nicholas Birns and Juan E. De Castro
Crime Fiction as World Literature, edited by David Damrosch, Theo D'haen and Louise Nilsson

Danish Literature as World Literature,
edited by Dan Ringgaard and Mads Rosendahl Thomsen
From Paris to Tlön: Surrealism as World Literature, by Delia Ungureanu
American Literature as World Literature, edited by Jeffrey R. Di Leo
Romanian Literature as World Literature, edited by Mircea Martin,
Christian Moraru, and Andrei Terian
Brazilian Literature as World Literature, edited by Eduardo F. Coutinho
Dutch and Flemish Literature as World Literature, edited by Theo D'haen
Afropolitan Literature as World Literature, edited by James Hodapp
Francophone Literature as World Literature, edited by Christian Moraru,
Nicole Simek, and Bertrand Westphal
Bulgarian Literature as World Literature,
edited by Mihaela P. Harper and Dimitar Kambourov
Philosophy as World Literature, edited by Jeffrey R. Di Leo
Turkish Literature as World Literature, edited by Burcu Alkan and Çimen Günay-Erkol
Elena Ferrante as World Literature, by Stiliana Milkova
Multilingual Literature as World Literature,
edited by Jane Hiddleston and Wen-chin Ouyang
Persian Literature as World Literature, edited by Mostafa Abedinifard,
Omid Azadibougar, and Amirhossein Vafa
Mexican Literature as World Literature, edited by Ignacio M. Sánchez Prado
Beyond English: World Literature and India, by Bhavya Tiwari
Graphic Novels and Comics as World Literature,
edited by James Hodapp (forthcoming)
Feminism as World Literature, edited by Robin Truth Goodman (forthcoming)
Modern Irish Literature as World Literature,
edited by Christopher Langlois (forthcoming)
African Literatures as World Literature,
edited by Alexander Fyfe and Madhu Krishnan (forthcoming)
Taiwanese Literature as World Literature,
edited by Pei-yin Lin and Wen-chi Li (forthcoming)

Beyond English

World Literature and India

Bhavya Tiwari

BLOOMSBURY ACADEMIC
NEW YORK • LONDON • OXFORD • NEW DELHI • SYDNEY

BLOOMSBURY ACADEMIC
Bloomsbury Publishing Inc
1385 Broadway, New York, NY 10018, USA
50 Bedford Square, London, WC1B 3DP, UK
29 Earlsfort Terrace, Dublin 2, Ireland

BLOOMSBURY, BLOOMSBURY ACADEMIC and the Diana logo are trademarks of Bloomsbury Publishing Plc

First published in the United States of America 2022
This paperback edition published 2023

Copyright © by Bhavya Tiwari, 2022

For legal purposes the Acknowledgments on pp. viii–ix constitute an extension of this copyright page.

Cover design by Simon Levy

All rights reserved. No part of this publication may be reproduced or transmitted in any form or by any means, electronic or mechanical, including photocopying, recording, or any information storage or retrieval system, without prior permission in writing from the publishers.

Bloomsbury Publishing Inc does not have any control over, or responsibility for, any third-party websites referred to or in this book. All internet addresses given in this book were correct at the time of going to press. The author and publisher regret any inconvenience caused if addresses have changed or sites have ceased to exist, but can accept no responsibility for any such changes.

A catalog record for this book is available from the Library of Congress.

ISBN: HB: 978-1-5013-3464-1
PB: 978-1-5013-8687-9
ePDF: 978-1-5013-3466-5
eBook: 978-1-5013-3465-8

Series: Literatures as World Literature

Typeset by Deanta Global Publishing Services, Chennai, India

To find out more about our authors and books visit www.bloomsbury.com and sign up for our newsletters.

Contents

Acknowledgments	viii
Note on Translation	x
Introduction: Beyond English	1
1 Why World Literature?	9
Vishva Sahitya	11
Universalism, *Sahitya*, and *Sahit*	24
Translation and *Vishva Sahitya*	28
2 Here Is World Literature	35
The World-making of the English *Gitanjali*	37
Tagore's Translations, World-making, and *Gitanjali* in Prose-poems	46
World-making of *Gitanjali* in Spanish	56
3 The World Is in the Lyrics	63
The World in Lyrics	65
The World-making of *Chhayavaad*	74
World versus *Vishva Sahitya* in Hindi	82
4 (Woman) Author and the World	89
World-making versus *Vishva*	92
Varma's *Sahitya* and *Vishva*	101
5 World in Translation, World in the Original	115
Chemmeen's *Vishva* in India and Beyond	118
To Compare, to World	125
World-making of Small Things	131
India in the Original, India in Translation	137
Coda: World Literature and India	143
Notes	153
Bibliography	183
Index	195

Acknowledgments

Scholarship does not thrive in penury. This project would not have been feasible without the generous support of the University of Houston, my home institution, at various stages. The most notable assistance came from my university just before Covid-19 hit the world. In early 2020, I received the Provost's 50-in-5 grant that allowed me to workshop my manuscript. I am grateful to my manuscript workshop readers Hosam Aboul-Ela, S. Shankar, and Francesca Orsini for providing feedback that gave depth to my book. I am also thankful for the critical responses given on the manuscript by the Bloomsbury reviewers. I am especially grateful to the reviewer, who indicated the timelines by which I could finish the recommended revisions.

Many ideas presented in this book were first conceptualized for sharing at the annual conference of American Comparative Literature Association (ACLA). The ACLA has been my intellectual home for more than a decade. I am grateful for all the valuable comments and questions raised by fellow comparatists on my conference papers at various ACLAs. A version of the discussion addressed in this book on Rabindranath Tagore, and T. S. Pillai was published in *The Routledge Companion to World Literature*, and the *Journal of World Literature* respectively.

Ideally, teaching and scholarship should go hand in hand. At a time, when full-time academic positions have become rare jewels, I feel incredibly lucky to have one in an institution that prides itself for being one of the most diverse campuses in North America. Many authors addressed in this book are regularly taught by me on my campus. Because my students are interested in literary worlds and languages beyond their own, my research has benefited from teaching them.

I am glad that I have friends like Julie-Françoise Tolliver, Emran El-Badawi, Emire Cihan Yüksel, Hosam Aboul-Ela, and Abdel Razzaq Takriti in Houston. They have supported my work in various capacities. I am also grateful to Lois Zamora, Thomas Beebee, Hannah Chapelle Wojciehowski, and David Damrosch for providing mentorship at various moments in my life.

I am lucky that I am often able to discuss my writing process with my dad, Vimal Yogi Tiwari, who brainstormed with me the title of this book. I am glad that he is present in my life. Though Ankit Jha, my husband, thinks he will not be mentioned in the acknowledgment, he does not know that writing this book would have been a tedious task without him. His "teatime" at 4:00 p.m., and our evening strolls marked the end of my day's work. I am grateful for those daily punctuations.

This book is for my parents, Supriya Yogi Tiwari, Vimal Yogi Tiwari, my teachers at Jadavpur University and the United States, and for comparative literature.

Note on Translation

All translations are mine unless otherwise indicated. Wherever possible, I have provided the original, or translated, and transliterated the original, either in the body of the text or in the chapter endnotes. I have tried to maintain consistency while transliterating Bengali, Sanskrit, and Hindi words. Readers fluent in any one of those languages and aware of the language politics in South Asia can, however, find places where they might disagree with me. I have explained my rationale in notes. Since most South Asian languages do not have the concept of capital letters, I decided to capitalize all the letters in the titles of Hindi, and Bengali works. For Spanish titles, I followed the general practice of capitalizing the first letter, and proper nouns in the titles.

Introduction

Beyond English

Beyond English: World Literature and India centers on the possibilities and pitfalls of comparatively reading the world in and around a text in translation and in the original. It seeks to shift the debates on world literature that currently hinge on the model of circulation and global capital by deeply engaging with the ideas of the "world" and world-making. I argue that the numerous Indic words for world (such as *vishva, jagat, sansār, duniyā, bhūgōl, jahān, lok*) offer a nuanced understating of world and world-making that is antithetical to a commodified and standardized monolingual globe. By focusing on the nuances hidden in the concept and meaning of the words "*jagat*," "*sansār*," and "*vishva*," I strive to challenge in the book the artificial divide between what it means to compare and to world in the fields of comparative literature and world literature studies. While doing so, I go beyond the hegemony of English in many scholarly discussions on world literature, and instead speak of multilingual contexts by analyzing and comparing the histories and cultures of production, translation, and reception that surround texts' presence in the world.

The book identifies world-making in a text as an existential actuality, a process of creating, making, and remaking different worlds, that is in conversation with the vagaries of human nature, where the author, critic, translator, reader, and publisher are all involved. As a result, my inquiry in this book stresses the importance of contextualizing a text in its immediate world culture, where the focus is not on some abstract theoretical concept of world literature, but a real dialogue with the universe, world, or *vishva* in a text with a world, *jagat*, and *sansār* around that text. Since this book argues for reading and analyzing the cultural histories and paratexts of multilingual literary worlds in the original and in translation, it constantly investigates the polemics of translation, as well as the politics of reading a text in the original in a specific location in a world, which as we will see can be differently understood under the terms "*vishva*," "*jagat*," "*sansār*," and "world."

The chapters present close readings of Rabindranath Tagore's essay on *vishva sahitya* or world literature in Hindi, English, and Bengali: Tagore's world-making of the poetry collection *Gitanjali* in English; the *chhayavaad* or shadowism poets' world-making and their desire for a new world in Hindi; Mahadevi Varma's split *vishva* in literary worlds; and comparative analysis of world-makings of Malayalam author Thakazhi Sivasankara Pillai's *Chemmeen* and Arundhati Roy's *The God of Small Things* in the original and in translation. Through these authors and texts, the book suggests that ideas of a world and of world-making reflect authors' intentions to be part of a universe (*vishva*); a conflict between the world (universe or *vishva*) in a text and the literary world (*jagat*, and *sansār*) around the text; authors' desire for a new re-ordering and reconfiguration of material and nonmaterial worlds (*vishva, jagat, sansār*); and one author's conscious choice to bifurcate her literary world (*vishva*).

My analysis of the different words for "world" in Indic languages as used by the abovementioned authors assist me to elaborate and critique world literature. Chapter 1, for instance, analyzes Tagore's usage of words for world, such as *sansār, vishva*, and *jagat* in his *vishva sahitya* lecture. The analysis merges as well as reverses the ideas of comparative literature and world literature. Further, Tagore's preference for "world literature" over "comparative literature" is indicative of his desire for a supranational unity in a particular moment in time, exhibited in joy and empathy through the world-makings of the *vishva* in literature. Chapter 2 argues that it is in the realization of *vishva sahitya*, through the various world-makings of the *vishva* in the text, whether in the original or in translation, that a slice of a world, *jagat*, and *sansār* in a specific time and place can be understood. Thus, even when Tagore imagines a *vishva sahitya* that is ideal because it centers on the indestructible *vishva* or universe, it is the pursuit of that *vishva* in the concrete *material* world, *jagat*, and *sansār* that supports our understating, whereabouts, politics, and purpose of world literature. This is explained in the book by doing a comparative analysis of various versions of *Gitanjali* in translation and in the original.

One of the ways to appreciate the subtle differences for the word "world" in some Indic languages, as used in this book, is to know that *sansār* is relationship-bound, and *jagat* is place-bound. Both the words are translated as "world" in English. *Sansār*, however, is cyclic, a manifestation of illusions or *maya* created by living beings in a *jagat*. Just as there are many *sansārs* so are there many *jagats*. Unlike *vishva* that is an ever-present universe, a world, and a constant, *sansār* is an encapsulation of the cycles of pain, joy, life, and death. Each being is bound by the *maya* of their *sansār* as played out in the *jagat*, indicative of a *location* where the *maya* is carried out. *Sansār* reflects the numerous intertwined relationships that living beings form with one another in a *jagat*. Those interspersed relationships are a summation of material, emotional, physical, economical, and philosophical realities of simply being in a *jagat*, or a world. *Sansār* exists because there is a relationship between entities, living or nonliving, in a *jagat*. The word "*sansār*," when etymologically broken down, is formed of two words. The "*sa*" refers to "together," and "*saar*" suggests the "synoptic meaning" of something. By definition then the world or *sansār* cannot be experienced alone in a world or *jagat*, because it is a summation of connections and disconnections among entities in a particular place. Throughout the book, I use the words "*jagat*," and "*sansār*" alongside the word "world" to suggest how they differ from the *vishva* or universe in the text. Accordingly, I ask ontological questions about the epistemes of the disciplinary boundaries between comparative literature and world literature. I also gesture toward translation's seminal, but often ignored, position in reinvigorating debates on the future of comparative literature—a future that needs to be worldly.

Beyond English: World Literature and India critiques the recent scholarly discourses on world literature and India by highlighting two things. First, in most South Asian languages, there is no exact translation for the English word "translation." Translation is often expressed as *rūpāntar, anuvād, bhashantar,* and *tarjumā*, meaning "change in the form," "speaking after," "change in the language," and "interpretation," respectively. These words for "translation" are intimately connected with how the *world, universe,* or *vishva* in a text is being interpreted. Second, the concept of "world" itself is varied and is not always the opposite of the "globe," as evidenced through various terms (*vishva, jagat, sansār,* etc.) which cannot be reduced to the English word "world" or "globe." The word "*vishva*" can be translated as both "universe" and "world." *Vishva* is both worldly and unworldly. *Sansār* and *jagat*, on the other hand, do not reflect the entire *universe*; nor are they beyond the material.

Thus, by emphasizing and restoring faith in the analysis of the "world" in world literature through the Indic concepts for the word "world" in and around a text, and by taking the politics of originals as seriously as those of translations, the book proposes a shift in scholarly debates on comparative literature and world literature. For example, the chapter following the analysis of Tagore's *vishva sahitya* and world-makings of *Gitanjalis* complicates the tension between the *vishva* in *chhayavaad* poems and the *jagat, sansār,* and world around the *vishva* in the *chhayavaad* lyrics. Chapter 3 does this by emphasizing the politics of world-making and canonization of the original in the original language synchronically and diachronically. Further, through a comparative reading of the worlds created by modern Hindi poets such as Mahadevi Varma, Sumitranandan Pant, and Suryakant Nirala in their lyrics, Chapter 3 addresses the question of canonization, and genre in world literature or *vishva sahitya* debates: something that Tagore did not consider while speaking on *vishva sahitya*. Chapter 4 suggests that the question of canonization, non-canonization, and the difficulty of reading the *vishva* of a female author in the world, *jagat*, and *sansār* can be tackled in creative ways. In this chapter, I argue that if female authors such as Varma are to be included in the debates on *vishva sahitya*, whether in the original or in translation, then comparatists need to go against the grain in reading their works. The final chapter of the book suggests that instead of dwelling on the divide between the original and the translation, and between comparative literature and world literature, the comparative analysis of world-makings of the original and translation in different worlds, *jagat*, and *sansār* is a rewarding endeavor. As an example, I compare the world-makings of the Malayalam novel *Chemmeen* with English novel *The God of Small Things*. The chapter also highlights how Indian Writings in English and Indian Writings in English Translation present an *Indian vishva* for *a* world, *jagat*, and *sansār* in the original and in translation.

The emphasis on "world" in world literature is certainly strategic in this book because, in the last few years, world literature has been conveniently assumed to be a literature that is a product of a circulatory model in translation, and in the original when it is in English, on the back of global capital. The result is that currently we have an iteration of world literature that is an expression of the politics of globalization and a globe that leans heavily toward Anglophone centers. Scholarly discussions—especially but not only in English—often utter very little about the *world* and *literature* in world literature that is beyond English. This means that even well-meaning critiques of world literature end up perpetuating versions of world literature that are focused on a globalized Anglophone world literature.[1] Thus, for instance, while arguing for analyzing the "world" in world literature, Pheng Cheah's strategy is to read the world-making of mostly postcolonial novels that in the *original* are in English. Or, when Baidik Bhattacharya discusses world literature, he ends up arguing that Anglophone postcolonial literature *is* world literature.

Undoubtedly, the discussions on what is a world literature, what gets included in world literature (whether in translation or in the original), and what undermines that world literature are relevant for teaching and research. More so, because (as Stefan Helgesson and Pieter Vermeulen have recently reminded us) most of the earlier discussions of world literature took place specifically in Germany, and postmillennial interventions on world literature continue to flourish in Anglophone and North American contexts, where English does not have the same competition as it would, say, in many parts of multilingual Europe or in South Asia.[2] Consequently, Pascal Casanova's "rise to global fame undeniably coincided with the English translation of her book in 2004,"[3] and Franco Moretti's multivolume work on the novel in Italian was eclipsed by his English-language work.[4] Even scholars who have argued against the institutionalization of world literature have addressed readers who are primarily well versed in Euro-American literary traditions.[5] Franco Moretti calls world literature a problem, Emily Apter invokes untranslatability as a fulcrum for re-orienting comparative literature, the Warwick Research Collective suggests that peripheral literatures are getting appropriated in capitalist centers, and Aamir Mufti makes the justifiable call to "Forget English." These perspectives all reflect a crisis of a globalized world literature *in* English, not necessarily of the entire world or *vishva, jagat,* and *sansār,* because globalization itself has varied outcomes in different parts of the world.[6]

Beyond English: World Literature and India counters the globalized and narrow conception of *world* and *literature* in world literature in English by doing comparative work on literary texts in *more than one* language. Throughout the book, I have made use of a range of canonical and noncanonical para-textual materials, genres, magazines, translations, and author personalities in the original and translation to suggest a way forward in our discussions on comparative literature and world literature. In fact, in order to adequately expand and provide resolutions on the debates on world literature and India, I have consciously chosen authors and literary works that present inherent contradictions, either with each other or in their immediate and distant literary worlds and canons, in the original and translation. Each chapter in the book highlights that tension and contradiction, adds a new flavor to the meaning of the concept of *vishva sahitya,* and argues that world literature is neither an elliptical refraction of national literatures gaining in translation in time and space[7] nor is it merely a legacy of orientalism, monitoring translations and literary expressions in the global market.[8] Instead, this book illustrates that world literature is a construct of the *vishva,* universe, or world in *sahitya*[9] (literature), in *jagat* (world), and *sansār* (world), in translation or in the original, always through world-makings at a specific location.¹⁰ As a whole, all the chapters emphasize and complicate the very idea of world-making, illuminating the tension between the indestructible but malleable *vishva*, universe, or world in *sahitya* and the material world (*jagat*, and *sansār*) around that *sahitya* by situating the world of and in a text synchronically and diachronically.

Further, by engaging with a range of materials such as poetry, letters, critical commentaries, novels, essays, periodicals, and film in the original and translation, my book ends up providing unique perspectives on world literature. First, it makes a rich archival contribution that is relatively ignored in debates on world literature, subsequently changing the nature of research questions on the future of comparative literature and world literature in India and beyond. Second, unlike scholarly works that debate world literature and postcolonial authors by studying authors as object of study who write and gain *only* in English, my book positions authors writing in Bengali, Hindi, English, and Malayalam as *theorists themselves* of *vishva sahitya*. This strategy helps in organically tackling questions of language, canonization, translation, genre, and gender in world literary debates from a new vantage point that is not exclusively Anglophone-centered. The authors, critics, and translators in this book actively engage with their immediate world, *jagat*, and *sansār* in more than one language; and they care about the poetics of literature. Third, by "going beyond English," without treating other languages addressed in this book as peripheral or secondary to English or each other, the book escapes the unproductive circle of reading "native" literary traditions as always competing with English. Thus, for instance, there is a lot new to learn about modernism as a world literary movement when we look at *chhayavaad* Hindi poets struggling in their immediate world, where Hindi is trying to create a mark as a language. Similarly, new questions about the concept of Indian literature and world literature can be asked when reading a Malayalam text like *Chemmeen* in translation and in the original, while encountering the text in more than one mode.

Undoubtedly, India's multilingual contexts set translations and comparativisms as preconditions to the study of any literature in more than one language and mode. Besides, India as a nation contradicts the very idea of constructing a national literary canon as a theoretical framework often used as an organizing principle for the study of literature in research projects. In some degrees, by doing away with the notion of "nation" and "Indian literature" in my book, I open up the possibility of going beyond the postcolonial frameworks that have often privileged a certain type of narrative in the colonizer's language in the guise of "ethnic" literature in the late twentieth and twenty-first centuries, especially in the Anglo-American academia. Since the book does not engage exclusively with Anglophone texts, it also frees the discussion of literature in India from the Prospero-Caliban model, forging a new understanding of translation, and literature in the immediate worlds in different languages within India.

Indeed, through analyzing and comparing world-makings in Bengali, Hindi, Malayalam, and English, I demonstrate that authors and critics use various Indic words for "world" (in their literary texts and in critical commentaries on *sahitya* or literature) in ways that complicate the world, universe, or *vishva* in a text. As indicated in the course of the book, various words for "world" indicate a complex web of human beings' connections with different and varying aspects of the world, and those relations cannot simply be reduced to products of a monolingual global capitalism. The desire for a/the world and world-making by Indian authors addressed in the narrative arc of this book indicates not some rootless cosmopolitanism that is a product of globalization, nor a simple search by peripheral writers for acceptance in the metropole, but an argument for a new world reality in the discussions on *vishva sahitya* or world literature.

To a casual observer world literature often means coalescing it as a sum total of all the literary traditions under the sun. Such an assessment reduces world literature into an object that is impossible to study, or worse marks world literature as a body of literary texts that could be qualified with adjectives such as "masterworks," "noncanonical," or "canonical." In a multilingual country like India, this approach would almost always privilege one language or movement over the other, without comprehensively evaluating individual literary traditions. But if world literature is taken as a method, it provides an opportunity to study the ontology and epistemology of literature, its very being, and its perpetual becoming in a specific world. Such a world literature becomes a study of world-making that is almost never oblivious to the social, economic, and political contexts that bleed into the *vishva* in a literary text in the world, *jagat*, and *sansār*, as examined through the works of Tagore, Varma, *chhayavaad* poets, Pillai, and Roy.

Beyond English: World Literature and India is curious about the processes of world-making of authors, and creation of different worlds in literary movements, and genres in translation and in the original. The study of this kind of literary dynamism in the book produces theoretical ideas on world literature that are poetically and politically active, worldly, and almost never a solitary monologue in time and space. In this respect, the book suggests that world literature and literatures in India be assessed through comparative and translational lenses that do not operate on local-global, center-periphery, and distant-close reading models, but rather on theorizing the *world*, and by zooming on the small through the means of a case-study approach that is multilingual. Such approach and discussion emphasize the worldliness of a world literature that are centered on a humanism, literature, and a reconfiguration of the relationships of human beings within a world. By doing so in this book, I encourage comparatists to carry discussions of world literature through South Asian literary traditions that are beyond the hegemony of English—or, to put it polemically, where English happens to be just another language that is among and not beyond other languages.

1

Why World Literature?

In 1905, the British partitioned Bengal into two halves—East Bengal and West Bengal—on the pretext that the state had become unmanageable. In those days Bengal comprised the present-day states of Assam, Bihar, Orissa, and West Bengal of India, as well as the entirety of Bangladesh. The British wanted to divide and rule Bengal on the basis of religious and linguistic identities concentrated in various pockets of the state. Consequently, a strong wave of patriotism hit British India. There were widespread protests against the British, and a strong ideological divide emerged among the "moderate" and "extremist" members of the Indian Congress on the issue of addressing and responding to the partition. Though Bengal was eventually reunited in 1911, Bihar and Orissa became separate states. Delhi was announced as the new capital of the British Empire in India. Kolkata was no longer the capital of British India. The fact that today the official state languages of Bihar, Orissa, Assam, and West Bengal are Hindi, Odia, Bengali, and Assamese (respectively) is a striking reminder of the extraordinary linguistic, literary, and cultural diversity that the British were encountering in various parts of India. Clearly, politically and socially speaking, a great deal had happened between 1905 and 1911 in British India. It was during these times, exactly a year and a half after Bengal was partitioned, that Rabindranath Tagore was asked by the National Council of Education (NCE) to give a series of lectures on comparative literature, where he inaugurated the concept of *vishva sahitya*, or world literature.

It is uncertain whether the lecture series was on the discipline of comparative literature, or on the *act* of comparing literatures in British India. Considering that NCE's goal was to subvert the British education model in India, it could certainly have been the latter. Tagore's lecture on *vishva sahitya*, however, operated as a double-edged sword, for it was just not about the act of comparing literatures in the immediate imperial world, but also about the purpose of a discipline like comparative literature, which he chose to translate as *vishva sahitya* (world literature) in Bengali. Here it would be helpful to recall that the NCE's function was to provide a channel for modern education outside of the curricula and system shaped by British interests, thereby resisting efforts by the governor general of British India to separate wealthy Indians from their native traditions through English education.[1] Indeed, a number of acts and laws were passed in the years leading up to the NCE's establishment. For instance, the Vernacular Press Act was passed in 1878 that created a huge unrest in British India. The purpose of the act was to curb Indian vernacular newspapers from criticizing British policies. Important to note here is that the law did not apply to English newspapers published in India. Though the law was repealed in 1881, the reverberations of mistrust in the British administration only continued. As a result, in 1904, when the Indian Universities Act was passed, the most urgent concern of the NCE had become protecting education in vernacular or *bhasha*[2] traditions. Further, a number of indigenous educational institutions had opened up in the beginning of the twentieth century in the cities formerly known as Madras, Bombay, and Calcutta. These institutions imparted education that was anti-Macaulay in spirit while also encouraging nationalist sentiments. The Vernacular Press Act, the Indian Universities Act, and the partition of Bengal in 1905 created distrust among Indians for even the most liberal and progressive British officials serving in India.

Moreover, by early 1900s, the social reforms brought by Brahmo Samaj[3]—a theistic movement within Hinduism that discarded the authority of Vedas and meaningless rituals, and believed in the universal spirit, Brahman—had started to bear fruit in Bengal and beyond. Tagore's family had played a central role in the Brahmo Samaj movement, which was founded in Bengal in 1828 by Raja Ram Mohan Roy. In fact, Rabindranath Tagore himself became an active member of Brahmo Samaj in the early twentieth century. Brahmo Samaj's liberalism and universalism appealed to Tagore's worldview. It was during these times that Tagore, for the lecture series, spoke on topics that ranged from world literature and literary creation to the sense of beauty in literature. These lectures (along with others) appeared in Bengali magazines, journals, and periodicals, and were later anthologized in 1907 as *Sahitya*.[4] They inaugurated Tagore's position as a literary critic and scholar of a multilingual culture in British India.

Accordingly, in this chapter, I examine the significance and purpose of *vishva sahitya* or world literature for Tagore, and his defiant act of translating "comparative literature" as "world literature." The act of translating "comparative literature" as "world literature," I argue, has roots in Tagore's beliefs in the *ānand* (joy) and *ātmīyatā* (empathy) of the *vishva mānav* (universe/universal/world-human/man)[5] in world-making the universe, world, or *vishva* in *sahitya*. While in the *vishva sahitya* essay Tagore does not directly speak of translation's role in conceptualizing world literature, this chapter emphasizes that by translating "comparative literature" as "world literature," Tagore imagines a world literature where translation and *vishva mānav* go hand in hand to experience different worlds of literature. I explain this later in the chapter by pointing out that for Tagore the word "*vishva*" in *vishva sahitya* is not *jagat* or *sansār*—words that could all be translated into English as "world." Tagore's careful choice of the word "*vishva*" over other synonyms for the word "world" available to him in Indian languages and his complete abandoning of the word "*tulnātamak*" for "comparative" suggest that Tagore considered *vishva sahitya* beyond nations, authors, humans, and history. For him, the transcendent nature of *vishva sahitya* echoed the principles of Brahmo Samaj, where humanism and spiritualism came together to engage with the universal spirit.

Yet, as I indicate in the following pages, it was in the realization of *vishva sahitya* that a slice of a world (*jagat,* and *sansār*) in literature of a specific time and place could be understood by the *vishva mānav*. By contextualizing Tagore's lecture-cum-essay "Visva Sahitya"[6] in its immediate sociohistorical milieu, by putting it in conversation with his other essays on literary criticism, and by doing a close reading of the text, this chapter then offers to readers Tagore's purpose of world literature, and his methodology for doing world literature in a multilingual world, where the act of translation and comparison is centered on the kinship of *vishva mānav* and world-making the *vishva* in *sahitya*.

Vishva Sahitya

Apart from his vocation as a creative writer, Tagore wrote several political essays in the last decade of the nineteenth century.[7] In 1880, he wrote his first political pamphlet, which he later disowned.[8] In 1898, he also addressed the Bengal Provincial Conference, where he spoke against the Sedition Bill. From 1893 to the first decade of the twentieth century, Tagore had written approximately thirty-five major political essays that were collected in books with titles such as *Ātmāshakti* (Self-empowerment), *Swadesh* (Our Country), *Bharatvarsha* (India), and *Raja Praja* (Rulers and Subjects).[9] He had also given a lecture in 1895 at the annual meeting of the Bengal Academy of Literature, titled "Bengali National

Literature,"[10] and in his 1904 essay "Swadeshi Samaj"[11] he had asked people to set up parallel governments on their own in villages instead of begging Britishers for freedom. Tagore's political and social essays, his position as a peerless creative author, and his family's cultural influence in Bengal made him a fitting advocate to speak for the NCE's aims. Before Tagore lectured for the NCE, he had also engaged in the political world through his writings. Further, in 1901, Tagore had also started working to establish his university, Visva Bharati, at Shantiniketan. He later founded this university in 1921, using his Nobel Prize money.

As the director of the Bengali Studies of the NCE, and an important member of the Brahmo Samaj with a keen interest in education and an array of political and creative writings behind him, Tagore must have seemed the perfect choice to give lectures on comparative literature, literary criticism, and education in British India. For Tagore, lecturing at NCE while he was actively working to establish his own university presented a perfect opportunity to reiterate his educational ideals and comment on the purpose of literary studies in a world that was rife with comparisons between native and British education.

Suitably, at the inauguration of the NCE in February 1907, Tagore introduced the idea of *vishva sahitya* or world literature to his audience. Though *vishva* can be translated as "universe" or "universal," and some scholars and translators[12] have used these terms in the past while translating Tagore's *vishva sahitya* essay from Bengali into English, the most common practice is to interpret *vishva sahitya* as world literature. In recent years, the original title of Tagore's essay has often been left untranslated in the body and title of the English versions of the essay, as well as in scholarship on *vishva sahitya*. This perhaps says something about the contestations one has to make when speaking of world literature in English. To return to Tagore's 1907 lecture, as if to tease those who had invited him to speak on comparative literature, Tagore chooses to *translate* the English phrase "comparative literature" as world literature by declaring: "You have called the topic I have been entrusted to discuss as 'Comparative Literature' in English. In Bangla I shall call it Visva Sahitya (world literature)."[13] Tagore's decision to use the Bengali nomenclature *vishva sahitya* for comparative literature—which translates as world literature in most Indian languages, including English—is significant.

Tagore's twofold desire to rename and re-translate comparative literature as *vishva sahitya* reflects a change in his own political and spiritual positions. In addition, the translation of comparative literature as world literature also acts as an indicator of what Tagore did to *Gitanjali* while self-translating it, which I address in detail in the next chapter. Most importantly, however, the translation of comparative literature as *vishva sahitya* in Bengali, first, suggests Tagore's conscious distancing from the word "*tulnā*"—a word that is prevalent in many Indian languages for the word "comparison"—when it came to doing literary studies in British India, where the fervor of nationalism was fomenting. Second, the renaming and re-translating of comparative literature as world literature highlights translation in *vishva sahitya* as dependent on the kinship of the *vishva mānav*, and world-making that encourages personal engagement with the universe or *vishva* in literature, or *sahitya*.

Further, the choice to distance himself from the word "*tulnā*" had roots in Tagore's change in political and literary worldview. In the last phase of his political writings, Tagore had considerably revised his initial position on the ideas of nationhood and nationalism. For him, nationalism nurtured baser passions of greed, cruelty, and hatred in human beings. He had begun criticizing the nationalist agenda, and the criticisms only became more severe as time passed. I will analyze some of those reservations by looking at Tagore's "Nationalism in India," published in 1917, later in the chapter. It is, however, noteworthy here that at the time Tagore delivered his lecture on *vishva sahitya*, comparative literature as a discipline had not yet formally taken root in South Asia. Sisir Kumar Das and Sukanta Chaudhuri note that the lecture shows no awareness by Tagore of any scholarly debate on comparative literature, nor of the problem of influence studies that formed the core of comparative literature studies at the beginning of the discipline in the West.[14] Das and Chaudhuri's observation about the lack of awareness displayed by Tagore about the discipline of comparative literature could be accurate.

I say *could be* because though comparative literature as a discipline had not formally taken root, comparative methodologies and comparative practices in the name of comparative studies, comparative religion, and comparative philology were thriving around the world, including in India, when Tagore lectured on *vishva sahitya*. In fact, the foundation of oriental studies was based on, to some extent, comparisons or *tulnā*. Besides, Tagore read widely. Since he lived in British India—specifically in Kolkata, which was the epicenter for many literary exchanges—it is likely that Tagore would have come across Matthew Arnold's remarks[15] on the connections between literary traditions, which are only comprehensible through comparisons.

Arnold's remarks, often cited by comparative literature scholars, were delivered in 1857 for the Oxford Inaugural Lecture, and Tagore was quite familiar with British Romantic and Victorian literature and authors. Further, Arnold's remarks that there is connection everywhere, and that "no single event, no single literature"[16] can be "adequately comprehended except in its relation to other events, to other literatures,"[17] is not far in spirit from Tagore's thoughts in "Visva Sahitya." In addition, etymologically and conceptually speaking, the word "comparative" (or *tulnātamak* in many Indian languages, including Bengali) formed, and continues to form, the basis for examining literary connections and assessments in multilingual India. The word "*tulnātamak*" carries in itself the word "*tulnā*," meaning comparison, as I indicated before. Historically speaking, comparisons of two or more poets in courtly as well as public gatherings have always been a part of literary cultures in the Indian subcontinent.

In fact, comparison of one writer with another is so ubiquitous in Indian literary criticism and literary circles that one often finds random poetic adages that compare and contrast poets. For instance, in a famous Sanskrit poetic adage,[18] the speaker compares the ancient Sanskrit poets Kalidas, Bharavi, and Dandi with each other, only to declare that Magh, a seventh-century poet, is better than all of them because his poetic skills are superior to theirs. This kind of comparison was not restricted to Sanskrit poets, and it is also visible in other premodern and modern literary criticisms. Take for example the fact that the spirit of comparatively studying, assessing, and judging poets in the fifteenth- and sixteenth-century North Indian literary world often led to pitting of Tulsidas against Surdas, while supporters of both of these poets severely criticized Keshavdas.[19]

To emphasize the point on *tulnā*, let us take Tagore's work. In his essay "Sakuntala," published in Bengali in 1902,[20] Tagore compared the characters Shakuntala[21] (from Kalidas's *Shakuntala*) and Miranda (from Shakespeare's *The Tempest*). The English translation of the same essay appears in an English version of the Sanskrit play, with a preface stating that this rendition of *Shakuntala* is being created solely for presenting it on the stage for an English audience. Tagore's translated essay, which appears as "Sakuntala: Its Inner Meaning,"[22] in 1920, carried the subtitle—"Its Inner Meaning"—that was absent in the original. While the essay is about Shakuntala the character, both the Bengali and English versions begin with some sort of Goethe's response to the translated Sanskrit play, indicating that Tagore was quite familiar with Goethe's work and understood the reach of translation in different linguistic communities. More specifically, the 1920 English translation begins with a quatrain by Goethe on *Shakuntala*, the Bengali version does not. In the essay, Tagore dismisses Miranda's simplicity as artificial, and Shakuntala's as natural, in just a handful of sentences. Though comparing Kalidas with Shakespeare was not new at that time, it is noticeable that in this essay Tagore reaches the conclusion that Shakuntala is a better-crafted character than Miranda by means of a hurried comparison.

What I mean by that is that in the essay Tagore declares in a few sentences, without thoroughly engaging with the play *The Tempest*, that Miranda's simplicity has roots in her ignorance as it has never clashed with knowledge of the world.[23] In contrast, Shakuntala knows her world; Tagore explains this by engaging with the play to emphasize that her simplicity is deep-seated, just like her purity.[24] At the heart of such comparisons (or rather *tulnā*), whether it is Tagore or some other author, often the intention is to declare one writer better than the other,[25] or one character better than some other. These comparisons are not necessarily aimed at knowing the other more fully through comparisons, as Arnold envisioned in his Oxford remarks; Arnold, interestingly, also wanted to correct mistakes about others through the act of comparison. So, it is possible that Tagore might have not known the existence of the discipline of comparative literature, or the works of Hugó Meltzl, the Transylvanian Hungarian who founded *Acta Comparationis Litterarum Universarum* (perhaps the first comparative literature journal) in 1877. Nonetheless, Tagore was culturally, historically, and linguistically aware of the perils and traditions of comparisons for assessing the "best" and the "worst" that are sometimes inherent in the word "*tulnātamak*" in many Indian languages, including Bengali, when he spoke of *vishva sahitya*.

For Tagore in 1907, then, the concept of *tulnātamak sahitya* or comparative literature was too narrow, as it could easily lead to comparisons that promoted regionalism, provincialism, or sectarianism. It could also promote nationalism in British India based on what would be perceived as "native" and "foreign" cultures. An antidote to these problems was *vishva sahitya*—an expansive category in spirit and nature that argued for literature not as a property of any creed, race, or nation, but as a treasure of the entire universe or *vishva*, where world-making by human beings was emphasized. Indeed, for a long time, the old model of comparative literature in North America and Europe was based on influence, imitation, and reception studies among a handful of European literatures, where the "donor" was considered "superior" to the "receiver."[26] Tagore was, therefore, not wrong in his instincts for advocating for *vishva sahitya*.

Additionally, such comparisons, in a multilingual context like India where one language, culture, or literary tradition is deemed superior to the other, could imply a juxtaposition of isolated events and literary texts as "prominent" and could also involve reductive comparisons between literatures, where any literary or linguistic tradition could have acted as "donor" to another. An example of unintentionally reductive comparison is in fact visible in the 1929 Hindi translation[27] of Tagore's *vishva sahitya* essay by Vanshidhar Vidyalankar. In an otherwise excellent translation of Tagore's essay, Vidyalankar replaces the word "Bangla" with Hindi[28] in the sentence where Tagore announces that *in* "Bangla" he will call comparative literature *vishva sahitya*. In doing so, without realizing, Vidyalankar gives the impression that the poet is rejecting the English name of comparative literature and choosing to call it *vishva sahitya* in Hindi, instead of Bengali. Technically speaking, *vishva sahitya* will remain as it is in Hindi,[29] but the translator's choice to replace the name of one language with the other in a multilingual context exemplifies the kind of comparative linguistic and cultural chauvinism between a donor and receiver of which Tagore was wary. Further, the replacement of "Bangla" with "Hindi" is especially pertinent in the 1920s and 1930s, when many were lobbying to make Hindi the national language of a prospective independent India. At the same time, replacing "Bangla" with Hindi could also be read as an exegesis of Tagore's "Visva Sahitya," where universalism is also marked by particularism—something that will become clear when I analyze the words "*jagat*," and "*sansār*" in the context of *vishva sahitya*, *vishva mānav*, and world-making.

Undoubtedly, the position of literature and language was of utmost importance for Tagore's *vishva mānav* in *vishva sahitya*, as this position presented the opportunity to create worlds and engage with those worlds in the most personal manner. In fact, Tagore reveals his intentions of calling comparative literature world literature after spending three-fourths of his lecture on the merits and joys of finding oneself in others, then explaining the three kinds of connections human beings make with each other and the world. Here, he uses the word "*jagat*" for world. These three connections in the world or *jagat* are based on intellect, need, and joy. Tagore proposes literature as the sole entity that provides *ānand*, or joy, because it inherently involves deep engagement with the self and others through the process of world-making the *vishva* in literature. Tagore, to that effect, opens his lecture by remarking that all the "talents that we possess within ourselves are only for reaching out to everyone else. Through such relationships we realize ourselves, we attain truth. Otherwise, it does not matter whether I am or anything else is."[30] By the time Tagore introduces *vishva sahitya*, he makes abundantly clear to his audience that literature is constantly in the making, where demolition and remaking of literary trends express the "eternal ideal"[31] of human being's "nature and self-expression,"[32] and the ideal that "also embodies the hull which guides the literature of a new age."[33] For Tagore, if "we judge literature according to that ideal then we have made use of all humanity's powers of discretion."[34] In this way, without yet naming *vishva sahitya*, Tagore sets the stage to emphasize literature's role for *vishva mānav* in *vishva sahitya* for countering petty provincialism, arrogance, and a mere replacement of one author by the other.

If literature and *vishva mānav* take center stage for Tagore in *vishva sahitya*, so do different kinds of readers and critics in the process of world-making. Calling the world, *vishva*, universe of and in literatures whole, and better than the narrow and fragmented worlds that humans can see (a reference to his famous poem "Where the Mind Is Without Fear" from the English *Gitanjali*), Tagore declares that not all individuals have the "broadness of feeling or discretion, neither do all societies"[35] to experience the world of literature fully. As an example of that lack of breadth, Tagore suggests that when "craftiness takes the place of art, pride substitutes glory and Tennyson is replaced by Kipling."[36] Indeed, the juxtaposition of Tennyson with Kipling is important because Kipling had just been awarded the Nobel Prize in 1907, the year Tagore delivered the "Visva Sahitya" lecture. By bringing Tennyson and Kipling together, Tagore indicates that the true experience of the world of literature is not possible if looked through the prism of awards. This observation by Tagore later turns out to be an irony, because in 1913 Tagore was awarded the Nobel Prize, and his fate and readership changed forever. I examine his work post-Nobel Prize in the next chapter.

Nevertheless, the Tennyson-Kipling example is significant as it comes just before Tagore declares his intentions of speaking and translating comparative literature as world literature. Thus, for Tagore, *vishva sahitya* is not a popularity contest, or being awarded the Nobel Prize, or a mere transplantation of one author by another, even if the NCE must have aimed their educational goals otherwise in British idea at the height of nationalism. After explaining the ethos of *vishva sahitya*, without naming it, Tagore announces: "Now is the time for me to come to the main point—and this is it—to see literature through the mirror of nation, time and people is to diminish it, not see it fully."[37] Indeed, for Tagore, to look at a piece of literature of a nation was insufficient, as he did not believe in the concept of nation and nationalism. In this regard, Partha Chatterjee suggests[38] that for Tagore, the difference between "nation" (*desh*) and "my nation" (*svadesh*) relied on *ātmāshakti* (the force of self-making). Being born in a nation, for Tagore, did not indicate a right to the things that the nation offered. In order for an individual to claim a nation as *svadesh*, their relationship with the nation must be "personal and quotidian."[39] Similarly, any claim on a piece of literature as one's own, or belonging to a particular nation or time, was unacceptable for Tagore. In his view, someone could only belong to a piece of literature if they engage with it personally through world-making. On the contrary, literature could not be anyone's property, because it offers the universe or world, or *vishva*, that is for all.

This is why, after emphasizing the different kinds of readers and the importance of literature, Tagore goes on to laud compositions that show literature as a temple that the *vishva-mānav* (universal man)[40] has built. In this temple, "writers have come from all times and all nations to work as labourers,"[41] and "the plan of the building is not available,"[42] but "whatever is wrong is immediately demolished."[43] Tagore considers artists and authors to be in some sort of divine frenzy as they perpetually engage in world-making by building, dismantling, and rebuilding literature. Calling writers laborers, Tagore suggests that each author integrate their "own composition into the whole and thereby complete the invisible plan."[44] In his "Visva Sahitya," writing in a highly philosophical and symbolic language which is very near to that of his creative works, Tagore describes literature as the single unifying force that brings the reader and the writer, the ancient and the modern together, by engaging in a play between the universal and particulars. Certainly, central to Tagore's literary theory of universalism and particularism in *vishva sahitya* is the concept of *sahit* (togetherness that brings general good); he rejects outright the doctrine of art for art's sake.

To reiterate, it is only after warning those who might be inclined toward replacing Alfred Tennyson with the newly awarded Nobel Laureate Rudyard Kipling, assigning a critical role for readers in assessing literature based on connections, describing authors as laborers who are working for an invisible plan of world-making, emphasizing the role of *vishva mānav*, and diving into the Upanishadic philosophy of the cosmos and the human self that Tagore launches his *vishva sahitya*. Tagore declares that he has been entrusted to discuss what is referred in English as "comparative literature." He adds, that in Bengali he will "call it Visva Sahitya (world literature)."[45] For Tagore, literature offers the potentiality to observe human beings expressing themselves, where readers have an active role in discerning what "is truly worthy of observing in literature,"[46] and this worthiness is not based on prizes, popularity, and glory, but on empathy that touches the animate and inanimate world. Tagore emphasizes empathy and kinship as central to *vishva mānav*, *vishva sahitya*, and world-making by giving concrete examples of texts like the Ramayana and Mahabharata, which exist in several competing and often supplemental versions that have touched the souls of all human beings.

Choosing texts such as Ramayana and Mahabharata that have hundreds of translations and renditions in various languages and cultures, while explicating his *vishva sahitya*, Tagore suggests the limitless potential of *vishva mānav* in world-making of literature. These texts, Tagore declares, live forever in different contradictory forms and iterations through "tales and fables, *kirtans* and *panchalis*; Ram–Lakshman appear to prop up the most insignificant actions of the pettiest of men."[47] Furthering empathy as fundamental to *vishva sahitya*, *vishva mānav*, and world-making, Tagore draws on the universality of *bhāva* (emotions), suggesting that all human beings are capable of understanding, personally engaging with, and transforming the beauty in the *vishva* of *sahitya*. Tagore proposes that "the monsoons that bless"[48] human beings have led to the composition of "many rains of songs and showers of poetry,"[49] which have in turn produced "so many *Meghdutams*, so many Vidyapatis."[50] Describing all texts as writerly, and authors as world-makers living in each and every human being, Tagore acknowledges that there cannot be just one text (*Meghdutam*) or one poet (Vidyapati); there are several texts and poets like them. Advancing the real connection of literature with the lives of human beings, and connecting the pains and joys that human beings experience in their homes with those of characters from myths and epics, Tagore emphasizes that through literature, human beings advance, surpass, and intensify themselves, and burnish themselves with a halo of brightness as they struggle on.[51] Tagore calls this particular ability to experience literature through empathy a response to "an augmented thought-creation, a second *samsara*[52] (universe) of literary composition that surrounds this worldly *samsara*."[53]

Indeed, if the experience of empathy as visible in personalized world-making is contingent on the play between the universal and the particular that is central to *vishva sahitya* and *vishva mānav*, the tangible world around/of literature with that of the intangible world in literature is dependent on the interpretation of the word "world." It is worth noting that unlike the English word "world," words such as "*sansār*," "*duniyā*," "*lok*," "*vishva*," "*jagat*," and '*jahān*," to name a few, are used for "world" in many Indian languages. Each of these words indicates a specific type of relation that the individual, community, or collective has with the mortal or immortal world, which in turn contextualizes the meaning of "world." For instance, the word "*sansār*" or "*samsara*"[54] that Tagore uses first in the quoted section means the world that is formed out of empathy and connection that the literary compositions surrounding human beings entailed. The second time he uses the same word, Tagore means a world that is a result of the cosmic *maya* (illusion) which is forever at play in the universe. The *sansār* of literary composition, no matter how whole it might appear to the human eye, is only an illusion of the cosmic *sansār* or world-making. Throughout "Visva Sahitya," though hard to discern in various English translations of this essay, Tagore plays with different words for "world," sometimes using them as adjectives or simply combining different noun words for "world," in order to add a new meaning to the world and to *vishva sahitya*.

In the Bengali version of the essay, the words "*sansār*" and "*jagat*" often exist as nouns. For instance, in the very first paragraph of the essay, where Tagore explains the three kinds of connections that link human beings to the reality of this world, he uses the word "*jagat*" for "world." He proceeds in the next few lines to speak of kings and authorities who have thought of themselves as owning the *jagat*, or of situations where human beings have felt disrespected by *sansār*. Significantly, throughout the essay, the reader never gets the impression that human beings can own or be disrespected by *vishva*. For Tagore, the *vishva* is bigger than *sansār* and *jagat*. Whenever Tagore speaks of *vishva* it is either conjugated with *jagat* as in *vishvajagat* (universe/universal-world), *mānav* as in *vishvamānav* (universe/universal-human) or *sahitya* as in *vishvasahitya* (universe/universal-literature). The word "*vishva*," as mentioned before, can be translated as "universe," or "universal," or "world." However, when *vishva* is joined with *jagat*, *mānav*, and *sahitya*, the resulting nouns transcend the limits of what can be known by a human. In these cases, *vishva* becomes an adjective as well as a noun. Sometimes Tagore also adds two words for "world" together, as in *jagatsansār* (world-world); this is a common practice in many Indian languages. Note that *jagat* and *sansār* can be known, but they are neither universal nor the universe. They can also not be translated into "universe," like *vishva* can. In short, for Tagore, *vishva* is all-encompassing, like the universal spirit of Brahman.

That is why when Tagore speaks of the world *of* literature, or the world *of* human beings, he uses the words "*sansār*" or "*jagat*." It is only toward the end of the essay, when he explains the world *in* literature, that he uses the word "*vishva*" as *vishvasahitya* or *vishva sahitya*. Interestingly, he arrives at *vishva sahitya* after speaking of the *vishva mānav*. Unlike an ordinary *mānav*, the *vishva mānav* is in tune with the Brahman or the universal spirit. This is because both *jagat* and *sansār* can be created and destroyed by *mānavs* (humans), as they are a manifestation of *maya*. On the other hand, *vishva* is indestructible because it carries within itself the Brahman, the universal spirit that is present in the *vishva mānav*. What needs to be stressed here is that the indestructible *vishva* carries within itself the *maya*-filled *sansār* and *jagat*. For Tagore, it is the potential of literature as offering *vishva* or universe that cannot be owned and destroyed by anyone that is significant for renouncing comparative or *tulnātamak* literature in favor of *vishva sahitya*. In fact, for him, the *vishva* in *sahitya* offers the endless possibilities of various world-makings of *jagats* and *sansārs* of the *vishva mānav*, which eventually create *vishva sahitya*.

To sum up, despite Tagore's esoteric language and his notion of a divine plan that can be traced in his association with the Brahmo Samaj, a concrete definition of *vishva sahitya* can be gauged: a universal or a universe that has particulars, a world that is ideally one but also different because of the individual's world-making, as evidenced in Tagore's examples of many Ramayanas, Mahabharatas, *Meghdutam*, and Vidyapatis. Since Tagore's *vishva sahitya* is dependent on the interaction and collaboration of human beings, rich and poor, who sing their own songs during monsoons, it is a particular concept with multiple meanings; hence, it lends itself to many comparisons, resulting in a layered world, *sansār*, or *jagat* in *vishva*, universe, and world. Simultaneously, the particular also has an ideal in the Tagorean world; the ideal audience member is a sensitive viewer who experiences the same *bhāvas* that the author felt while creating that world.

Conversely, for Tagore, this does not mean that all the other emotions are invalidated, because in his view, studying literary works is equivalent to engaging with the history of the *vishva mānav* who continue to build the temple of literature, as indicated in "Visva Sahitya." Since the temple of literature is always a work-in-progress, its association with history becomes fundamental for understanding the world-making of *sansār*, or *jagat* in *vishva sahitya*. Just after introducing *vishva sahitya*, Tagore elaborates that if the study of history is focused on a mere change from one ruler to another (e.g., Akbar and Elizabeth, as he mentions), or focused on a single region such as Gujarat, then this history is piecemeal and can only satisfy readers' curiosity for information, rather than acquainting readers with the history of human beings. Similarly, Tagore explains what is worth considering in world literature:

> How man expresses his joy in literature, how and in what form the human soul chooses to manifest its diverse, variegated, multiple images of self-expression, that is the only thing worth considering in world literature. Literature must actually enter the world—whether it pleases to express itself in the form of the

diseased, the accomplished, or the ascetic person—to know how far man can find his kinship in the world, and to what extent he can realize truth. It will not do to know it as an artificial construct; it is a world in itself. Its essence exceeds the individual's grasp. It is in continuous creation, like the material universe itself, but in the innermost core of that unfinished creation is a perfected ideal that remains unmoving.[55]

For Tagore, as can be seen in the quoted paragraph, *vishva sahitya* or world literature is not a particular type of selected literature nor is it a sum of all the world's literary traditions. It is a slice of a world, *sansār*, or *jagat*, that is part of a world in progress toward becoming whole, a *vishva*, a universe. Tagore uses the word "*jagat*" to speak of world in the above quoted section. By default, then, *vishva sahitya* is varied and multiple. Its goal is to allow human beings to find kinship in the world, and it is in this quest for the *vishva mānav* and world-making that *vishva sahitya* exists. Because world literature is not an artificial construct, and it is dependent on a particular individual's capacity or world-making, the pursuit of a lasting kinship is never complete. Though this unrealized goal of a lasting kinship of world literature with the material world (*sansār* or *jagat*) might seem unfinished, it is this very characteristic of world-making in world literature that is central to its core when Tagore translates comparative literature as *vishva sahitya*, which as *vishva sahitya* is incomparable.

Tagore explains this point by bringing in a myriad of professions in the next few sentences of his lecture. Suggesting that the invisible *rasa* (creative and connecting sap) flows through everybody—the grocer, the blacksmith, the laborer, the merchant, and the homemakers as they go about their work in the world—Tagore reminds his audience that all human beings are at the end of the day creators, engaged in a world of *maya*, and thus, we are all actors in a play doing our bit of world-making. Using highly philosophical language to illustrate his belief in universal consciousness or *vishva ātmā*, an Upanishadic notion, he emphasizes that without knowing all the parts, it is impossible to comprehend the whole. Since no one can know all the parts of *jagat* and *sansār*, the knowledge of the whole, that is the *vishva* (and, by extension, of the part) remains incomplete. Hence, for Tagore, the practice of judging and comparing authors, literary texts, translations, literary traditions, or time periods on a one-on-one comparative basis (even in the context of *jagat*, and *sansār*) is an artificial construct that simply can be reduced to a list based on the philosophy of replacement of one author with another, as seen in the previous Tennyson and Kipling example.

To that effect, in a dramatic twist in the essay, while connecting the study of *vishva sahitya* with the material, and the particular to the universal and universe, through the literary and the concept of *rasa*, Tagore declares:

> Do not so much as imagine that I will show you the way to such a world literature. Each of us must make his way forward according to his own means and abilities. All I have wanted to say is that just as the world is not merely the sum of your plough field, plus my plough field, plus his plough field—because to know the world that way is only to know it with a yokel-like parochialism—similarly world literature is not merely the sum of your writings, plus my writing, plus his writings. We generally see literature in this limited, provincial manner. To free oneself of that regional narrowness and resolve to see the universal being in world literature, to apprehend such totality in every writer's work, and to see its interconnectedness with every man's attempt at self-expression—that is the objective we need to pledge ourselves to.[56]

To understand the implications of these metaphors, we should recall that the birth of the NCE took place at a tumultuous time when the British administration had divided the state of Bengal into East and West Bengal. The real motive of the British, however, was to separate Hindus and Muslims into two different geographical regions, with the Muslim population predominating in the Eastern part of Bengal. Tagore is countering this policy by using the ecological metaphors of earth and land, emphasizing the organic connectedness that exists beyond geographical—or religious or linguistic—boundaries when it comes to literature and other art forms. For him, *vishva sahitya* is the ability to see the world as a unified whole, a universe, despite parts of the world, *sansār* and *jagat*, being different from each other.

For Tagore, *vishva sahitya* does not refer to a particular set of literary texts from different parts of the world, but rather the opportunity to develop kinships with the *vishva mānav*. This possibility is provided by literature or *sahitya* which carries the universe or *vishva*, and various worlds of the *vishva mānav* as in *jag, jagat, duniyā, bhūgōl, jahān, sansār, lok*, and so on. Clearly, by refusing to lecture on a topic that he was initially given, renaming it and translating it, introducing as *vishva sahitya*, and then declining to give an exact definition of the term that he had just introduced, Tagore makes quite a statement in front of an audience who perhaps must have expected a direct fiery rebuke of colonial powers, policies, and education in the name of comparative literature and comparisons.

Instead, Tagore instructs his audience to look at any piece of literature as the universe or world, a *vishva* that is as much theirs as someone else's, because it is universal and carries in itself the ideal of pursuing kinship and world-making for fellow human beings.

Universalism, *Sahitya*, and *Sahit*

As pointed out earlier, Tagore's notion of *vishva sahitya* did not emerge in a vacuum. Central to his *vishva sahitya* is the belief that *vishva mānav* can come together because of the universalism that can be experienced through the world-making of the universe or *vishva* in *sahitya* in the world, *sansār*, and *jagat*. For Tagore, the *sansār* and *jagat* were themselves not monolithic, apolitical, or singular at any location.[57] In fact, *sansār* and *jagat* have the potential to become one with the world, universe, and *vishva* because of human being's personal engagement with literature. This is only possible because the concept of universalism in *vishva sahitya* is deeply connected with a belief in togetherness and goodness for all, which in turn is embedded in the word "*sahitya*." In the next few pages of this chapter, I highlight how universalism, *sahitya*, *sahit*, and translation are connected with *vishva mānav* and *vishva sahitya*.

The fact that universalism had become important to Tagore was visible in 1907, the year Tagore spoke of *vishva sahitya*. That year, Tagore started serializing his novel *Gora* in a Bengali magazine, *Prabashi*. In the novel, Tagore's defense of universalism that has roots in the Brahmo philosophy is clearly visible. Through the central character Gora in the novel, Tagore points out the quandary for the liberal Brahmo Samaj movement, which had to negotiate between Hindu nationalism and oppressive imperial colonial rule. A victim of an 1857 mutiny, Gora, whose name literally means "white" in many Indian languages, is adopted by an upper-caste Hindu Brahmin household. Without knowledge of his Irish parents, Gora, a white young man, not only supports regressive tenets of Hinduism in order to support a Hindu-Indian national identity; he is also blind to caste discrimination and poverty. However, Gora's orthodox worldview of nationalism and Hinduism crashes when his adoptive father Krishna Dayal, who with time had also become an orthodox Hindu, reveals to Gora on his deathbed that he was adopted. Suddenly, the narrator points out that Gora had no parents, no lineage, no country, and no god. The only thing that was left to him was vast negation.[58]

Vast negation is nothing but an echo of the Sanskrit phrase "*neti neti*," which means "not this, not that" or "neither this, nor that." The concept of *neti neti* can be found in the Upanishads, which persuade one to use rationality to understand the nature of Brahman, the universal spirit, by focusing on what is not Brahman. Consequently, in one of the most significant moments in the novel, specifically toward the end, Gora relinquishes his upper-caste Hindu identity and accepts a universal identity.[59] He declares to Paresh Babu, a sympathetic member of the Brahmo Samaj: "Today I am free . . . to-day I am really an Indian! In me there is no longer any opposition between Hindu, Mussulman, and Christian. To-day every caste in India is my caste, the food of all is my food!"[60] Certainly, only after the *maya* of Gora's world-making of *sansār* and *jagat* breaks down is he able to appreciate the sympathy and kinship among all humans by becoming a *vishva mānav*.

Indeed, by 1907, Tagore had completely retreated from nationalism to universalism.[61] David Kopf suggests that in a 1908 lecture given to a gathering of Brahmo Samaj, Tagore reminded his audience that if Indians and English people were just to stand apart, only mutual repugnance could grow.[62] The lecture is significant because Tagore, for the first time, in strong words, critiques caste discrimination and suggests that even if the British leave, India would not have cured its social defects.[63] Further, when Tagore took over the editorship of the Bengali magazine *Tattvabodhini* in 1911, he started promoting his ideals of universalism through essays and articles in the magazine. The idea that literature could foment universalism and empathy in the world, *vishva*, or universe was not new for Tagore, because he believed in the *sahit* of *sahitya*, which I explain later. Even during his nationalist period—specifically, in 1895, by taking the example of his home-state Bengal[64]—Tagore suggested that English education had revitalized the Bengali mind, which was now free to judge what was good for it. This of course did not mean he discouraged education in Bengali language and literature; had Tagore been critical of indigenous languages, he would never refer comparative literature as *vishva sahitya* in Bengali but would instead use the term "world literature" in English. On the contrary, Tagore was acutely aware that the development of Bengali prose had a great deal to do with translation from Sanskrit and English, and that Fort William College of Kolkata—an institution of oriental studies—had played an integral role in this development.

If the nature of home (here referring exclusively to Bengali culture and Bengali literature) was in a dynamic cultural exchange, the concept of nation[65] was an empty rhetoric that was always up for grabs by the orthodox. The concepts of nation, nation-building, and nationalism had never appealed to Tagore. He had directly started criticizing the call for nationalism in 1907. In fact, while visiting the United States a decade after his *vishva sahitya* lecture, Tagore would go on to criticize the nation-building process by Indians in British India in his lecture "Nationalism in India."[66] In this lecture, Tagore asserted that India's problems were not political, but social. "Nationalism in India," along with other essays that critique nationalism as a global movement in the post–First World War world, was published in the collection titled *Nationalism* in 1917. In "Nationalism in India," Tagore declares: "I am not against one nation in particular, but against the general idea of all nations. What is the Nation?"[67] He goes on to add that a nation is the "aspect of a whole people as an organized power,"[68] a mechanical organization that "incessantly keeps up the insistence of the population on becoming strong and efficient."[69]

For Tagore, the concept of nation had the power and allure to divert human beings from the path of goodness or *sahit*. He insisted, in this essay, that a belief in nation and nationalism turned people into perpetuating slavery, robbing human rights of fellow men and women, and abusing others in the pursuit of wealth and power. He criticizes nationalism in a powerful single sentence: "Nationalism is a great menace."[70] Tagore indicates that nationalism is based on exclusion, whether in terms of political or social orders of caste, race, language, and ethnicity; it occurs not just in India but all around the world, and it needs to be severely criticized. For Tagore, then, literature, as seen in *vishva sahitya*, was the only true means through which the concept of nation could be challenged. Through literature, *svadesh*[71] could intermingle, and world-makings could intertwine and interlace with *vishva mānav*. Indeed, with universalism in the universe, *vishva*, or world becoming central to Tagore's philosophy against nationalism, *sahitya* lent itself to creating empathy.

The word "*sahitya*," used in many modern Indian languages, is usually translated as "literature" in English. But *sahitya* does not have the same resonance as the word "literature" in English. Unlike the English word, which loosely means anything written and printed, *sahitya* carries in itself the word "*sahit*"— which can mean, as indicated before, being together for the general good. Tagore elaborates on the meaning of *sahitya* by suggesting[72] that words together (*sahit*) with each other create literature (*sahitya*), which indicates that the word "*sahitya*" connotes the emotion (or *bhāva*) of union. This union, for Tagore, is not just between *bhāvas*, languages, and texts; rather, it is a connection between one human being and another, between the present and the past, between what is close and what is distant. Only in *sahitya* does such a multidimensional meeting of world-makings and human beings become possible, thereby making kinship between *vishva mānav* viable. In fact, Tagore explicitly states that "*sahitatvā* or union is the main ingredient of sahitya;[73] it unites the isolated, and installs itself wherever it finds union."[74] As seen through the concept of *vishva sahitya*, for Tagore, literature represented the highest form of communication and connection with one soul to other for the *sahit* of humanity. Thus, he regarded the term "comparative literature" as too confining, as it undermined the organic connections between and among all *sahitya* that is the *vishva*.

Suggesting that the highest function of human intellect consists in forging bonds with others, in "Visva Sahitya," where the transcendence of the self results in a discovery and union with the other, Tagore sees love and joy at the heart of forging bonds with others. Although Tagore begins his lecture on *vishva sahitya* by emphasizing a supranational universality of literature, toward the end he offers a much more particular account, where the sum total of works composed by different individuals cannot qualify as world literature. As he concludes his lecture to the Council, Tagore modulates the universalism of his approach, acknowledging that each work is a whole and yet also part of something very particular. Even as they echo Upanishadic philosophy, Tagore's ideas, on the surface, also sound similar to what the 77-year-old Goethe had said to his young disciple Johann Peter Eckermann in 1827:

> I am more and more convinced . . . that poetry is the universal possession of mankind, revealing itself everywhere and at all times in hundreds and hundreds of men . . . I therefore like to look about me in foreign nations, and advise everyone to do the same. National literature is now a rather unmeaning term; the epoch of world literature is at hand.[75]

Through their respective concepts of *vishva sahitya* and *weltliteratur*, both Tagore and Goethe highlight the ineffectiveness of parochial regionalism or nationalism that ignores the cross-cultural connections between languages and literatures. But Goethe emphasized the term "world literature" in 1827, following the collapse of Napoleon's imperial ambitions in Europe, to project the role of literature as an instrument for peace and cross-connections between nations.[76] When Goethe began addressing the issue of *weltliteratur*, Germany was not a politically unified country, and he saw in literature the universal elements that could bring nations and communities together. Goethe's paradigm of *weltliteratur* is rooted in Germany's historical and political ethos of the 1820s and 1830s. He believed that Germans had a role to play in the era of world literature, and he enjoyed looking for himself in foreign literatures.

In contrast to Goethe's *weltliteratur,* Rabindranath Tagore's concept of *vishva sahitya* does not deem any nation, region, language, literary tradition, or ethnic group as having a special role. Tagore's idea of *vishva sahitya* stems from the colonial realities of his times; his belief in the universal spirit, *sahitya, vishva mānav, vishva, jagat,* and *sansār*; and his own cosmopolitan upbringing in a Bengali household, where he perhaps saw himself playing a special role—not from any particular ethnic or national group. As an artist engaged in continuous world-making of the material universe, without knowing the divine plan, Tagore becomes one of the laborers, a *vishva mānav* working for *vishva sahitya.* No wonder that he wrote in his memoir that "East and West met in friendship in my own person,"[77] and declared, "thus it has been given me to realize in my own life the meaning of my name."[78] Rabi/Ravi means sun in many modern Indian languages. Certainly, by the time Tagore delivered his lecture on *vishva sahitya*, he had entered the world of worldly literary criticism, he had a particular philosophy about translation and universalism that I analyze in the next section, and he was thinking of translating his *Gitanjali.* Indeed, *Gitanjali* caught Tagore in one of his most spiritual modes. Further, the intellectual milieu in which *Gitanjali* appeared in Europe was also in a critical phase. The shadow of the First World War was hanging on the horizon; *Gitanjali* perhaps soothed readers' tense spirits, and Tagore was welcomed as a prophet of peace from the East. Tagore, too, heartily accepted his role, since he believed in the universal spirit of Brahman and in the work of the *vishva mānav.* But just as translation of comparative literature as *vishva sahitya* requires thoughtful explanation, Tagore's translation of the Bengali *Gitanjali* into English language raises questions that need to be resolved, which I address in the next chapter.

To come back, however, to *vishva sahitya,* it is necessary to add a few points about the position of translation in the universalism of *sahitya,* and its association with the *vishva mānav, vishva sahitya,* and world-making.

Translation and *Vishva Sahitya*

Even before the "Visva Sahitya" lecture, where he decided to translate comparative literature as world literature, Tagore had been actively involved in the translation and study of German, French, Sanskrit, Bengali, and English literatures. As a young adult, Tagore had also published his translations of literatures in *Bharati*, a literary magazine started by his brother in 1877. The family-run magazine also published works that Tagore's siblings and cousins had translated from French and English into Bengali. Tagore's interest in the world of literatures was matched by his interest in the world of languages. For instance, Tagore took interest in German culture in his teens when he started to learn German[79] and "tried to read Goethe's *Faust* in the original."[80] The bilingual edition of Goethe's *Faust* that has Tagore's markings is preserved in Santiniketan at Visva Bharati. Tagore's interest in Goethe went deeper than merely reading "a few lines of the original text."[81] He published an article on Goethe in the journal *Bharati* in 1878, and it is also believed that he translated some poems by the German poet Heinrich Heine into Bengali.[82] In fact, in 1974, *Desh*, a Bengali journal, serialized a debate between scholars on whether Tagore translated Heine into Bengali from German or from English.[83]

Further, the times in which Tagore grew up and was living centered on the potentiality of translated text to break boundaries and change society. In the early nineteenth century, Raja Ram Mohan Roy had translated several texts that were holy to the Hindus in order to prove that idolatry was not in the books that the priestly caste revered, obeyed, and fiercely defended.[84] For Roy, translation was a necessary tool with which he emphasized the significance of Brahman, the universal spirit. Tagore had witnessed the change brought in society because of Brahmo Samaj. Moreover, literatures, languages, cultures, and translations were a living and breathing part of world-making when Tagore spoke of *vishva mānav*, which in turn played a significant role in his conception of *vishva sahitya*. Since *vishva sahitya* is contingent on human relations as manifesting in the world-making of the *vishva* in *sahitya* in world, *sansār*, and *jagat*, where literature is the joining force for *vishva mānav* for the *sahit* of everyone, translation becomes the linchpin for its conception. Translation for Tagore, however, was not an exact rendition of the original. It could not be. Since world, *sansār*, and *jagat* are varied and multiple, just like world-making, only the sap or *rasa* of them could be rendered in translation by the labor-artist or *vishva mānav* who was engaged in world-making.

Though Tagore did not directly speak of translation theory per se, except in some parts of *Anubād-Charchā*,[85] he was an avid translator. Tagore wrote *Anubād-Charchā* for his students in 1917; in the "Introduction," he mentions that a word-to-word rendition between two languages is not possible. He takes the example of Bengali and English to explain that expressions in both of these languages are different, so a search for equivalence in words is not productive.[86] Indeed, an implementation of this translation practice is seen in Tagore's English *Gitanjali*. Tagore did not hesitate to make changes to the original poems when he was translating the Bengali *Gitanjali* into English. This was mainly for two reasons. First, fidelity is not the most important criterion that marks a good literary translation in many South Asian contexts.[87] Translating is not an act of betrayal, but one of homage. Note that in almost all Indian languages, as indicated earlier, the nearest words to translation are *bhashantar* (change in language), *anuvād* (speaking after), *rūpāntar* (change in form), and *tarjumā* (paraphrase). Often, the translation is referred to as a *chhaya* (shadow) of the original. Translation, then, is understood as rewriting and recontextualizing of world-making the *vishva* in *sahitya*. Second, Tagore believed in the universal spirit that existed in *sahitya* and brought *vishva mānav* together in the *vishva*. Since the sap of a text could be realized by the *vishva mānav* in *vishva sahitya* through world-making, the *vishva* in the text, as seen in Tagore's examples of Ramayana and Mahabharata, rendering one language into another did not present a problem of fidelity.

To elaborate these points, let me give an example[88] that is not from the lecture *vishva sahitya*. In a 1934 letter to Helen Meyer-Franck about her translations of his poems into German, Tagore praises that the new versions read like the original, so that one forgets they are translations.[89] Even two decades before writing to Meyer-Franck, Tagore had written in 1911 to Ramananda Chatterji, the founder and magazine editor of *Modern Review* (established in 1907). In the letter, Tagore discusses his ideas about translation, describing it as something that could be rendered quickly in prose:

> Coomaraswamy was here in the ashram. He desires to translate some of my poems, so I hastily rendered three or four of them into the plainest prose in order to help him. If Coomaraswamy writes something based on these, you must publish it in *Modern Review*. I have no objection provided it passes through his hands. Ajit translated a few—these are with Coomaraswamy too, and whatever he considers worth printing, you may publish. But it would not be proper for my name to be given as translator after Coomaraswamy has scrubbed and polished a mockery of a translation.[90]

Ananda Coomaraswamy was a Sri Lankan Tamil philosopher and a scholar. Like Ajit Chakravarty, a teacher at Shantiniketan, Coomaraswamy had tried his hand at translating Tagore's poems. Coomaraswamy did not know Bengali well enough, so he sought Tagore's help with the task. Tagore paraphrases the sap (*rasa*, as many scholars would say) of the poem into plain prose swiftly. He has no objections if the translations are published, and he thinks that he should not be identified as a translator of these verses.[91]

Tagore's translational practice had something to do with the cultural and literary milieu of that time. Translation activity before the mid-nineteenth century was radically different in Bengal.[92] A free translation of Mahabharata and Ramayana from Sanskrit into Bengali had already led to a profusion of Sanskrit words in the colloquial Bengali language by the eighteenth century. With the establishment of the Vernacular Committee in 1851 by the efforts of some Indian and British officials, a new trend began. The Vernacular Committee, later changed to Vernacular Society, aimed to produce translations of English texts into Bengali while adapting them into the new culture. In the process, not only British texts but also literatures available in English from other languages received attention through translation, leading to the production of prose in a similar vein in Bengali. The society's activities also had a significant role in the development of the actual Bengali language, which in turn led to the production of many literary pieces in prose in the next few decades. With respect to poetry, during the second half of the nineteenth century, and the first few decades of the twentieth century to a certain extent, one comes across a large number of poems that are called adaptations, literally "*chhaya abalambane* (in the shadow of), and quite often the language is mentioned, but not the name of the poet or the poem."[93]

This attitude toward translation of poetry not only acknowledges that there are differences that need to be decoded from one literary system and encoded into another but also expresses a belief in universalistic notions of poetry in general, where literature is regarded as a common shared endeavor rather than an intellectual property of the individual who created it.[94] This is exactly what Tagore had in mind when he spoke of *vishva sahitya*, *vishva mānav*, and world-making. Further, in "Literary Creation,"[95] one of the lectures that he delivered for NCE, Tagore mentions that in human society, "the thoughts of one mind strive to find fulfillment in another, thereby so shaping our ideas that they are no longer exclusive to the original thinker."[96] Though Tagore does not directly specify the role of translation in establishing kinship within his "Visva Sahitya," he does directly discuss translation's crucial role in the development of Bengali prose elsewhere.[97]

Moreover, Tagore speaks of "one literature, of essences and truths, but what lends a different dimension to his theory of essences and truths is the fact that they are contingent on human relations,"[98] or kinship, as suggested through the literary examples he gives in "Visva Sahitya." In addition to that, in "Literary Creation," Tagore confesses that his "idea adjusts itself somewhat to the particular mind of the particular friend in whom it secretly seeks fulfillment."[99] He adds that what is said is always "shaped by the conjunction of speaker and listener."[100] Hence, the concept of *vishva sahitya* in Tagore's mind is open-ended, idealistic in spirit, and therefore incomplete. It is within this framework that the translational norm must "also be open-ended enough to include free adaptations of poems that can belong anywhere and to all."[101]

Tagore's idea of *vishva sahitya* and translation was also prevalent among his contemporary poet-translators. The first attempt to anthologize world poetry in Bengali, *Tirtharenu*, was undertaken in 1908 by the poet-translator Satyendranath Dutta, who at that time seemed unsure of the end product. Tagore describes Dutta's translations in *Tirtharenu* as *sristikarya* (creative acts) rather than *silpakarya* (artifacts), adding that the translated poems had taken shelter in the branches of the original to blossom in all their beauty and *rasa*.[102] Tagore wrote to Dutta that the poems were both a translation and a new poem. This belief—that a translated poem could exist independently as a piece in the never-ending project of *vishva sahitya*—accounts for the liberties Tagore took in many of his translations, and specifically in *Gitanjali*, which I address in the next chapter. Since the never-ending project of *vishva sahitya* is dependent on the layered and multifaceted understanding of the word "world" and world-making by the *vishva mānav*, an inherent comparative study of the unfinished world literature that gives *ānand* or joy is also at the core of Tagore's idea of *vishva sahitya*.

It is for this reason that Tagore's *vishva sahitya* has become a call for doing comparative literature in multilingual India, where languages and cultures differ within every few miles, and preferring one over the other as "donor" or "receiver" can create grossly unjust and unfair comparisons. As a result, India's first department of comparative literature recognizes Tagore's *vishva sahitya* as fundamental for doing comparative literature in India. The department was established at Jadavpur University in 1956, in Kolkata, almost five decades after Tagore had given his *vishva sahitya* talk at the university's parent body, the NCE. Further, the constitution of the Comparative Literature Association of India states its objectives as follows: "To promote the ideal of one world by appreciation of Comparative Literature beyond national frontiers, and in pursuance thereof to rise above separate identities of single national literatures so that the all-embracing concept of Viswa-Sahitya as visualized by Tagore or Goethe's

Weltliteratur may be realized as a measure of international understanding."[103] Among comparative literature scholars of India, Tagore is regarded as nothing less than the founder of the discipline,[104] which was still in its infancy in the West in 1907 when he delivered his *vishva sahitya* talk.

Since Tagore, notable comparatists have tried to think about a paradigm that would help in making sense of the linguistic and literary diversity of India, which could often be seen as a microcosm of the world. For instance, Amiya Dev, who also taught at Jadavpur University, suggested the idea of forming comparative Indian literature as a discipline in the 1980s.[105] This suggestion was prompted by the talk of creating an Indian literature in translation that was proposed in the 1960s and 1970s by Sujit Mukherjee,[106] V. K. Gokak,[107] and others. Gurbhagat Singh had rejected Dev's idea because, according to him, the ideology behind such a discipline sacrifices multiple and diverse expressions in favor of a homogenized Indian literature/identity.[108]

Moreover, if history and politics play central roles in forming notions about literature and literary canons, the literary historiographies of India, from a practical point of view, would vary from region to region, state to state; comparative literature departments should vary accordingly and relatively, which would favor Gurbhagat Singh's argument. The core point to realize in these debates is that a comparative literature that is also not a *vishva sahitya* does not make sense in India. As I have elaborated in this chapter, Tagore knew what kind of comparative literary study to practice in the multilingual and multicultural world, *sansār*, and *jagat* of India—one that was the *vishva*, not a *tulnātmak sahitya*—that aspired for *sahit* through *ānand* in its world-making.

The purpose of world literature for Tagore is not a rootless eco-touristy cosmopolitanism that operates in a handful of global languages. Nor is Tagore's *vishva sahitya* founded on comparing fictitious national literary traditions, where a few authors become representative of literary canons (Tennyson, Kipling, or Vidyapati, to use Tagore's examples). Since Tagore does not believe in the concept of nation, but *svadesh*, *vishva sahitya* does not project the glorification of a location and language in or of the world. Rather, it encourages world-making through personally engaging with *sahitya*. *Vishva sahitya* shuns cultural imperialism at all levels by making translations and transcreations part of the *ānand* of literary study, necessary for connecting different manifestations of world-making of the *vishva* in *sahitya* in world, *sansār*, and *jagat* for the *vishva mānav*. No wonder that in a letter written to Charles Freer Andrews in 1920, Tagore writes that for so long he was working "under the delusion that"[109] his mission was to establish an Indian university, where Indian cultures in all their varieties could be reflected, but traveling to Europe made him realize that the call of Visva Bharati at Shantiniketan is the "invitation of India to the rest of the world."[110] Quite aptly, in 1921, Tagore formally launched his university with the motto "Where the Whole World Meets in a Single Nest."[111] The word used for world is *vishva* in the original Sanskrit quote used by Tagore. The cozy image of a nest, an indestructible *vishva* that nurtures the diverse world, might seem idealistic and simple, but looked through the world in literature, *vishva sahitya* emphasizes the immense potentiality of world-making of the *vishva mānav* united through the universal spirit of Brahman in translation and in the original. In short, for Tagore, the purpose and methodology for doing world literature is in *ānand*, world-making, and *ātmīyatā* or empathy of the *vishva mānav*, found not in an exact rendition of an original, but in the sap of the *vishva* in *sahitya*.

2

Here Is World Literature

When Tagore spoke of *vishva sahitya*, he did not necessarily think of pedagogical and scholarly implications of teaching world literature in a classroom or university, whether in India or elsewhere. That is why he did not argue in his *vishva sahitya* essay that the world-makings of Ramayana, Mahabharata, and *Meghdutam* could also be analyzed to arrive at conclusions other than *ānand* or joy. For instance, one can think of countless ramifications of literary canons for marginal voices, consequences of cultural propaganda disseminated through literature, repercussions of the politics of prizes in consolidating traditions, or implications of uneven power dynamics among literary traditions in different languages. Undoubtedly, world-making does not always tell a joyful tale, nor is it an arbitrary exercise, whether in India or beyond, as examined in this chapter. It is true that Tagore was keenly aware that *vishva sahitya* should not center on replacing one author with the other (recall his example of Tennyson and Kipling) or focus on glorification based on prizes and recognition. Nevertheless, specifically, while speaking of *vishva sahitya*, Tagore did not imagine a consequence of world-making other than joy in literary and cultural histories and traditions.

In all fairness, Tagore cannot be blamed. He had other concerns in his mind when he inaugurated *vishva sahitya*. For him, the universal and the particular present in the indestructible *vishva* in literature or *sahitya* through quotidian world-making in the original, or translation becomes a call to combat nationalism, and shunning literary comparisons based on nation-state encourages universalism that is for the good of all. Indeed, it was with these ideas of *sahit*, *ānand*, and universalism in *vishva sahitya* that Tagore self-translated and published his Bengali *Gitanjali* into English in 1912. *Vishva sahitya*, as analyzed in the previous chapter, is the world-makings of the *vishva* in *sahitya* by *vishva mānav* for the *sahit* and *ānand*, where the sap of a translation is no different from an original in different literary systems. Consequently, the material and cultural analysis of the world (*jagat*, and *sansār*, to use words from Tagore's essay) of *sahitya*, whether in the original or translation, presents a perfect scholarly opportunity to pinpoint in concrete terms the whereabouts of world literature. The analysis and examination of the world-making of a text, and the world that surrounds a text, also invite interventions (if and when needed) while speaking of world literature. It is with this goal—that is, to illustrate the whereabouts of world literature and the politics of a world around a text—that I analyze Tagore's *Gitanjali* in this chapter.

By taking the example of Tagore's *Gitanjali*, which was published a few years after his *vishva sahitya* lecture, I argue that the world-making of the *vishva* in *sahitya* directly engages with debates on the location, literary canons, and power dynamics among languages—something that Tagore did not consider when speaking on *vishva sahitya*. Even though Tagore thought of *vishva sahitya*, and definitely of his *Gitanjali*, as operating outside the realms of the *maya* or illusion of world, *jagat*, and *sansār*, it is in the very analysis of the *maya* that surrounds a text that is central for a comparatist for speaking against and for (and sometimes both) world literature. Moreover, speaking of the *maya* of world, *jagat*, *sansār*, and location in world literature encourages a discussion of world literature itself being a construct[1] that is not necessarily as apolitical as Tagore imagined it to be in his *vishva sahitya* essay. In fact, an analysis of world literature as a construct informs readers of linguistic and literary underpinnings, debates on literary canons, and power dynamics that operate synchronically and diachronically in literary frameworks relative to locations. These issues remain central to discussions on literature, whether the *sahitya* is Tagore's *vishva sahitya* or not, and whether that *sahitya* (or literature) is being taught in a classroom or argued in a research monograph; in the original or in translation; in single, comparative, or world literary frameworks.

In addition to the previous reasons, the purpose for taking *Gitanjali* to speak about the whereabouts of world literature and the significance of a world, *jagat*, and *sansār* around a text for its world-making is threefold. First, in recent scholarship on Tagore, the desire is to introduce Tagore as a world author of multiple genres. For instance, *The Essential Tagore* (published in 2011) includes English translations of Tagore's Bengali works in various genres such as plays, autobiography, stories, songs, prose, poetry letters, and so on.[2] Poetry is suggested as just one of the facets of Tagore's works. However, in places like Bengal and elsewhere Tagore continues to be foremost known as *vishva kavi* (world poet). In addition, *The Norton Anthology of World Literature* completely does away with Tagore's poetry and introduces readers to his short stories, such as "Punishment" and "Kabuliwala."[3]

In these contexts, then, to talk about *Gitanjali*, as I do in this chapter, is to highlight the worldliness of world-making with respect to genres in world literary debates. Second, Tagore's dedication of his Bengali *Gitanjali* to his personal god and of the English translation to William Rothenstein indicate Tagore's strong beliefs in *vishva mānav*; Brahman; and the importance of the listener, reader, or receiver of a text. These beliefs are also expressed in "Literary Creation" and "Visva Sahitya." Subsequently, through his self-translation of *Gitanjali*, Tagore practices the very philosophy that he preaches in *vishva sahitya* for the *vishva mānav*. Third, the cultural and translation histories of a text in the world, *jagat*, and *sansār* present world-making as not an idealistic and simplistic activity of the *vishva mānav*, but rather as a strategy that can be used to study, teach, and critique world literature in multilingual contexts in the original and translation. This becomes clear when we see that Tagore actively participated in world-making a text in English that suited the taste of its time and that was also consistent with his philosophy of *sahitya*, translation, and universalism. In that sense, Tagore is not the colonized "other" of Edward Said's imagination, who has no agency.[4] In fact, Tagore appears to be someone who defies the Saidian binaries of self-other and Orient-Occident,[5] as seen in this chapter through the analysis of Bengali, English, and Spanish versions of a few verses from *Gitanjali*.

The World-making of the English *Gitanjali*

For many of the poems in the English *Gitanjali*, one has to look for the original not in the Bengali *Gitanjali* but in the three volumes of Tagore's Bengali verses: *Naivedya*, published in 1901; *Kheya*, published in 1906; and *Gitimalya*, published in 1914.[6] The famous opening poem from the English *Gitanjali* has been taken not from the first poem[7] in the Bengali *Gitanjali* that came out in 1910 (three years after the *vishva sahitya* lecture), but from Poem 23[8] in *Gitimalya*, a work that was published after the English as well as the Bengali *Gitanjali*. Thus, in a peculiar way, the translation has come before the two originals (English and Bengali). As a result, the two *Gitanjalis* are different. For instance, the first verse from the English *Gitanjali* begins as:

> Thou hast made me endless, such is
> thy pleasure. This frail vessel thou
> emptiest again and again, and fillest it
> ever with fresh life.[9]

This verse does not say anything about the speaker's pride or tears, in contrast to the first poem in the Bengali *Gitanjali*. As if the comparative textual analysis were not baffling enough in itself, the arrangement of the poems in English *Gitanjali* is neither chronological nor consistent with the order of their publication history. The poems are not even arranged with any thematic unity. Each English poem is self-contained, giving an impression that the collection is an anthology of Tagore's verses that he wrote over the entire decade. The very meaning of translation as rendering something "faithfully" is destabilized when comparing the two books by the same author. Yet, the poems are not so alien from their Bengali twins as to become completely new works, no matter in which collection, order, and timeline they might appear. They are a change in the form (*rūpāntar*) and language (*bhashantar*) that is spoken after (*anuvād*), and in some cases before, and paraphrased (*tarjumā*) to only become a shadow (*chhaya*) of some original, as I indicated in the previous chapter when discussing *vishva sahitya* and translation.

In contrast, the most recent English translation of *Gitanjali* by William Radice is remarkably different from Tagore's English *Gitanjali*.[10] First, for translation, Radice uses the manuscript that was preserved among the William Rothenstein papers at Harvard. As a result, the number of poems in Radice's book is 83 instead of 103. Further, the order of poems in the English translation of *Gitanjali*, published in 2011, differs from Tagore's English *Gitanjali*. One could argue that the new translation is literally and metaphorically a new book. Certainly, Radice thinks so.[11] Second, in this new translation of *Gitanjali*, Radice has tried to replicate the various forms and styles of original Bengali poems. This means that unlike Tagore's translations, which were prose translations of his Bengali lyrics in English, Radice has rendered sonnets as sonnets, ballets as ballets, and he has also found equivalent meters in English, when possible.[12] Finally, the book carries Tagore's translations in Appendix C, along with W. B. Yeats's Introduction, which was published in Tagore's self-translation in 1913. By providing all this material and information, Radice suggests that readers can come closer to "Tagore's original conception of the book."[13] However, it is important to note that Tagore's self-translations were not done with the goal of publishing them as a book, for which he received the Nobel Prize.

In fact, when Tagore translated his Bengali *Gitanjali* into English in 1912, he truly did not think of publishing it as a book, let alone receiving the Nobel Prize for it in 1913.[14] In his Nobel Prize acceptance speech, submitted to the Swedish Academy in 1921, Tagore mentions that when he opened the telegram, he could hardly believe what he read.[15] Tagore ends the speech, which he gave in Stockholm, by inviting the entire world to live in harmony in the name of love and humanity—very similar to his idea of *vishva sahitya*. The poet was unable to be physically present to receive the Nobel Prize in 1913. Tagore also did not know that within two decades of translating his *Gitanjali*, his thoughts would change and consolidate into an affirmation of what is often termed as untranslatability, which he would again later contradict when speaking about prose-poems. In a letter written to his friend Amiya Chakravorty in 1934, Tagore writes: "As I glanced through those [poems of *Gitanjali*], I found how carelessly I had once translated them. I feel ashamed today that I did not devote time enough to discern how the originals were divested of the value peculiar to themselves in the process of transference to another language."[16] Tagore's confession to Chakravorty that he was careless while translating his Bengali poems into English is antithetical to what he had written to his niece, Indira Devi, in 1913.

In the letter written to Indira Devi, Tagore describes the circumstances that led him to translate the Bengali *Gitanjali* into English. He writes that he was feeling well rested after a long vacation in the country house at Sealdah and did not have any energy to "sit down and write anything new,"[17] so he "took up the poems of *Gitanjali* and set"[18] himself "to translate them one by one."[19] Immediately after expressing his desire not to write anything new, Tagore reminds his niece that he did not, however, undertake this task in a spirit of reckless bravado. He had, in reality, only felt an impulsive urge to recapture through the medium of another language the feast of feelings and sentiments that his Bengali verses had ignited in him.[20] His remarks echo his ideas of world-making, translation, and *vishva sahitya* that I addressed in the earlier chapter. The letter gives insightful details about how the Bengali *Gitanjali* became the English *Gitanjali*, and it also insists that the act was not reckless, but a creative activity, where the poet and the translator merged while world-making. The letter is certainly of great documentary value for understanding the birth of the English *Gitanjali* as well as Tagore's later prose-poems in Bengali. Tagore continues the story-like narrative in the letter, telling his niece that he gradually filled the pages of a small exercise book, "and with it in my pocket I boarded the ship."[21] He adds:

> The idea of keeping it in my pocket was that when my mind became restless on the high seas, I could recline on a deck-chair and set myself to translate one or two poems from time to time. . . . Rothenstein already had an inkling of my

reputation as a poet from another Indian friend. Therefore, when in the course of conversation he expressed a desire to see some of my poems, I handed him my manuscript with some diffidence. I could hardly believe the opinion he expressed after going through it. He then made over the manuscript to Yeats. The story of what followed is known to you. From this explanation of mine you will see that I was not responsible for the offence, which was due mainly due to the force of circumstance.[22]

As can be seen from the quoted sections, Tagore was surprised to receive the praise for translating his poems from Bengali into English—an act that he had originally done, according to what he reveals to his niece in the letter, in order to keep his mind from getting restless on the sea. Further, the circumstances that led Tagore to the Nobel Prize are extraordinary and merit a brief discussion, too, because they shed light on world-making of *Gitanjali*, where Yeats, Pound, Tagore, and Rothenstein each played a significant role.

William Rothenstein first became impressed "with a short story of Tagore in translation. He asked if there were more, and someone sent him a few of Tagore's poems."[23] When Tagore was in London in June 1912, Rothenstein arranged a meeting at his home so that W. B. Yeats, H. G. Wells, and some other poets could meet him. During that gathering, Yeats read out some of Tagore's poems to the audience. The result: Tagore instantly became known in the London literary circle. At that time, "few people in the West were really prepared for a phenomenon like Rabindranath Tagore, coming from, of all places, India. At best they were ready for a Swami or an adept of the type 'discovered' and made famous by Madame Blavatsky. But what they found was a poet, speaking a language that was universal."[24] Ezra Pound was so impressed with Tagore that he quickly published an essay about his work, along with some of his forthcoming prose-poems from the self-translated English *Gitanjali*, in the December 1912 edition of *Poetry*. In his essay, Pound declared that the appearance of Tagore's self-translated poetry from Bengali into English was a significant event in the history not only of English poetry but of world poetry. There is no explanation of what world poetry is, but perhaps for Pound, here it means the non-Western world.

The essay introduces Tagore to Pound's immediate American audience as a Bengali poet, not an Indian poet, who is the best of the best. Pound writes that Bengal is a nation of fifty million people, and that the great age of Bengali literature is this age, which is synonymous with Rabindranath Tagore. Considering Tagore's position as a creative author and cultural critic in Bengal at that time, this is not an inaccurate assessment. Pound claims that Tagore's work has the same impact as that of Petrarch and classical Greek literature on European Renaissance literature, and he writes that readers' "intimate intercourse with Bengal is the opening of another period."[25] He ends his essay by announcing that the world fellowship[26] is now nearer because of Rabindranath Tagore. To demonstrate the prospect of world fellowship, Pound chooses the following poem by Tagore as an introductory poem for *Poetry*:

> Thou hast made me known to friends whom I knew
> not. Thou hast given me seats in homes not my
> own. Thou hast brought the distant near and made a
> brother of the stranger. I am uneasy at heart when I
> have to leave my accustomed shelter; I forgot that there
> abides the old in the new; and there also thou abidest.[27]

Establishing a poetic self of Tagore through the previous verse who is hesitant in the "new world," but confident that the new world is not that different from the old, Pound publishes the quoted poem and five others in a volume where Tagore is featured along with four American poets John Reed, Alice Corbin Henderson, Clark Ashton Smith, and George Sterling and the Irish poet W. B. Yeats.

It is important to note here that Pound had perhaps personally selected the poems out of the manuscript of English *Gitanjali*, which was not yet in print. Most likely, Tagore did not have a significant role in selecting these poems for publication in the American magazine. By publishing a poem that introduces Tagore as a "stranger," one who expresses unease about meeting a new readership that is not located in the poetic speaker's home, Pound acts as an interlocutor, a world-maker, or a *vishva mānav* (to use Tagore's terminology from *vishva sahitya*) for Tagore's *sahitya*, as well as a custodian of the vicissitudes of literary taste in Anglo-American poetic traditions. In fact, Pound had written in a letter to Harriet Monroe sometime in September 1912 that he would soon send her some poems by the very great Bengali poet, Rabindranath Tagore. Certainly, the quoted verses suggest that world poetry, whatever that might mean for Pound, will always be double-edged; it will be what makes someone feel inadequate, whether at home or beyond. Tagore feels like a "stranger" to his new non-Bengali audience, but the new readers of Tagore in English are also strangers to him. Pound called Tagore's poems "the sensation of the winter,"[28] and he wrote that W. B. Yeats was writing an introduction for them.

Yeats did write that "Introduction," which highlights his world-making of Tagore's *Gitanjali*. If we look at the "Introduction" of the English *Gitanjali*, published by Macmillan a few months after Pound's pronouncements in *Poetry*, we see that it opens with Yeats recounting a confession he had made to a Bengali medical doctor. Yeats writes:

> I know no German, yet if a translation of a German poet had moved me, I would go to the British Museum and find book in English that would tell me something of his life, and of the history of his thought. But though these prose translations from Rabindranath Tagore have stirred my blood as nothing has for years, I shall not know anything of his life, and of the movements of thought that have made them possible, if some Indian traveller will not tell me.[29]

Yeats's inability to find any books about Tagore and the history of his thought in English in the British Museum suggests that at that time, modern and contemporary literature by Indian authors, specifically in translation, was not easily available. It also indicates an abundance of European texts relative to other literary traditions in the British Museum. Since the colonial center has no materials focused on Tagore, Yeats cannot know anything about his contemporary counterparts in India unless he gains access, not through texts, but through people traveling from India to England (or vice versa). Calling Yeats's mesmerized response to Tagore's poetry "natural," the Bengali doctor informs him that there are many poets in India, but no one is like Tagore in India or even in Europe, for his poetry is sung from the west of India to Burma, wherever Bengali is spoken.[30]

For Pound, Tagore's poetry became an event in the history of world poetry, but simultaneously a sensation of a season—meaning, something that might not last long considering that literary tastes change, especially perhaps if the poet and the readers remain "strangers" to each other. Pound started criticizing Tagore's philosophy as early as April of 1913, but Yeats saw something more personal for his world-making in Tagore's work. In his "Introduction," for instance, Yeats writes that he carried the translations of Tagore's verses wherever he went, including railway trains, buses, and restaurants, and often had to close the book "lest some stranger would see"[31] that he was very moved by them. "These lyrics,"[32] he adds, "in the original,"[33] display a world "that I have dreamed all my life long."[34] Some of these remarks by Yeats sound similar to the sentiments expressed by Tagore about literature in his *vishva sahitya* lecture. When Tagore spoke of people singing and telling tales of Mahabharata and Ramayana in his *vishva sahitya* talk, and making them as their own, he did not mean they were all chanting in Sanskrit. Yeats, too, did not know Bengali, but he situates Tagore alongside authors and traditions that he holds dear.

Displaying a sketch of Tagore by Rothenstein next to the title page, the "Introduction" by Yeats compares Tagore's poems with Chaucer's forerunners and the writings of Renaissance European saints and painters. Yeats considers *Gitanjali* as holding a world whose civilization is unbroken, and "where poetry and religion are the same thing."[35] He adds that the verses in *Gitanjali* "will not lie in little well-printed books upon ladies' tables . . . but as the generations pass, travelers will hum them."[36] Yeats's "Introduction" is important as he is world-making Tagore on three levels. First, Yeats uses the figure of the Bengali doctor, a native informant, to emphasize Tagore's position as an exceptional poet at his home and beyond. The Bengali doctor presents Tagore as someone who already has a massive following beyond India while also introducing him as unique and incomparable. Second, the doctor validates Yeats's bodily sensations in response to the beauty of Tagore's poetry as obvious and universal responses. Third, Yeats's "Introduction" marks the prose translations by Tagore as untouched by anyone else, and which in the original carries a dream for which Yeats has always longed.

The readers arrive at these conclusions after Yeats describes the conversation between himself and a Bengali doctor. Though centuries apart, in a way, Yeats's response can be compared with the Oriental scholar William Jones's "Preface," published in 1789, to his translation of the Sanskrit play *Shakuntala* to analyze the similarities between their world-makings of two different authors at separate times in literary history. In this preface, Jones writes that a Brahmin assured him that the *natakas* (plays) were not histories:

> [*Natakas*] abounded with fables; that they were extremely popular works, and consisted of conversations in prose and verse, held before ancient Rájás in their publick assemblies, on an infinite variety of subjects, and in various dialects of India: this definition gave me no very distinct idea; but I concluded that they were dialogues on moral or literary topicks; whilst other Europeans, whom I consulted, had understood from the natives that they were discourses on dancing, musick, or poetry. At length a very sensible Bráhmen, named Ráchácánt, who had long been attentive to English manners, removed all my doubts, and gave me no less delight than surprise, by telling me that our nation had compositions of the same sort, which were publickly represented at Calcutta in the cold season, and bore the name, as he had been informed, of plays. Resolving at my leisure to read the best of them, I asked which of their Nátacs was most universally esteemed;

and he answered without hesitation, Sacontalá, supporting his opinion, as usual among the Pandits, by a couplet to this effect: "The ring of Sacontalá, in which the fourth act, and four stanzas of that act, are eminently brilliant, displays all the rich exuberances of Calidása's genius." I soon procured a correct copy of it; and, assisted by my teacher Rámalóchan, began with translating it verbally into Latin, which bears so great a resemblance to Sanscrit, that it is more convenient than any modern language for a scrupulous interlineary version: I then turned it word for word into English, and afterwards, without adding or suppressing any material sentence, disengaged from the stiffness of a foreign idiom, and prepared the faithful translation of the Indian drama, which I now present to the publick as a most pleasing and authentick picture of old Hindû manners, and one of the greatest curiosities that the literature of Asia has yet brought to light.[37]

Jones informs his readers that plays are extremely popular in India, and that they are in prose and verse, touching on various topics, and in many dialects of India. Though Jones uses the word "dialect" here, he means languages.[38] For earlier orientalist scholars, Sanskrit was *the* language, and all other languages of India were dialects. Just as Yeats had to rely on some "Indian traveller" to tell him about Tagore, Jones had to wait until he met a "sensible" Brahmin familiar with the English manners to quell all his doubts by educating him about the plays, and about Kalidas's *Shakuntala*, the greatest among all of the plays. Note that the "sensible" Brahmin uses a couplet to emphasize the brilliance of Kalidas; I indicate this in the preceding chapter, where I engage with the meaning of comparison in the Indian context. The meeting with the Brahmin, and the couplet quoted by him, lead Jones to declare that his discovery and "faithful" work on *Shakuntala* is the greatest piece of literature from Asia that has so far remained hidden. Jones intimates that his readers can now have the most authentic and exclusive idea about Hindu manners, not Indian manners. Jones, hence, presents *Shakuntala* as an exclusive Hindu experience.

Yeats, too, becomes a champion of Tagore for his English audience, as he saw him someone whose poetry was already sung beyond India, wherever Bengali was spoken. Yeats's well-meaning introduction to Tagore's self-translated English *Gitanjali* marks a shift, where the attention is not on Sanskrit, but on modern Bengali in translation, and where Tagore is being associated with Chaucer and Renaissance authors and saints. At the same time, both Yeats and Jones use the figure of an Indian traveler or Brahmin to authorize the texts, verifying that people in the poet's own native country hold his work in high regard. In addition, Yeats and Jones give the impression that they now have exclusive access to the translations of Indian authors. In the process, Yeats and Jones also suggest their chance encounter either with the text in the original or through some intermediary. Despite the shift in focus from Sanskrit to modern Indian literature, for Yeats Bengali literature is not separate from religion and mystery; perhaps this is a legacy of Occident-Orient stereotypes. Just as Jones associates Hindu manners with the literary play *Shakuntala* and thinks of a Sanskrit play as the authoritative Indian play, Yeats looks at Bengali literature as religious in nature. Certainly, Yeats's "Introduction" to Tagore's English *Gitanjali* reveals his own personal interests, but at the same time it also demonstrates a new interest in reading the translation of modern Indian literature—albeit an interest that is still spiritual and religious in nature.

To come back to Yeats specifically, even before he had met Rabindranath Tagore, he was deeply engaged in the Dublin Theosophy Lodge as well as in astrological studies. In 1908,[39] Yeats wrote that Christianity revolted against nature-worshiping and reduced the human mind into a pebble, which is abstract, and where nothing is reflected. What the European Renaissance painters and poets had rediscovered in the landscapes—the voluptuous body and joyous movement—was already present in the depths of the souls of astrologers, spiritually enlightened people, and students immersed in Eastern contemplation.[40] When Rothenstein introduced Tagore's self-translation of *Gitanjali*, Yeats truly believed that he had finally arrived at something creative that was not marred by the nationalist propagandist literature. In fact, toward the end of the glorious introduction to Tagore's English *Gitanjali*, Yeats writes that "we"—possibly meaning Western, European, or Irish authors—write long books where not even a single page would make writing a pleasurable activity. That is because writing is governed by the same principle that underlies fights, politics, and money: a confidence in the general design plan. Tagore, on the other hand, like Indian civilization in general, is content to discover the soul and "willing to surrender to spontaneity."[41] No wonder Yeats was later disappointed to realize that Tagore's "surrender" to "spontaneity" was not always related to spirituality but was instead sometimes related to his approach toward translation and *sahitya* in *vishva sahitya*. In the following section, I explain how Tagore viewed the translation of *Gitanjali*, suggesting that he, too, like Yeats, actively encouraged a particular kind of world-making while translating his *Gitanjali*.

Tagore's Translations, World-making, and *Gitanjali* in Prose-poems

If Yeats was ready to accept Tagore as a wise man from the East, Tagore also played a role in shaping this image of himself by taking great liberties with his self-translations of *Gitanjali*, as well as the other poems that he translated into English after 1912. Many critics have noticed that after the unexpected success of Tagore's *Gitanjali*, which ran into twelve reprints before he was awarded the Nobel Prize, Tagore began to think that it was the devotional and mystic element that brought him literary success beyond India, and that ingredient was most suited for translation.

It was, however, not just his own work that he often rendered in spiritually leaning versions. After receiving the Nobel Prize in 1913, Tagore published a translation of Kabir, a sixteenth-century poet, which for many years remained the only available translation of Kabir in English. Tagore is often accused of translating Kabir's songs into prosaic English verses, similar to his own translation of *Gitanjali*, while possessing very little knowledge of the language of the original. Instead of keeping Kabir's poems open to several interpretations in English, Tagore showers on them his own personal religiosity and monotheistic interpretations of Hinduism.[42] Kabir's rather earthy use of language, sexual tension, and sharp humor gets transformed into loose, clichéd, mystical verse in Tagore's hands. Thus, a verse[43] by Kabir is paraphrased as follows:[44]

> Beloved come within my house, my body yearns for you.
> Every one says I am your woman, yet of this I have no assurance.
> For until we have slept in one bed, this love of ours remains unconsummated. I cannot eat, I cannot sleep; I am restless within and without. (You are to me) as the lustful man desires a woman, as the thirsty water. Isn't there any helpful soul who could take these words of mine to Hari? For now Kabir is delirious and expires without seeing him.[45]

Tagore translates the same verse as follows:

> My body and my mind are grieved
> for the want of Thee;
> O my Beloved! come to my house.
>   When people say I am Thy bride, I am
>   ashamed; for I have not touched

> Thy heart with my heart.
> Then what is this love of mine? I have
> no taste for food, I have no sleep;
> my heart is ever restless within
> doors and without.
> As water is to the thirsty, so is
> the lover to the bride. Who is there
> that will carry my news to my
> Beloved?
> Kabir is restless: he is dying for sight
> of Him.[46]

In the translated version by Tagore, the bold reference to consummation and yearning for the beloved's body is lost to the grieving mind and body that can only be satiated by the touch of "Thy heart with my heart." There is no reference to pain or grief in the original, just plain desire for the beloved's body. Further, the subjectivity of the speaker is separate from that of Kabir, who is perhaps just witnessing the longing of the speaker for "Hari," present in the original (as quoted in the endnote). In fact, it is unclear from the last line in the original if Kabir's deliriousness, after watching and/or hearing the desire of the speaker, is being further observed by a third person in the poem. All this is lost in Tagore's translation, including the beloved "Hari" replaced with "god," translated as "Thy," "Thee," and "Him." It is pertinent to question the reasons behind Tagore's preferring a spiritual world-making, just not of his own work but also of others.

Tagore's compulsion to translate the theme of divine in literature is well explained by Hiranmay Banerjee. Banerjee writes that in the beginnings of the twentieth century, Tagore had started to believe in his personal god directing the poet's creative life. Tagore called his personal god *jīvan devtā*[47] (the god of life force), who "controlled his activities,"[48] and was helping him create humanism through his *vishva sahitya*. Tagore was convinced that he was fulfilling the wish of his god through his creative output. In a poem written for his personal god in 1892, which he later translated, Tagore wonders if his personal god had chosen him in his mature moments so that he could offer his songs to *jīvan devtā* for his crown. Curiously, Tagore dedicated the poems in the Bengali *Gitanjali* to *jīvan devtā*. The very title "*Gitanjali*" means an offering of songs. Hiranmay Banerjee suggests that the concept of *jīvan devtā* had inspired Tagore to pour out poetry in some of his most difficult times, especially after the death of his wife and daughter.[49] Three entire books of poems—*Gitanjali, Gitali,* and *Gitimalya*—are addressed to *jīvan devtā*.

If the Bengali *Gitanjali, Gitali,* and *Gitimalya* are dedicated to Tagore's personal god, the English *Gitanjali* and *The Gardener* are dedicated to William Rothenstein and W. B. Yeats, respectively, who played an important role in introducing Tagore to his European readers. The dedications indicate Tagore's ideas about the eventual reception as well as the intended readership of his creative work. For Tagore, art was always for someone; that someone helped in world-making art's world. Tagore had also long ago realized that universality as a quality could only be applied to literature when world-making was particular, as indicated in through the concept of *vishva sahitya* in earlier chapter.

Tagore also thought that authors have the greatest potential to cross languages, cultural barriers, and even individual tastes when their work is published in translation. This, too, is evident in his *vishva sahitya* essay, as well as other works where he argued that the world of literature was the real world because it moved toward perfection, though perfection is never realized.[50] If a part of the world, *jagat,* and *sansār* was primed to view Tagore as a religious and spiritual poet because of his *Gitanjali*—dedicated to *jīvan devtā* in the original—he did not see any harm in taking liberties with his work for the *sahit, ānand,* and universalism of that world in translation. Indeed, in "Literary Creation," Tagore writes that authors try to mold their work to meet the "nature of the person to whom it is offered."[51] He also claims that writers express their thoughts to their friends, community, society, and sometimes to the eternal human spirit. Literature bears a testimony not only "of the writer but of those for whom it is written,"[52] suggesting that dedications and readership are important. He adds that literature, like the material world, speaks not only of itself but also of the world that surrounds it. In fact, as Tagore remarks, it is often the strength of the surrounding world—that is, *jagat* and *sansār*—that sustains a piece of literature, rather than its own strength.[53] Hence, his choice to dedicate his English *Gitanjali* to Rothenstein, and *The Gardener* to Yeats, is significant, because these two individuals (along with Pound) played an important role in sustaining the *vishva* in his *Gitanjali* in the world in English and beyond. If and when *vishva sahitya* needs to be studied, critiqued, argued for or against as a construct or an axiom, the world, *jagat,* and *sansār* of that location and its world-making need to be analyzed and examined.

In addition, Tagore's liberties when translating his lyrical Bengali *Gitanjali* into English prose-poems stem from his specific ideas about translating poetry, as addressed in the previous chapter, and his growing interest in the genre of prose-poems. Thus, Tagore is actively participating in world-making the *vishva* in his text in the world, *jagat*, and *sansār* around his text. Before Tagore tried his hand at translating his lyrical Bengali *Gitanjali* as prose-poems into English, Tagore's admirers, including Ajit Chakravarty, Roby Datta, Ananda K. Coomaraswamy, and Sister Nivedita, had translated his work. Additionally, between 1909 and 1912, English translations of some of Tagore's short stories and poems appeared in *The Modern Review*, a well-known literary journal in Kolkata at that time.[54] Similarly, in London, Roby Datta published some of Tagore's poems in translation along with many other European and Sanskrit poets in 1909 in his *Echoes from East and West*. In the "Preface" to his anthology, Datta writes that he kept the word order of the original, but rendered the translated verses in the equivalent metrical form in English in order to preserve the "true genius of the English language."[55] At the time, Roby Datta was a student at Cambridge; he later became a well-known teacher of English Literature at Calcutta University and a skilled translator who evidently anticipated a favorable reaction from Tagore.[56] But when Datta presented the poet with a copy of his lyrical translations of poems, Tagore was not pleased.

Tagore's interest in self-translating was furthered by William Rothenstein's request in 1911. In a letter written to Tagore in February of 1911, Rothenstein reminds Tagore that he would be grateful to receive translations of Tagore's short stories and verses. Before 1912, Tagore had not formally commented on others' translations of his work.[57] In 1912, Tagore wrote to his friend Pamathalal Sen, an Oxford-educated Brahmo leader: "I don't think my poems can be rendered properly into English . . . certainly not in rhymed verse. Maybe it can be done in plain prose. When I go to England I shall try my hand at it."[58] The letter written to Pamathalal Sen is significant as it marks the first time Tagore seriously considered translating his work before reaching London in the summer of 1912. The letter also indicates the active role Tagore takes in world-making the poems in his English *Gitanjali,* as well as his growing interest in prose-poems. As explained by Tagore in the letter written to his niece quoted in the beginning of this chapter, the translation and publication of the English *Gitanjali* as a book did happen suddenly, but Tagore's underlying impulse to world-make himself in mystical prose-poems was not spontaneous. By 1912, Tagore was dissatisfied with Ajit Chakravarty's and Roby Datta's translations of his poems. He strongly disapproved of the metrical translations, and he preferred lucid prose renderings of his verses. What is more important to pay attention to is his desire and resolution to self-translate in order to justify the creativity and the *vishva* in his *Gitanjali* to the world, *jagat*, and *sansār*, which according to him were continuously misrepresented by translators in English. The English *Gitanjali* resulted both from Tagore's dislike for the translations made by admirers of his work, and from his own developing creative interest in prose-poems.[59]

Despite the discrepancy between the first Bengali and English poem from the two *Gitanjalis* that I indicated earlier in the chapter, there are several poems that are rendered close to the original. Tagore was able to translate the *rasa* or sap of the poems, as suggested in the previous chapter when I discussed his ideas about *vishva sahitya*. For instance, both the Tagore poems, Poem 18 in the Bengali *Gitanjali* and its English counterpart and Poem 22, are very close to each other. I produce here a few lines of both the poems, followed by my translation of the Bengali verse:

In the deep shadows of the rainy July, with
secret steps, thou walkest, silent as night,
eluding all watchers.
  To-day the morning has closed its
eyes, heedless of the insistent calls of
the loud east wind, and a thick veil has
been drawn over the ever-wakeful blue
sky.[60]

আজি শ্রাবণ-ঘন-গহন-মোহে
গোপন তব চরণ ফেলে
নিশার মতো নীরব ওহে
সবার দিঠি এড়ায়ে এলে।
প্রভাত আজি মুদেছে আঁখি,
বাতাস বৃথা যেতেছে ডাকি,
নিলাজ নীল আকাশ ঢাকি
নিবিড় মেঘ কে দিল মেলে।[61]

In March 1913, Ezra Pound had declared the previous poem beautiful and stated that he did not find Tagore's usage of "thou" and "thy" odd;[62] Pound himself was using these archaic English words while translating poems from European languages. Even in its English reincarnation, with the archaic English "thou" and "walkest" that remind one of the King James Bible, the poem conveys a longing for the beloved, who is the only "solitary" traveler in the "deserted streets" on a day when the ever-prying "blue sky" is covered with a thick veil of monsoon clouds. The extraordinariness of the meeting is conveyed and emphasized by

Tagore in the English version through the single-worded last line of the first stanza, "sky," and the final brief line of the last stanza, "a dream," suggesting the unreality of the moment offered by a chance occurrence.

In the Bengali version, however, the longing, the extraordinariness of the event, the meeting, and the secrecy of the solitary traveler are conveyed through a layer of sonorous semantics,[63] which evoke the auditory and visual arrival of the monsoon clouds in the "shameless blue sky,"[64] and the solitary traveler on the street[65] through alliteration and internal rhyme. Although the metrical rhyme scheme and rhythm are lost in the English version (as they would be in any language), it is difficult to overlook that the Bengali poem's central theme (the dream-like moment) comes across via the effective short last lines of the two-stanza prose-poem—even when the two poems are not chronologically compatible in the two books.

Further, Tagore can be close to the original, and an effective prose-poem poet, even when he likes to add religious and spiritual overtones. To illustrate, take Poem 3 in the English *Gitanjali*. This poem begins as follows:

> I know not how thou singest, my master! I
> ever listen in silent amazement.[66]

In the Bengali *Gitanjali*, the foregoing poem's counterpart is Poem 22:

> তুমি   কেমন করে গান কর যে গুণী,
>   অবাক হয়ে শুনি, কেবল শুনি ।[67]

Translation:

> Let me hear how you sing,
> enrapt let me hear, only hear.

When comparing the two Tagore poems, it is not hard to observe the similarities. I have provided my translation of Bengali verse into English so that Tagore's English version can be evaluated. Both poems express a sense of wonder and amazement at the extraordinary skills of the singer in captivating the enraptured heart of the poet, who is already in a trance. In that respect, the translation is thematically very close to the original. In the Bengali version, though, there is no indication that the singer is a "master" of the poetic speaker. Bengali is most of the time a genderless language where verbs and pronouns do not specify gender in a sentence; hence, what was just a play between two ungendered people in Bengali, via the pronouns "you" and "I," takes an austere gendered tone with a word such as "master," that almost give a biblical overtone to the English afterlife of the poem.

Certainly, Tagore has not been able to please everyone with his translation. Dismissing Tagore's translational efforts, Sujit Mukherjee writes that the English *Gitanjali*'s unique position and reception were the "result of the author endeavoring to be his own translator,"[68] which culminated in a transformation rather than a translation of the work. On *Gitanjali*'s translation, Mukherjee adds, "Rabindranath Tagore himself must share part of the blame in conspiring with the rest of the world to perpetuate the myth of this work being a 'translation.'"[69] Nevertheless, one major comparative literature critic, Buddhadeva Bose, softened his earlier criticisms. Having formerly described the English *Gitanjali* as just an *offering*—a sacrifice—in English, a miracle of translation, where the miracle is not in survival, but in reincarnation on a foreign soil, lacking the "sensual metrical arrangements of the original,"[70] Bose writes that he now partially agrees with the self-translations. The Bengali *Gitanjali*'s mellifluous rhyme scheme and lyricism are greatly acknowledged and often compared with Tagore's dry prose translations of the English *Gitanjali*, done in an Edwardian diction that no longer appeals to modern readers. Attributing the genesis of *Gitanjali* to a sincere creative impulse, Bose, a self-translator himself, believes that if Tagore had been obliged to be led by another poet or even a translator, this impulse would not have carried him far.[71]

However, unlike many authors who are happy to read a translated reflection of themselves in foreign literatures, Tagore not only disliked others' translations of his work into English; he also remained unhappy with his self-translation[72] and world-making of the *vishva* in his *sahitya*. Even after Yeats voiced appreciation for Tagore's translation of *Gitanjali* at the dinner party arranged by Rothenstein, Tagore remained continuously wary of the reception of his translation—perhaps justifiably so. In a letter written to his friend Kshiti Mohan Sen in June 1912, he remarks, "People here have taken to my work with such excessive enthusiasm that I cannot really accept it. My impression is that when a place from which nothing is expected somehow produces something, even an ordinary thing, people are amazed—that is that state of mind here."[73] It is noteworthy that after making this observation—which clearly suggests the Occident-Orient conflict, a legacy of the dying nineteenth century—Tagore looks at his journey to England as some sort of divine pilgrimage that God has intended for him:

> It was for this that my God dragged me to this country at my age—for it is literature, art and suchlike that are the real bridges uniting one country with another. Maybe from all this I should eliminate my personal self and humbly acknowledge the best in my writing without hesitation. . . . I feel as if God is

expressing His own gladness through others' praise of my work; it is as if He has brought me from East to West in order to make me aware of the fact of his gladness.... I am preparing myself to submit to the honour with my forehead touching the dust.[74]

Notice in the previous letter that Tagore, quite appropriately, thinks of literature and art as the only uniting forces between nations, and he admits that he should eliminate his "personal self and humbly acknowledge" the success of his work. Throughout the previous passage, one can see some resonance with Tagore's idea of *vishva sahitya* as unifying force; he acknowledges that the European perception of his work may reflect the Occident-Orient conflict, but he also voices hope that literature can transcend the East-West divide. Further, he thinks that literature is an agent of God that can bring unification, where he should not be excessively appreciated—ideas that I examined through *vishva sahitya* in Chapter 1. In that unification, he views himself as a chosen one, perhaps a *vishva mānav*, who could foment friendship between the East and the West.

Tagore believed his enthusiastic acceptance in England to be part of some divine plan, a viewpoint visible even in the letter that he wrote to Yeats after he sent off the introduction to *Gitanjali*:

> It has been such a great joy to me to think that things that I wrote in a tongue not known to you should at last fall in your hands and that you should accept them with so much enjoyment and love.... What my soul offered to my master in the solitude of an obscure corner of the world must be brought before the altar of man where hearts come together and tongues mingle like the right and the left palms if hands joined in the acts of adoration.... My heart fills with gratitude and I write to you this letter to say the appreciation from a man like you comes to me not only as a reward for my lifelong devotion to literature but as a token that my songs have been acceptable to Him, and He has led me over the sea to this country to speak to me His approval of my works through your precious friendship.[75]

This passage is replete with sentiments suggesting Tagore's gratitude toward Yeats and God. The letter also shows Tagore's firm faith in his personal god, guiding his life as *vishva mānav* and his work for the noble purpose of *vishva sahitya*. It is important, however, that Tagore mentions his verses having originally been written in a language unknown to Yeats "in the solitude of an obscure corner of the world,"[76] as though the word, *jagat*, and *sansār* of Bengal's millions of people had vanished from his own view as well as from Yeats's eyes. The letter also indicates Tagore's realization that his self-translations brought him an unprecedented glory and instant fame in English,[77] where hearts came together and tongues mingled in acts of adoration.

Conversely, Tagore's response to Yeats contrasts sharply with a letter that he wrote in 1932 to his lifelong friend William Rothenstein. Tagore writes:

> Poets are proverbially vain and I am no exception. Therefore if I cherish even an exaggerated notion of the value of my own poems which are in Bengali I am sure you will half humorously tolerate it. But I am no such fool as to claim an exorbitant price for my English which is a borrowed acquisition coming late in my life. . . . But yet sometimes I feel almost ashamed that I whose undoubted claim has been recognized by my countrymen to a sovereignty in our own world of letters should have waited till it was discovered by the outside world in its own true majesty and environment, that I should ever go out of my way to court attention of others having their own language for their enjoyment and use. At least it is never the function of a poet to personally help in the transportation of his poems to an alien form. . . . However, you must own that you alone were to blame for this and not myself.[78]

A careful reader will notice that Tagore still suffers from the pangs of translating *Gitanjali*, even two decades after receiving the Nobel Prize. He almost feels that he went out of his way to speak in a language that he acquired later in his life (which is untrue), and he laments the fact that though his literary genius was recognized in his own home, it was only celebrated by the world once he was "discovered" by the outside world because Tagore went out of his way to translate it. And then, as if this confession was not more than enough, he makes his friend a partner in crime in his glorious fame. Regardless of Tagore's complicated association with the self-translation of the *vishva* in *Gitanjali*, he used translation as a creative, humanistic, and self-marketing enterprise to connect with his immediate world, *jagat*, and *sansār*.

As a young child Tagore had translated the entire text of *Macbeth* into Bengali verse. Later in life, he took translation to another level. Tagore spontaneously paraphrased Kalidas's work and extracts from the Upanishads, and toward the last stages of his life he produced a version of Eliot's "Journey of the Magi" in Bengali[79]—not just because he admired Eliot, but because he was continuing the experimentation with the prose-poem form that he had begun in his English *Gitanjali*. Tagore is one of the very few poets from his era who took on the task of disseminating his own work via translation. Goethe had certainly enjoyed his French reception, and he once claimed that he preferred reading his *Faust* in French over reading it in German, but he did not translate it. Baudelaire, on the other hand, had made Poe a great man in France, but left it to Swinburne and Symons to bring his own work to England.[80] Tagore, a *vishva mānav* in his mind, took the mission on himself. Indeed, to appreciate Tagore and his *Gitanjalis*, one must be open to reading him as practicing the philosophy of *sahit*, *ānand*, and *vishva mānav* of *vishva sahitya*. In fact, as Tagore wrote in a letter to his friend Ajit Chakravarty in 1913, to "be less at home in English may turn out to be an advantage especially in the matter of translating shorter lyrics,"[81] which he was planning to translate as prose-poems. Tagore's remark indicates his idea of *vishva sahitya*, where a translation is a shadow. At the same time, the observation suggests Tagore's creative interest in prose-poems.

Whether the English *Gitanjali* should be considered only a product of translation is an issue of great debate. Sometimes Tagore called the poems translations, only to later contradict himself in letters written to his well-wishers. The Nobel Prize citation announcement declares that Tagore was recognized for the award "because of his profoundly sensitive, fresh and beautiful verse, by which, with consummate skill, he has made his poetic thought, expressed in his own English words, a part of the literature of the West."[82] The citation echoes the Orient-Occident relations that I have discussed at few points in this chapter. It also suggests that the Nobel Prize committee affirmed Tagore's own view of his poetry as a bridge between the East and the West, expressed in a few letters quoted in the chapter. Nevertheless, the citation does not directly say anything about the translations being from Bengali, as if agreeing with Tagore's ideas on translation and *vishva sahitya*, but instead emphasizes that Tagore expressed "his poetic thought" in "his own English words." Further, the phrase "a part of the literature of the West" suggests that the Nobel Prize was awarded because Tagore's work added value to the Western canon (whatever that Western canon meant then). Tagore himself remained uncertain about the nature of his English *Gitanjali*, though we know that he did not consider being awarded the Nobel Prize as *vishva sahitya* (as suggested in the earlier chapter with Tagore's example of Tennyson-Kipling). The *vishvas* in his *Gitanjalis*, however, do constitute what *he* meant by *vishva sahitya*.

Despite Tagore's conflicting remarks about his prose translations of *Gitanjali* in English, it represents a milestone in Tagore's poetic career. The English *Gitanjali* is indeed a collection of his short verses rendered as prose-poems, a genre he later inaugurated in Bengali literature with the publications of *Lipika*, published in 1922, and *Punascha*, published in 1932. In fact, in a lecture titled "The Prose Poem,"[83] delivered at Shantiniketan in 1939 and published in 1940, Tagore mentions that poetry expresses itself better when free from ornamentations such as rhyme and meter. He writes: "I had translated my *Gitanjali* into English prose."[84] Many distinguished English poets, he writes, accepted his work as part of "their own literature,"[85] suggesting that he had transcended all superficial boundaries and become part of *their* world, *jagat*, and *sansār*. The effusive praise embarrassed Tagore, as the English *Gitanjali* did not have what he then thought was poetic then: rhyme and meter. But since the world, or *jagat*, or *sansār*, was able to extract *ānand* from his prose-poems, the poetic sap of the *vishva* in his *Gitanjali*, Tagore continued to actively translate his poems into English. In fact, he declares in this lecture that a prose *Gitanjali* was "no loss; on the contrary, a verse translation"[86] would have been "condemned and held unworthy of esteem."[87] We might pause here and ask: unworthy by whom, and for whom? By his *jīvan devtā*? Or, by the world, *jagat*, and *sansār* that surrounded the *vishva* in *Gitanjali*, whether that world be in Bengali, in English, or, say, in Spanish?

World-making of *Gitanjali* in Spanish

Gitanjali's entry as a book into Indian languages was slower than the growth of its popularity in European languages. In that respect, Spanish presents a fascinating example, for it offers the possibility of a south-south dialogue that possibly circumvents the center of the British Empire. Moreover, Spanish's identity as the language of Spain—a colonizing power—and a language of the majority of Latin American countries that were once colonized puts it in equivalence with English. However, Spanish's position in the United States and beyond might not always be at par with English, making it a language of the Global South. Further, for many thinkers and poets in Latin America, Tagore presented as the first contact with India, and vice versa. Indeed, Tagore's connection with Latin America is significant considering that he had been to Latin America even before he had visited many parts of India. For instance, Tagore visited Kerala for the first time in 1922,[88] just two years before he visited South America. By 1922, Tagore had been to Europe twice, and he had already become quite popular in the European literary circles. The first Spanish translation of *Gitanjali* had become available in 1915.

In contrast to his European translations, the first Hindi translation of *Gitanjali* appeared in 1921.[89] By then the book had already been translated into German, Spanish, French, and Danish. In fact, during the years 1914–24, there were more translations of *Gitanjali* in a book format in German than in Hindi, more in Spanish than in Nepali, and more in French than in Kannada. *Gitanjali*'s translations in a book format first appeared in Marathi in 1917, in Gujarati in 1918, and in Malayalam in 1926.[90] Further, a number of these published translations of *Gitanjali* were made into Indian languages from Tagore's English *Gitanjali*—not from the Bengali original.[91] Conversely, Tagore's presence in Spanish can be traced back to 1915, where his fame had reached countries like Chile and other Latin American countries.[92] For example, Gabriela Mistral described being inspired by the Bible, Tagore, and Tolstoy. Pablo Neruda was inspired by Tagore as well; and his famous poem "En mi cielo al crepúsculo eres como una nube" (Poem XVI) published in 1924 bears strong similarities with Tagore's song in Spanish: "Tú eres la nube crepuscular del cielo / de mis fantasías," poem XXX of *The Gardener*.[93] Octavio Paz argued[94] that Tagore's popularity in Latin America cannot solely be explained by the affinities that exist between the Latin American world and the "Indo-occidental baroque" of the Bengali nor by the fact that Tagore was from the Orient. Paz claimed that the true explanation of Tagore's success lies in the magnetic power of his poems. The younger generation read them with same fervor with which their grandparents had read great Romantic poetry a hundred years back. He adds that an entire generation in Mexico grew up reading an anthology prepared by the educator José Vasconcelos in 1920, which included the translated works of Tagore along with selections from Dante, Cervantes, Plato, Tolstoy, and Goethe.[95] Perhaps Mistral's interest in Tagore, too, solidified from the fact that Tagore had been canonized by José Vasconcelos.

However, Tagore's presence in Europe and Latin America defies simple summarization.[96] Howard Young points out:

> First of all, one must acknowledge his enormous popularity; extensively translated and widely reprinted, Tagore's books have sold better than many Spanish-language poets. During World War II, long after Tagore's idolatry faded in Europe, Latin Americans, including members of the working classes in Argentina, Uruguay, and Chile, continued to read *Gitanjali* and *The Gardener*, and in Spain today poets still compete for the Rabindranath Tagore prize for poetry.[97]

Indeed, Tagore's presence in Latin America has been enormous. As Paz remarks, Tagore was the first substantial acquaintance from the "Orient" for many Latin Americans. A look at Tagore's world-making in Latin America unavoidably leads to his most visible association with Victoria Ocampo, who singlehandedly and consistently published his short stories, poems, and essays in *Sur* and *La Nación*. A rich correspondence between the two had ensued once Tagore returned to India after living for some time in Ocampo's house in Argentina. Just after his trip, Tagore wrote and dedicated a collection of prose-poems for her. In a letter written in October 1925 that accompanied the book *Purabi*, published the same year, Tagore wrote to Ocampo:

> I am sending to you a Bengali book of poems which I wish I could place in your hands personally. I have dedicated it to you though you will never be able to know what it contains. A large number of poems in this book were written while I was in San Isidro. My readers who will understand these poems will never know who my Vijaya is with whom they are associated. I hope this book will have the chance of a longer time with you than its author had.[98]

It is a well-known fact in Bengal that the two had struck up a deep friendship. Ocampo writes to Tagore in 1925 that she is working on his play *Red Oleanders* and that one of her friends in Italy, Dario Niccodermi, writes plays and stages them. Tagore would be much impressed by *Red Oleanders*.[99] Ocampo's letter is replete with sentiments that show a strange mix of literary and personal interests. But Ocampo remained Tagore's faithful publicist in Latin America for her entire life. The archives of *La Nación* and *Sur* reveal that Tagore was published and republished.[100] For many Tagore readers in India—specifically, in Bengal—Argentina became known as the land where Tagore's muse "Vijaya" lived. In addition, after the success of *Gitanjali*, for many Spanish and Latin American poets Tagore became the new Oriental artist and philosopher to follow—even after his fame had declined in Europe.

The first Spanish translation of Tagore's *Gitanjali* was prepared by Zenobia Camprubí de Jiménez from English, with Juan Ramón Jiménez's assistance. The two had fallen in love with each other while translating Tagore, and they remained his most ardent translators, publishing no fewer than twenty-two Spanish versions of his work from 1915 to 1965.[101] The couple's translations of Tagore were warmly received by critics and readers alike. In fact, the growing demand for Tagore translations inspired other translators to enter the competition. Beginning in 1917, the couple printed warnings on the books noting that they were the only translators authorized by Rabindranath Tagore to publish his works in Spanish; nonetheless, the pirated translations of Tagore's books only increased.

Howard Young is right in suggesting that Tagore's success worked "as a two-edged sword for his Spanish mediators."[102] On the one hand, the couple received steady 5–10 percent translation royalties from Macmillan; on the other hand, Tagore's books sold in the thousands, while Juan Ramón Jiménez had to accept "the fact that his books collected dust on shelves."[103] Young points out that the early translations done by the couple reflected in tone, style, and diction "the best of Juan Ramón Jiménez,"[104] whose "own preoccupations with the dualities of earth and sky, finite and infinite, were similar to Tagore's."[105] Young adds that while Tagore was a poet who had translated his poems into a foreign mode of speech, keeping it close to the Edwardian diction, Jiménez was a poet "translating into a language whose dominant lyrical discourse he had helped to fashion."[106]

The desire to create a more robust connection between Spanish and Bengali is visible in a 1918 letter written to Tagore by Zenobia Camprubí de Jiménez. She writes that it has been three years since the couple translated *Gitanjali* and that she would like to visit India. She requests that Tagore or some of his friends help the couple develop a new edition in Spanish that would be produced after understanding the Bengali lyrics. She further writes in the letter that the couple does not know Bengali—in fact, no one in Spain does—but there is so much similarity between India and Andalusia that Tagore is more deeply felt there than in Europe and America, where he is widely read. The letter also lists out all the English works of Tagore that the couple has read. Indeed, Juan Ramón Jiménez was so impressed by Tagore's "The Post Office" that he composed a new piece inspired by it.[107] Curiously, soon after the Jiménez couple brought out their translation of *Gitanjali* in 1915, a rival translation, *Gitanjalí: poemas místicos*, became available in Mexico in 1918, rendered by Pedro Requena Legarreta with a prologue by Joaquín Méndez Rivas. Possibly, the letter by Zenobia Camprubí de Jiménez was written to "better" the Spanish edition to compete with the new translation published in Mexico.

Unlike the Jiménez translation, which did not discuss any problems encountered by the translators in rendering Tagore's English verses into Spanish, the prologue by Méndez Rivas informs readers that Requena Legarreta encountered two obstacles while translating. First, the poems were not an *exact* translation from the original, even when translated by the poet himself—something that the Jiménez version did not stress. Second, the poems had their roots in Upanishadic philosophy and mysticism. Méndez Rivas describes[108] how Requena Legarreta overcame these obstacles by spending many hours in the study of the philosophy of the Upanishads, which is very different from the other translations of Tagore in Spanish. Along with this, he analyzed Bengali rhythm, cadence, prosodic values, and meter; Bengali is essentially a euphonic language and is propitious to rhyme. This is in part why the Spanish compositions are closer to the original,[109] meaning Bengali here, not English. Another reason, Méndez Rivas writes, is that Tagore himself gave Requena Legarreta several interviews in New York and provided helpful information. Tagore had traveled to the United States after receiving the Nobel Prize in the 1910s. Méndez Rivas writes that the translator had several interviews with Tagore in New York and gathered prosodic and metrical knowledge of Bengali by familiarizing himself with Upanishadic philosophy and theology.

Let us compare the first few lines of Poem 3 in Jiménez and Requena Legarreta's translations with Tagore's Poem 3 in the English *Gitanjali* to see its two Spanish afterlives. I have already compared a few lines of this poem, which features as Poem 22 in Bengali *Gitanjali*, with the English version in the earlier part of this chapter.

Jiménez:

¿Cómo cantas Tú, Señor? ¡Siem-
pre te escucho mudo de asombro![110]

Requena Legarreta:

Yo no sé como cantas, dueno mío;
Absorto escucho tu cancíon diviana;[111]

Tagore:

I know not how thou singest, my master! I
ever listen in silent amazement.[112]

Both the translators use the informal "you" in their verses as evident through corresponding informal verbs. Though Jiménez's version directly speaks to God right in the beginning, with an informal but capital "Tú" ("¿Cómo cantas Tú, Señor?"), Requena Legarreta's version addresses God in the final line with the word "Señor" ("A mi pecho, Señor, ha cautivado/ tu inagotable música sublime!").[113] Both the poems are a close afterlife of the English version, but unlike Bengali, which was able to conceal theology, the identity of the speaker, and gender, Spanish is as helpless as English. One could argue that there is no need to assess the Spanish versions with Bengali, when writing a research monograph or teaching students, as they owe their life to the English translation or world-making done by the poet himself. Even if the world-making and translation was not done by the poet in English, one could question whether comparing

Spanish verses with Bengali is really needed. Then again, a purist could argue to only read *Gitanjali* in Bengali, and never compare it with any other language. Equally, an argument could be made that there is so much to read in Bengali, just *Forget English!*[114] Possibly, comparing Spanish versions with each other in this particular section of the chapter by itself is enough. Though, according to Tagore's concept of *vishva sahitya*, even that would be pointless. Joy or *ānand* is beyond language. Of course, if one wishes to speak of literature, comparing and analyzing *Gitanjalis* in various locations, timelines, and languages is central to arrive at conclusions that are not unworldly.

Certainly, there is no doubt that Tagore's reception in Europe and the United States, and *Gitanjali*'s success, was partly based on the fact that he was perceived as a wise Oriental poet singing songs when the world was on the brink of the First World War. He, too, played a big role in validating that perception. By the time Tagore visited South America in the 1920s, he had acquired a dubious reputation—almost that of a mystic or a prophet.[115] Ocampo, for instance, refers to Tagore as "*Gurudeva*" (teacher) in her letters. She was not alone in being mesmerized by Tagore; Ocampo wrote in her long piece *Tagore Centenary Volume* in 1961 that the Theosophists came in great numbers, imagining that Tagore was one of them, and one unknown lady insisted on seeing Tagore immediately because she wanted to have her dreams interpreted. In her dreams she had seen an elephant, and since Tagore was coming from India where elephants existed, she assumed that Tagore would know the meaning of these dreams.[116] Tagore himself wrote in 1927 that after one of his lectures, he "was approached by one who wished to learn from me personal secrets about some other individual whom I had never known."[117] In Brazil, writes Cecilia Meireles, Tagore had become such a familiar name that some people confused him with other old European poets.[118] After all, Yeats, too, was reminded of old dead European poets and saints when reading Tagore. Meireles recalls an occasion where Tagore's poetry was being discussed and a fairly famous person was calmly heard to announce that "Tagore isn't alive today . . . he's a very old poet, far away back in the past,"[119] even though he was a living modern Indian poet writing in Bengali and English. Like the Mahabharata, Ramayana, and *Meghdutam* (all cited by Tagore in his *vishva sahitya* essay), *Gitanjali* and Tagore had come to belong to everyone, dead and alive.

For Tagore, as illustrated in Chapter 1, *vishva sahitya* emphasized the importance of the multiplicity of the text through various world-makings so that all human beings' expressions could find a place and a sense of kinship in the *vishva* of the *sahitya* in world, *jagat*, and *sansār*. Clearly, then, the whereabouts of world literature for a literary scholar are *not* exactly in the indestructible *vishva*, but in location(s), timestamp(s), and language(s) of literature(s). Since world-making is not apolitical but indicative of factors that sustain the universal and particular of a world synchronically and diachronically, in translation, or in the original, it is the study of a world *around* and *in* a text that *is* world literature. For instance, in order to, understand and appreciate *Gitanjali*—whether just in Bengali, or English, or Spanish, or some other literary tradition—the world *around* it, and the world *in* it, becomes important. In that sense, the *vishva* analyzed through the close reading of verses is significant. Moreover, since world-makings of that *vishva* in world, *jagat*, and *sansār* are not flat, comparisons of translations, originals, languages, timelines, and timestamps are required. Could world literature, then, be a nebulous category, a malady of American consumerism,[120] or a mindless pursuit of an ideal? Definitely not. World literature is tangible, comparable, and graspable because it exists in the original(s) as well as translation(s), in *jagat* and *sansār*, through the *vishva* in *sahitya*.

3

The World Is in the Lyrics

Not everyone can be a Nobel laureate. None of the *chhayavaad*[1] poets who thrived[2] at the height of European high modernism—Jaishankar Prasad, Suryakant Tripathi Nirala, Sumitranandan Pant, and Mahadevi Varma—became a Pound, Eliot, Yeats, or Tagore, nor is their poetry seen as exhibiting modernist sensibilities.[3] In fact, as I will indicate in this chapter, most *chhayavaad* poets were not even read by their immediate critics as Tagore's *vishva mānavs* engaged in some sort of world-making for *vishva sahitya*. Instead, these critics read the *chhayavaad* poets as anachronistically following British romantics or poorly imitating Tagore. To complicate matters, sometimes *chhayavaad* poets accused each other of plagiarizing Tagore from Bengali into Hindi. For instance, Suryakant Tripathi Nirala and Sumitranandan Pant bitterly argued over which one of them had copied Tagore and initiated *mukta-chhand* (free verse) in Hindi poetry[4]—something that suggests Tagore's immense popularity in early twentieth century Indian literary contexts.

Certainly, very few authors have opportunities like Tagore, who actively participated in the world-making of *Gitanjali* as a text celebrating the universal spirit when modernism was gaining strength in Europe. Neither are most authors self-translators nor do many have the fortune to acquire the iconic status of Kalidas, Tennyson, or Vidyapati in their respective worlds, while living or dead. For Tagore, since *vishva sahitya* was beyond the material world of *jagat* and *sansār*, the replacement of one author over the other in a literary canon was unacceptable. In fact, he hardly thought of a literary canon when he spoke of authors and *vishva sahitya*. Regardless, world-making is neither arbitrary nor unworldly. As explained in Chapter 2, world-making is intricately intertwined with a universe or *vishva* in a text and a world, or *jagat*, and *sansār* around a text.

Besides, in some instances, the *vishva* or universe in a text can be in a disagreement with the immediate world, *jagat*, and *sansār* around that text. This disagreement makes the world-making of that text contentious, as I suggest in this chapter through analysis of *chhayavaad* lyrics, where the question is not then about the politics of translation[5] but rather the politics of world-making of the original in the original language at the place of its origin. Clearly, nowhere do the consequences of world-making become more apparent than in the canonization of texts, authors, genres, and literary movements. This is true regardless of a text's position in comparative, or world literary debates, in translation or in the original, whether in a classroom setting or in published monographs, in India or beyond. Correspondingly, the world-making of a *vishva* or universe in a text at the place of its origin (and elsewhere) not only bears the key to the text's eventual existence, or the opposite in a world, *jagat*, and *sansār*; this world-making also offers reasons for synchronic and diachronic trends in literary studies regarding authors, genres, and literary movements in a particular world. Further, despite the unquestionable temporality of canonization and non-canonization of literary texts, awareness and knowledge of the nitty gritty of (non)-canonization thicken the world (universe or *vishva*) in a literary text and even literary movements. In this respect, lyric poetry—as I emphasize in this chapter by discussing the world in the lyrics of *chhayavaad* poets—is a rich source for theorizing on the worldliness of world-making, canonization, non-canonization, and the world in a text in world literary debates in translation or in the original. This is because lyrics are often thrice removed from the worldliness of theorizations, whether in translation or in the original.[6]

First, lyrics are usually assumed to be subjective expressions that engage with a world created by the poetic speaker in a specific moment. For instance, *chhayavaad* poets were criticized for this by their immediate critics in Hindi. The personalized utterances are often assumed to be bound to the world in a lyric, even though each time a lyric is read by someone its meaning multiplies and changes in time and space. In addition, lyrics, by virtue of their brevity, produce personalized world-makings within minutes of being read that could go unrecorded, unless one is working on a publication or teaching a class. Second, usually, when it comes to lyric poetry, the emphasis is on who is doing the *speaking* rather than who is doing the *listening*. In turn, this emphasis produces an immediate mirage between the world, universe in a text, and the immediate world around a text as the boundaries between listener(s) and speaker(s) in and outside the lyric world are constantly shifting and blurred. Undeniably, a novel could produce the same effects, but the generic world in a novel is usually denser and more tangible than that of a lyric because of its scale, plotlines, and characters.

Third, in the realm of world literature or comparative literature debates, poetry has often been ignored when it comes to theorizing poetics or disciplinary concerns, probably because of its assumed untranslatability.[7] Moreover, the stress placed on the inability to accurately translate lyric poems because of their formal elements (rhyme, meter, etc.,) puts them in a disadvantaged position compared to novels and short stories. This disadvantage is certainly conspicuous when literary systems are hesitant to accept translations as change in language, speaking after, change in form, paraphrase, or shadow of the original, as explained in earlier chapters. Translations, when not understood as rewriting and recontextualizing of world-making processes, posit relentless and often meaningless debates on fidelity.

One could argue, then, that as a genre, poetry is neither used for justifying nor defending disciplinary practices of comparative literature or world literature. Hence, these days, poetry's role in world-making and canonizing is minimal; it is at the periphery. Yet the sheer centrality and intensity of the world, or *vishva*, in a lyric makes this genre critical for discussing tensions between world-making and a world in a text, and that text's eventual canonization or non-canonization. In addition, as I suggest by analyzing *chhayavaad* lyrics, any potential conflict between world-making and the world or universe or *vishva* in a lyric throws light on the shadow canons, hyper-canons, and counter-canons[8] of a literary tradition. Understandably, such discussions might not lead to the *ānand* or joy that Tagore held dear in *vishva sahitya*. Still, the rich potentiality of the *vishva* or world in the lyrics suggests the continuous tussle between the world in a text and the world around that text. This perpetual tussle emphasizes the delicate dance that a comparatist might have to do when speaking for or against world literature in a specific location and timeframe, whether in India or elsewhere, in the original or in translation, in Hindi or beyond English.

The World in Lyrics

The most striking feature of *chhayavaad* verses is their focus on the subjectivity of the poetic "I," which was mostly absent in the preceding movement. In fact, *chhayavaad* poets are identified as writing "Meiṅ-Shailī" (I-style)[9] lyrics. Often in these lyrics, the poetic "I" directly speaks to animate or inanimate objects in an emotive voice. Sometimes the addressee is tangible, sometimes not. *Chhayavaad* was a loosely connected literary movement in Hindi that thrived during the years between the two world wars, though lyrics that could be characterized as *chhayavaad* had started emerging before the First World War. The movement did not have a formal manifesto (like the Progressive Writers of India) or any organized meetings to further their poetic outlook. Unlike literary movements such as *Dvivedi Yug* that were identified and named after authors, *chhayavaad* was named after a style seen in lyrics produced in Hindi in the early twentieth century. As Sumitranandan Pant recalls,[10] the four prominent poets of this movement—Prasad, Pant, Nirala, and Varma—were responding to the call of their age, without knowing that they belonged together as a group, by composing lyrics that used the subjective "I." They were identifying the call of the age as expressing, to use Pant's words, the *"nayā mānushyatava"* (new humanism) of a world that is negotiating *"vishva chetnā "* (world psyche) and *"vishva jīvan"* (world life) in their *"vyaktivādī"* (individualistic) poems. However, many critics of *chhayavaad* criticized the "I-style" poetry as self-obsessed and abstruse, even long after the movement had subsided.

In fact, while defending *chhayavaad* in the 1960s, Pant reminds his readers that to not see *chhayavaad* touched by the knowledge of worldwide companionships[11] and the background of world powers[12] would be unjust toward the newness of the subjective "I" in the *chhayavaad* poems. He further adds that such misreading only perpetuates the dogma according to which the poems were negatively judged at the time.[13] Pant adds that the time in which *chhayavaad* took shape was the age when nationalism had changed into internationalism, and when the poet's role was to speak of a *"vishva ātmā"* (world spirit) that was supported by the innovations in science that made possible a *"vishva sānyojan."*[14] Significant to note, even in the 1960s Pant is highlighting and explaining the basic principles of *chhayavaad*, such as that unlike the poet-saints of the *bhakti* traditions, who sought for a god in their souls, the *chhayavaad* poets looked for a *"vishva ātmā"* and searched for a *"vishva jīvan."* The purpose of Pant's detailed explanation of the philosophy of *chhayavaad* (when the movement had already faded away) is twofold. First, though *chhayavaad* had faded away by mid-1940, many critics continued to attack *chhayavaad* as escapist in nature.[15] In fact, Varma, like Pant here, published her defense of *chhayavaad* when the movement was already dead. Second, like Nirala, Pant had joined the Progressive Writers' Association in the 1930s. This organization encouraged realism in literature. This put Pant in an awkward aesthetic position, considering that most of the criticism hurled at *chhayavaad* came from progressive writers. Both Pant and Varma argued that the subjective "I" in *chhayavaad* lyrics was voicing the real concerns of the people by appealing to the subtle emotions in human beings, and in that respect was not very different from the basic tenets of realism in progressive writing.[16]

For Pant, and Varma, then, *chhayavaad* represented the humanism of the twentieth century that is centered on the subjective "I" in the lyrics, eager to organically engage with the world at large, and committed to remaking a new world, as I will explain in this chapter. The subjectivity in the *chhayavaad* lyrics is, hence, not abstract or escapist in nature, as their critics claimed. Rather, this lyric subjectivity speaks of the condition of humanity in general in the early twentieth century, which was eager for a change. Moreover, for Varma, and Pant, the subjective lyrics were not encouraging the humanism of the past, where the poets connected with the divine within, or saw the divine in the other. Nor was the poetic "I" in *chhayavaad* lyrics romantically interested in some mysterious beloved who is a divine figure. Instead, the poetic "I" is keen on making a new world.[17] To that effect, Pant remarks in the 1960s that the "I" and "You" pronouns used in *chhayavaad* poems express the search for new values, ideas, and feelings that was characteristic of the new humanism.[18] Indeed, the new humanism and the poetic "I" in the *chhayavaad* lyrics arose in response to the changes taking place in the world, *jagat*, and *sansār*, whether in India or beyond. The early twentieth century, as indicated in earlier chapters while discussing Tagore's *vishva sahitya*, brought political and social upheavals in India. In addition, the world was at the brink of the First World War when *chhayavaad* poems started to emerge in Hindi. Consequently, for the *chhayavaad* poets the *concept of the world* expressed via the poetic "I" in their lyrics acquired a new meaning while offering a possibility of fresh beginnings.

Many poems of the *chhayavaad* poets, as I indicate later, imagine a new world, address the world as their listener, or insist on reconstructing the world in which the poetic "I" lives. Since Hindi as well many other Indian languages are rich when it comes to synonyms for the word "world," the concept of world-making in *chhayavaad* lyrics presents a rich understanding of a new, transformed world. For instance, Pant's poems in *Pallav*, a collection that is often described as marking the formal beginning of *chhayavaad* movement, engage with various aspects of the world through the different words used for "world." The epigraph of Pant's *Pallav* begins with a quatrain that expresses that the "*jag*"[19] (world) is at the end of decaying autumn, and *Pallav* (fresh leaves on the branch of spring season) calls for a new affection. The collection includes poems such as "World Presence,"[20] "World Image,"[21] "World Clarinet,"[22] and "Life Carrier"[23] that either address the world (*vishva*) or speak of the beginning of a new world. For example, in "World Presence," first published in 1919, the poetic "I" suggests the flower as "the desire of the world, the laughter of the heart,"[24] but complicates the identity of flower by asking the flower: "O, flower, why you are no longer a flower?"[25] Pant uses the word "*vishva.*" Then, in "Life Carrier," first published in 1923, Pant addresses the world, or to be precise, *vishva*:

O, world! O world-worried heart!
Where is this life flowing?[26]

Describing the composed verses as restless that the world or *vishva* is not paying any attention to them, the speaker requests that "*dev*" or god should present himself soon. Another lyric, also published in 1923, titled "World Clarinet," suggests that the poets are transporting the sound of a world (Pant uses the word "*vishva*") clarinet, and they are carrying a world (Pant's usage is *jag*) of sorrows and happiness to people for eternity.[27] In all these verses, there is a constant play between the indestructible *vishva* and the forever-changing *jag*.

Varma's work, as I will emphasize in the next chapter in great detail, offers a rich source to contextualize the world in *chhayavaad* lyrics. Her position as a "woman-poet" adds an intriguing dimension to the first-person voice in her lyrics in Hindi, where verbs are always gendered. Thus, for instance, in Varma's "Desire,"[28] the speaker expresses a desire for a unique "*sansār*" (Varma's use):

This mad love desires,
a unique new world![29]

This new world or *sansār*, as presented by the poetic speaker, is the opposite of the existing world. Here, dreams become the watchmen, and rest is in burning. It is a new world that is described through surreal and sensual imagery—the sky sleeps in the sea, desires are measured with life's sensations, and eyes become the traders of tears. In addition, Varma's "Question"[30] begins with a declarative statement that small drops of "tears" bound in themselves deep "darkness-like pain" in this bright "star-like" varied "*sansār*," and ends with a hesitant question: "Is a chime not an entity somewhere?"[31] The second stanza identifies oceans made of small waves and rain of small droplets, suggesting that even the big deep ocean is made from smaller components. The final third stanza ends with the realization that everything is restricted in the world. The word used for "world" is *vishva*, so the listener, referred as "You" in the lyric, is also not peerlessly great:

> Who is not limited in this world?
> Even discoveries begin with limits!
> Why wouldn't you not live in petty breaths,
> are only you the greatest?[32]

If Varma's "Desire" is a poem of wanting a new world (Varma's use of word is *sansār*), her "Question" wonders why "You" cannot understand that the addressee ("You") is not beyond the limits of the world (her usage *vishva*). Two words are used for "world" in this short poem. The first word is *"sansār,"* used to contemplate the variety in the world. The second word is *"vishva,"* which could be translated as "universe" or "world," as explained in earlier chapters. *"Jag," "sansār," "lok," "duniyā,"* and *"vishva"* could all be translated into English as "world," but each of these words says something *about* the world in a lyric. *"Sansār"* and *"jag"* are physical spaces where *maya* or illusion manifests. *"Sansār"* can be intimate and small, as in familial relationships, or it could be massive, as in the individual's relationship with the world at large. *"Lok"* is a definite place in space and time and has a specific kind of *"maya."* For instance, heaven is a *"lok." "Vishva"* (which could also be read as globe in the previous poem) is also a *"lok"*; it is often called *"mrityo-lok"* (death-*lok*) because those who partake in its *maya* eventually die. *Vishva* or *mrityo-lok* exists specifically on the planet Earth. Ergo, when Varma writes in her poems that the poetic "I" wants a unique *"sansār"* and that the "You" of the poem is not boundless in *"vishva,"* she is re-envisioning a new world for the "I" and "You," though we do not know who they are. The personal and empathetic "I" in *chhayavaad* poems—specifically those by Varma, who uses "I" more often than any other *chhayavaad* poet—contains within itself a reworking and rearranging of relationships of a modern human being's individuality with the many facets of the world (I address this in the next chapter).

Correspondingly, many *chhayavaad* lyrics evoke new humanistic ideals of equality and gender through striking imagery of nature that connects and unites the world. This fresh world-making took new forms in Hindi lyrics. For instance, unlike their predecessors and contemporaries writing in Hindi, the *chhayavaad* poets emphasized the relationship between the speaker—the poetic "I"—and their natural surroundings in the most intimate fashion. Often the natural setting, even though small in scale, became a microcosm for the world. Thus,

Sumitranandan Pant writes in "World-reflection,"³³ first published in 1922 and then in *Pallav*:

> O! Smiling roses
> How did you get my childhood?—³⁴

In just two lines, the difference between the speaker and the listener, roses, is blurred. The roses possess the childhood of the speaker while they are smiling. The speaker connects the various changing stages of their life with the rose, and ends up by seeing the whole world, universe, or *vishva* reflected in these very roses:

> World-reflecting roses,
>   compassionate is still this change.³⁵

Thus, from roses that had mysteriously acquired the speaker's childhood to roses that are reflecting *vishva*, the word used by Pant, the lyric has tied the speaker, the indestructible world, and the roses together in time and space. In contrast, Mahadevi Varma in "Not My Smiling Lips—"³⁶ from her collection *Neerja* begins the lyric by suggesting that the focus should not be on the speaker's smiling lips, but on the string of tears of the world (*jag*). By using the refrain "don't touch my wet eyelids / look at the withered petals," the speaker insists that the addressee look at the dying flower petals rather than at the poetic "I." Midway through this lyric, the speaker addresses the listener as "beloved" and insists that instead of centering on the poetic speaker's personal constrains, the attention should be on the shackles of culture:

> Not my ties today, beloved
>   look at the chains of culture!
>   Don't touch my wet eyelids
>   look at the withered petals!³⁷

Unlike Pant's poem—where the boundaries between the speaker's childhood, the world, the universe, or *vishva*, and the roses quickly become blurred—Varma's lyric actively asks listeners to not gaze and touch the speaker's "smiling lips" or "wet eyelids" but instead to look at the "tears of the world [*jag*]" and "withered petals." Through a series of statements that often sound like commands to act, Varma's lyric continuously moves the listener's attention away from the speaker's subjectivity, either toward something as small as withered petals or as big as a tearful world. At one point in the lyric, the speaker suggests that the speaker's constraints should not be given any significance at all. Rather, cultural norms that limit and fetter the speaker should be scrutinized. Toward the end, Varma makes a dramatic turn. As if to elide the difference between a tearful world and the smiling lips, personal constraints and cultural restraints, Varma concludes the poem by merging the "listener" and the "speaker" as one:

> If, today, you are in me then "I" am in you
> > Now watch the painful moments!
> > Don't touch my wet eyelids
> > > look at the scattered petals![38]

Indeed, in both the lyrics the poetic self's subjectivity is intricately intertwined with the world (Varma uses *vishva* and *jag*). If the roses in Pant's poem become the *vishva* and a symbol of life's stages, in Varma's lyrics the speaker's smiling lips and wet eyelids are a suggestion to look at the tearful world or *jag*, and cultural restrictions that call for an elimination of any distinctions between the self and the other. Many critics of Varma, especially because of her position as a "woman poet," imagined the addressee in her lyrics to be a long-lost love or a divine figure. However, the "other," the listener(s), or the addressee in *chhayavaad* lyrics is continuously changing. It is not always a beloved or a divine figure. For instance, the speaker in Nirala's "Dwelling"[39] asks listeners:

Where—
Where is my place of dwelling?[40]

The poetic "I" adds that since the speaker has chosen the "I-style" expression in poems, the moment a fellow human being is seen in pain, the shadow of that grief finds a way into subjective poetic utterance,[41] suggesting that the difference between the poetic "I" and poetic "You" is superficial, like Varma's earlier verse.

A similar tone is seen in Nirala's "Breaking Stones,"[42] where the speaker observes a woman who breaks stones for a living in the scorching sun. The verse begins with an observation of a woman working, but it ends with the observer becoming an active speaker in the poem, who utters, "I break stones."[43] Indeed, Prasad writes that "Who is 'You'? And, who is 'I'?" are meaningless questions.[44] Instead, the human mind should be as vast as an ocean, forever expanding.

Further, the world in *chhayavaad* lyrics spoke of an intimate connection with nature, where the natural world provided a source of vision and emotional kinship.[45] In Varma's "Fall Steadily from the Horizon"[46] from *Neerja*, spring night is imagined as a companion of the world (her usage is *vishva*), cascading slowly from the horizon, touching the river water, and causing fragrant flowers to bloom. In the same volume, Varma's "What Messages Do the New Clouds Bring?"[47] personifies the animate and inanimate by describing the moment just before the rain, and the change this moment brings for flora, fauna, birds, earth, animals, and human beings. Each entity in the poem, living or nonliving, is responding to the rain personally, as in the classical Sanskrit poems from the *Rig Veda* or Kalidas's *Meghadut*.[48] Sometimes, this natural world also becomes a backdrop to speak of the erotic. For instance, "The Jasmine Bud,"[49] written in 1916—often identified as the first poem of Nirala, and later published in his first poetry collection *Parimal* in 1921—portrays a jasmine bud being woken up from sleep and made love to by her lover, wind. Though the bud is personified as a woman and the wind as a man, the poem breaks away from the earlier traditions. First, the natural world is personified with feelings, not simply described. Second, the personification of the natural world does not occur via mythical characters, as in the Braj poets. Finally, the heterosexual relationship between the wind and the bud is one of equality, where the bud is not "weak," and the wind is not "strong"; this is different from earlier Braj poems, which did not usually depict men and women as equals within sexual or romantic relationships.

Indeed, this portrayal of the relationship between a man and a woman in the world of *chhayavaad* lyrics was one of the most refreshing and lasting consequences of the movement, for it was based on new ideas of humanism and equality. In these lyrics, lovers were shown as soulmates and companions who could grow together and experience the world in harmony. The beloved is not only addressed as "*priyā*" (favorite), as in Varma's verse "Not My Smiling Lips—," but also as "*sakhī*" (companion) and "*sajnī*" (friend).[50] This kind of affection and companionship was different from the love that court poets in the Braj language conceived, where lovers were often portrayed as "*nāyaka*" (hero) and "*nāyikā*" (heroine), or in devotional verses "*priyā*," which only meant Krishna, or "*prabhū*" (lord) and "*svāmī*" (master). In *chhayavaad*, "no lordship is attached to the man."[51] Further, the word for love chosen by most *chhayavaad* poets is "*praṇay*," which suggests an attraction sustained by knowing the innermost being of the beloved.[52] Instead of sexual attraction in Radha-Krishna poetry in Braj, where Krishna clasps Radha to his breast, and lips meet lips, eyes meet eyes, and hearts join in bliss, the *chhayavaad* poets used various stages of love to create emotional eroticism.[53]

Since the *chhayavaad* poets emphasized emotional eroticism, they often focused on the abstract and the disembodied self. In one of his later poems,

"Experience,"[54] Pant imagines the arrival of a listener, who is described through the changes she brings about in the speaker as well in the outside world. The arrival of the listener (who is identified as a female through gendered verbs) evokes sweetness within the speaker, makes the flowers of his dreams blossom, spreads a fiery dignity, brings him a new perspective, and speaks words that are full of sweet sorrow. The reader, as well as the poetic "I," is left wondering whether the listener who brings all these physical and emotional changes in the speaker is actually a real being, or simply a process that leads to a poetic creation. Conversely, in Pant's poem "Human"[55] the speaker identifies natural phenomena such as starry nights, blossoming flowers, and bright daylight as symbols of shared humanism within the speaker, who sees them all and revels in the ecological and cosmic connections visible to all human beings.

It is true that engagement between the poetic "I" and the listener(s) is nothing new in lyric traditions around the world.[56] By definition, a lyric is a private utterance, often set to rhyme and rhythm, in the presence of an often oblivious listener who is privy to the vulnerabilities of the speaker. For Hegel, as Virginia Jackson and Yopie Prins write, the genre of the lyric is most difficult because it involves the poet's subjectivity at the center and moves the reader toward enlightenment through a historical progress.[57] Since the poet's subjectivity was the focus, for Hegel, the poetic "I" in the lyrics became the *actual* poet speaking.

In fact, as I will elaborate in the next section, many critics of *chhayavaad* poets assumed that Pant, Nirala, Prasad, and Varma were speaking of their personal experiences in these lyrics. This focus on the poetic "I" shifts attention from that which is being addressed, or suggested to be altered, in the world of the *chhayavaad* lyrics. Further, Jonathan Culler, Jackson, and Prins observe a lack of scholarship on the oblivious and neglected listener in the lyric.[58] Unable to come to a concise definition of lyric, Jackson and Prins declare lyric to be a "moving target" that keeps changing.[59] Certainly, as Jackson and Prins indicate, the historically arbitrary emphasis either on the speaker, listener, or lyricism itself creates a space to illuminate the uneven relationship between the speakers and listeners in literary traditions, synchronically and diachronically in world, *jagat*, and *sansār*. It is for this reason that the *chhayavaad* movement is important. This movement not only changed the course of poetry in modern Hindi by stressing the poetic "I's" experiences and emotions as the basis of art, it also brought intensity, humanism, and subjectivity to lyrics in Hindi, where the play between the deictic expressions (words such as *this, that, these, those, now, then,* and *here* that indicate the time, place, or situation in which a speaker is speaking) and pronouns "I" and "You" often transcended the fixed temporal spaces of the Puranas, Upanishads, and myths while insisting on a new world. Regardless, the immediate world-making of the world in the *chhayavaad* lyrics was contentious to say the least.

The World-making of *Chhayavaad*

The lyrics of *chhayavaad* poets took many readers by surprise. The uninhibited use of the poetic "I" in their lyrics was unique, though the movement was criticized as being a *chhaya* or shadow of Tagore and British romantics. Namvar Singh suggests that the word "*chhayavaad*" had become very popular by 1920 in various Hindi periodicals and magazines. In fact, in 1920, Mukutdhar Pandey published a series of four essays, titled "*Chhayavaad*," in *Sri Sharada* literary magazine. Singh points out, though, that Pandey's work cannot be said to be the first on *chhayavaad*.[60] In the four essays, Pandey identified *chhayavaad* with words such as mystical, mysterious, symbolic, and suggestive, depicting the interior world of the poet. The association of those words with the movement has continued since then, both in seriousness and in jest. For instance, in 1921, *Sarasvati*, the Hindi literary magazine, for the first time, published an essay on *chhayavaad* titled "*Chhayavaad* in Hindi,"[61] where a highly educated woman, her husband, and a painter converse with Pant about *chhayavaad*. The painter produces a white paper framed in gold. The painting, as the painter tells the woman and her husband, is based on Pant's poetry. The trio remark on the profundity of the (un)painted work that has the title "*chhaya*"[62] or shadow. When the painter is asked about the specifics of the poem that inspired the painting, the fictious Pant shows them a blank page. The essayist ends by mocking the *chhayavaad* poems as utterances of a nonsensical and unclear interiority that are based on the shadow of nothingness.

Singh remarks that this essay marks the first satire on the word "*chhayavaad*," meaning "producing a shadow," which at that time meant blindly following the British romantics and the Nobel laureate Tagore. According to this critique, the *chhayavaad* poets worked under the influence of Bengali poets, specifically Tagore, by producing subjective short lyric poems—but unlike Tagore's poems, their verses had no core and concrete basis in reality. Undoubtedly, by 1913, Tagore had become a revered figure for many authors in India. Hindi literary critics and authors admired Tagore, too, but saw the *chhayavaad* poets' short subjective lyrics as a poor imitation of Tagore's. Pandey's essay in *Sri Sharda*, as well as the essay published in *Sarasvati*, initiated the tradition of world-making the lyrical world of *chhayavaad* poets as immersed in mysticism and an ahistorical abstruse subjectivity that resulted from a poor imitation of Tagore. In fact, criticisms of *chhayavaad* poetry continued to be published in *Sarasvati* for many decades. Since its inception in 1900 at Allahabad, sponsored by a Bengali merchant, the periodical had played an important role in establishing standard Hindi by publishing entertaining debates on the literatures of India and the world. It successfully thrived until 1970 in Allahabad, which had become the center of Hindi literary circles[63] in the twentieth century.

Sarasvati's importance in world-making the *vishva* in *chhayavaad* lyrics as idiosyncratic and abstruse can be gauged by noting that all major Hindi authors who have now become "canonized" were published in this journal. In fact, Suryakant Nirala, one of the *chhayavaad* poets who was often critiqued by the Mahavir Prasad Dvivedi proponents, acknowledges[64] that Dvivedi, the editor of *Sarasvati*, had singlehandedly changed the fate of Hindi in the late nineteenth century and early twentieth century—a time when educated people were typically attracted to Urdu, and a large section of literary culture was devoted to Urdu aesthetics.[65] Indeed, in the beginning of the twentieth century, the magazine regularly featured pieces that supported making Hindi the national language. For instance, in an essay[66] published in March 1916, the anonymous author writes that for the last fifteen years, newspapers and various gatherings have suggested that Hindi could become the national language of an independent India. According to the writer, it is unnecessary to even debate whether Hindi or Urdu should be the national language; the writer focuses on Hindi's glowing capability to become the national language, suggesting that Urdu *cannot* be the national language.

Along with pieces on the Hindi-Urdu debate, the magazine also shows a clear awareness of the lack of modern verses in Hindi. In the June 1916 edition, the anonymous author of "Modern Hindi Poetry"[67] writes that it is shameful that Hindi does not have good poets who could be on par with poets like Tulsidas and Tagore. Tulsidas wrote in Avadhi in the fifteenth century, and Tagore, as we know, wrote in both Bengali and English. The essay identifies contemporary Hindi poetry to be of two kinds: meaningless couplets (a direct attack on poems in Braj language) or objective statements (critiquing poems by *Dvivedi* poets in modern Hindi). The essayist declares that the world of Hindi poetry is so flexible and immature that anyone can declare oneself to be an iconic poet, then suggests that perhaps Hindi is not fit as a language for writing poetry. Moreover, the essay connects the impossibility of writing good poetry in Hindi with a bigger problem. The author opines that perhaps in the modern age, people find the very genre of poetry a nuisance. This thought is contradicted a few lines later when the essayist muses that Tagore's poems in Bengali have proven that poetry in the modern literature can thrive. It is worth noting that Munshi Premchand's iconic Hindi short story[68] is published in the same issue, suggesting that Hindi prose was thriving and had a wide readership. The essay "Modern Hindi Poetry" is, thus, a rebuke of contemporary Hindi poetry, when *chhayavaad* was just beginning to emerge. It is unique because it questions the work of *Dvivedi* poets in a magazine that had become the mouthpiece for *Dvivedi* ideology, and it suggests the impotency of the Hindi language for composing good poetry with modernist sensibilities, by highlighting Tagore's work who was writing modern poetry in a neighboring language, Bengali.

Certainly, the *Dvivedi* poets were fighting a unique battle in the realm of poetry. They did not have a model in Hindi; they were fed up with the Braj language poems and couplets that were either devotional or sexual in nature; and they wanted to create parallel poetic content by writing poetry that was nationalistic, political, and focused on social evils of the times. For instance, *Dvivedi* poets were perhaps the first poets in Hindi who wrote on the plight of women as well as Dalits in the late nineteenth and early twentieth centuries. The Braj poets were not bothered about the concerns of mortal beings. Though *chhayavaad* poets were also rebelling against Braj poets, they were different from the *Dvivedi* poets, as they focused on the subjective expressions in their poems. This subjective engagement was considered juvenile by *Dvivedi* poets. As a result, when it came to *chhayavaad* poets, the leading literary magazine in Hindi, *Sarasvati*, was usually very cold. In fact, Prasad (who had written poems in Braj as well as in Hindi that aligned with the *Dvivedi* aesthetics), when refused publication in *Sarasvati*, started his own literary magazine, *Indu*, which became a platform to publish new *chhayavaad* poetry. Karine Schomer points out that by the 1920s, literary critics and writers reared in "the ideals of Mahavirprasad Dvivedi"[69] held positions in newly established Hindi departments in universities and literary magazines. Though they criticized Braj poetry as defunct and out of touch with the times, they also disliked *chhayavaad* poetry, which seemed to them obscure and unclear in its message. Pant's poetry was called "nonsense" many times in *Sarasvati*. The *Dvivedi* critics managing *Sarasvati* objected to *chhayavaad* poets to such an extent that it became a regular feature for some obscure *chhayavaad* poem to be taken apart and analyzed by pointing out syntactical errors, gender alterations, or the creation of compound words in the language.[70]

It was just not the *chhayavaad* poetry itself that was criticized; the figure of the new poet writing subjective lyrics also became a central target for satire. This was mainly because the poetic "I" in the lyrics was perceived as the actual poet—Pant, Nirala, Prasad, or Varma—speaking. For instance, one of the cartoons published in the magazine shows a long-haired poet (probably Pant or Nirala), frail in body and swathed in cloud of words such as "agony," "passion," and "tears," dramatically reciting a poem entitled "When Will You Come to Me, My Infinite Love?"[71] As a result, the *chhayavaad* movement generated vitriolic responses. For example, Ramchandra Shukla, a renowned critic of that time, commented on *chhayavaad* in what is often called the first book on the history of Hindi literature.[72] Shukla wrote that poetry in Kharī Bolī[73] was just finding its identity when suddenly Tagore's poetry became a big hit in the world and India, and these *chhayavaad* poets blindly copied Tagore's style, causing Hindi to lose its original path and destination. What Shukla meant was that the didactic element of the *Dvivedi* era was finding its niche in the Hindi poetic idiom by presenting itself as being different from Braj and Urdu language poets, when the escapist and romantic poetic "I," which in itself was a poor imitation of Tagore, became popular.

Tagore's *Gitanjali* had impressed the *chhayavaad* poets, just as it impressed many other readers. In fact, all of these poets were familiar with Tagore's work. In her work, published in 1956, Mahadevi Varma speaks of meeting Tagore in Shantiniketan. Varma writes that Tagore did not write anything that was unknown before, yet whatever he expressed always seemed new, and that under the shadow of Tagore the journey of her era began.[74] Grieving his death, Varma ends the essay by comparing herself to a small lamp that burns and gives light as a homage to the sun that has set in the figure of Tagore. Pant, Nirala, and Prasad were all mesmerized by Tagore (like the rest of the world at that time). Nirala, living in Bengal, had written several essays on Tagore. In fact, several Hindi translations of *Gitanjali* were published in *Sarasvati* along with regular advertisements of Bengali *Gitanjali* available in Hindi script. For example, in the 1916 January edition of *Sarasvati*, the ad by Indian Press informs readers about a Hindi *Gitanjali* that contains verses from the Bengali *Gitanjali* as well as other Bengali poems that were translated into the English *Gitanjali* in Hindi script. This means that all Bengali poems that were in the English and Bengali *Gitanjali* are available in *Devnagari* script. The book is advertised for people who understand and read Hindi, and speak Bengali, but do not read Bengali. Despite the tremendous awe that Tagore's poetry in Bengali generated among *Sarasvati* readers and *chhayavaad* poets, it would be a mistake to see *chhayavaad* as a movement simply influenced by Tagore's *Gitanjali*.[75] Take for example the fact that both Varma and Pant, though they respected Tagore's poetry, often pointed out how Hindi was different from Bengali in rhyme, meter, and sound. Nirala, who was well versed in Bengali, also wrote pieces that disagreed with Tagore's ideas on language. Pant in his *Pallav*, for instance, wrote a long introduction where he showed that the distinction between short and long vowels in Hindi and Bengali could not have helped in creating a mirror copy of Bengali verses in the Hindi lyrics of *chhayavaad*.

Karine Schomer observes that the scathing critiques of the *chhayavaad* poets published regularly in *Sarasvati* were mean personal attacks. She remarks that in one of the articles, published in 1921, the writer mocks the *chhayavaad* poems as being written in incommunicable language that relies on excessive imagination to say nothing. It was just not that these critics, who were mostly the old guard, criticized the poetic style of these new poets; they also harshly attacked the figure of the poet who practiced such art. As a case in point, take, for instance, the writer of "The Poet Mysterious"[76] in the August 1921 edition of *Sarasvati*, who writes that a shop in Kolkata produces mystical poets (a jab at Nirala) who are published in Hindi newspapers and magazines. In a mock interview of a young *chhayavaad* poet, the writer of "The Poet Mysterious," who uses the pseudonym *maujī* (meaning whimsical), asks how poetry is conceived. He remarks that a journal in Hindi recently published a sketch of a poet sitting next to a pond (probably criticizing Prasad, Nirala, and Pant) writing mystical poems, but the readers of *Sarasvati* are curious to know about the creative impulse that leads to these imaginative leaps. In response, the young poet (who, interestingly, is female) explains the importance of possessing a good pen and quietude before composing a verse about a pining woman.

Unlike Bengali, the verbs in Hindi are either masculine or feminine, and in some poems Nirala and Pant used a poetic "I" that spoke in feminine verbs; it became a common point of ridicule that these male poets wrote in female voices. Indeed, Pant's "Blanketed World"[77] or "A Drop of Ink,"[78] published in 1919, employs feminine verbs in the lyrics. The young female poet criticized in *Sarasvati* is not Mahadevi Varma, though she, too, became the butt of jokes in many later editions of *Sarasvati*. Varma was yet to become famous, though she was familiar with the poetry of Pant (who lived in Allahabad, where she had come to study). Many had assumed that the subjective *chhayavaad* lyrics—where the poetic "I" was speaking in both masculine and feminine voices, and which some considered excessively emotional—were written for young men and women and had nothing to do with the intense political and social movements in modern India as the nation sought to free itself from British rule. In fact, the *chhayavaad* poets were criticized for enclosing themselves in a world of fancy and for "trying to escape all the stresses and strains of the time."[79] Even after the movement had died out, some critics continued to attack *chhayavaad* poetry. For example, in late the 1940s, N. K. Devraj suggested that *chhayavaad* failed because of the topics the poets chose to write about. He wrote, "if *chhayavaad* poetry had not remained neutral to society, and had it not continued its subjective pleas to nature and the unknown beloved, it would have not fallen."[80] He adds that on the surface, it seems that these poets were copying Tagore by writing mystical and subjective poems, but Tagore's "mysticism was a result of a pre-World War"[81] ideology, whereas the *chhayavaad* poets were inspired more by Tagore's personality than by real-world problems.[82] For Devraj, *chhayavaad* poets' greatest disqualification is that they were not in touch with the problems of the world but, as I indicated before, the lyrical world in the *chhayavaad* lyrics was imagining a new world (*vishva*, *jagat*, and *sansār*), whose world-making was made contentious by the poets' immediate world.

The publication of *Pallav* became the official beginning as well as the first formal defense of the movement. Though the first collection of poems classified as *chhayavaad* had started appearing by 1918 in various Hindi journals—by Nirala who was writing from Bengal, Pant and Varma from Allahabad, and Prasad from Varanasi—a formal defense of the movement did not emerge until the publication of *Pallav* in 1926. It is for this reason that in his preface, humorously entitled "Advertisement,"[83] Pant responds to these personal attacks by writing that, out of childlike curiosity and excitement, he has left a small boat in an ocean of literature. Now he awaits the repercussions. He adds, in jest, that since his boat (*Pallav*) is light (a jab at those who called *chhayavaad* poetry flimsy and not in touch with the real world), it will not sink, and thus will not seem attractive to "holy" and "great" men. Pant uses the word "*mahāpurush*" (great men) to mock critics who favored the *Dvivedi*-style poetry, which he saw as nothing but didactic statements lacking any subjective engagement.

If the "Advertisement" is composed in a half-ironic tone by the young Pant, the "Introduction"[84] is written in a serious tone. In it, Pant leaves no stone unturned as he rationally criticizes the narrow world of Braj, with its unsecular and stifling expressions, and the ideologically driven poetry of the *Dvivedi* poets. Significantly, he does not mention Urdu traditions while establishing the *chhayavaad* poems as the new expression in Hindi; this is because the *chhayavaad* poets wanted to present themselves as the spokespeople of a new emerging Hindi, which was trying to free itself from *Dvivedi* poets as well as the Braj idioms. Emphasizing the importance of richness in expression, Pant writes that the present era demands a language that is not bookish, but one of human beings—a language in which "we laugh, fight, unite, and breathe; something that will be adept in showing the face of the psychological state of our nation."[85] Considering that Pant stresses that the poetic idiom of *chhayavaad* poets is colloquial and embedded in real lives of people, it is noteworthy that the poetry produced in modern Hindi by Pant and his contemporaries was dismissed by its critics as divorced from the realities of its time.

Certainly, the *chhayavaad* poets played an important role in establishing Hindi as a language of poetic idiom through the subjectivity in lyrics. The use of Hindi before the *chhayavaad* poets was equivalent to the use of Hindustani or Urdu. But in the nineteenth century, Kharī Bolī (rather than Braj or Avadhi, in Devnagari script) came to be regarded as the "standard Hindi," instead of Kaithi or Mahajani. This shift was brought about by the Fort Williams College in Kolkata and by higher- and middle-class and caste Hindus who created institutional spaces for Kharī Bolī, creating the first wave of activism in support of Hindi.[86] Initially, this activism occurred only in prose; poetry remained lifeless. In fact, Mahadevi Varma's "My Childhood Days"[87] describes how, while growing up, Varma was tutored to write poems in Braj. Her father was well versed in both Persian and Urdu (and studied English), and her mother knew Sanskrit and Braj, but there was "no influence of Hindi whatsoever."[88] Varma writes in the same essay that she stopped writing in Braj when she came to Allahabad for her education and saw Subhadra Kumari Chauhan, a then-hostel-mate and a poet, writing in Kharī Bolī. At that time, the *chhayavaad* poets were not only harshly criticized for the craft of their poetry; their choice to write poetry in Hindi in the I-style was not only a break from the immediate literary and historical past, but a protest and a voyage into the unknown "I" in the era of a collective national identity that wanted to establish an international solidarity in a new world. With the exception of Suryakant Nirala, the most prominent poets of this movement—Jaishankar Prasad, Sumitranandan Pant, and Mahadevi Varma—

did not always directly respond to these criticisms at the onset of the movement. As the movement gathered strength, and in some cases when it had already died from the contemporary Hindi literary scene, the poets spoke in its defense.

One instance of response to criticism appears in Mahadevi Varma's essay[89] on modern poet, published in 1942 as an introduction to her poems composed between 1936 and 1942 in the collection *Deepshikha*.[90] Here, Varma, who had been heavily attacked by critics like Devraj, explains the past and the present that the poets of her age had inherited. She elaborates that it was natural for people who had grown accustomed to the ostensible, ornate, and artificial tropes of Braj poetry to be disappointed with *chhayavaad* poetry, which was inspired by contemporary conditions and took advantage of common speech for the purpose of natural expression and ease in communication. Varma writes that the "new poetic language lacked flexibility and sounded harsh to ears accustomed to the sweetness of Braj Bhasha, and there was no virtuosity to its utterances."[91] Further, the narrative element in the Braj poetry had become so dominant—whether the poet was describing the romance of Krishna with Radha or the beauty of a woman from head to toe—that "all that is subtle and tender in the human being rebelled"[92] in *chhayavaad* poetry. Without openly denying the merit of her predecessors, Varma writes that most poetic works of that period used a language that was refined, "though stiff, and emotions were lofty though they lacked finesse,"[93] and "metre, though hardly new, seconded the mood of the poem and poetic themes were understandable and refined, even if they lacked mystery."[94]

The *chhayavaad* poets, writes Varma, were tired of the lifeless repetitions of concrete beauty, bored with the traditional set of poetic rules, and the idealistic and conventional language, and wanted to focus on the subtle. Though it is not clear what Varma means by subtle here, she does indicate that the *chhayavaad* poetic expressions were not like those of Braj, or their contemporaries writing poetry in Hindi that was didactic and objective. *Chhayavaad*, writes Varma,

> wanted to mould subtle perceptions of beauty along new metres in a way that could not match the highly strung rigidity of Khari Boli; thus its poets, like able goldsmiths, set themselves to measure every word in terms of sound, weight, and meaning, selecting each one carefully and sometimes creating new words to give their subtle feelings the tenderest of poetic bodies.[95]

It was because of the change that *chhayavaad* poets brought in their verses that they were able to touch the core of people. Through the essay Varma not only explains the historic, linguistic, and literary shifts in the late nineteenth and early twentieth centuries that led to the formation of modern Hindi language and literary traditions, the poet also recognizes the end of Braj as the dominant literary language and acknowledges Kharī Bolī as the poetic language of the *chhayavaad*. Note that in this essay, there is no mention of Hindi yet. There is also an inherent opposition to what both poetic traditions are offering. If Braj poetry is refined, lofty, and understandable, Kharī Bolī is flexible, fine, and mysterious. Above all, unlike Braj, Kharī Bolī offers to touch its readers personally because it is the language of the people, in which poetry about divine and mythical figures (such as Krishna and Radha) is not written.

On the one hand, Varma is touching upon the "I-style" that the *chhayavaad* poets employed, addressing the linguistic fracture that made Braj a relic of past and wanted Kharī Bolī the future of modern Hindi. On the other hand, she is criticizing her immediate predecessors as well as her contemporaries—the poets of *Dvivedi* era—whose works can be best characterized as "objective poetry of public statement, proclamation, nationalism, and social reform,"[96] and as lacking subtlety in intellect and compassion. In fact, during the times in which the *chhayavaad* poets wrote, the dominant norms were to compose poetry in Braj about love trysts between Radha and Krishna, describe the six seasons, describe a woman's beauty from head to toe, or compose devotional verses. Though changes in the country's social conditions had led to a decline in the support of Braj by generous patrons, it still remained attractive to many. In prosperous cities in the north of India, such as Kanpur, and Allahabad, the traditions of Braj poetry continued. Most notable in this respect are "The Connoisseur Society" of Kanpur, which supported Nathuram Sharma, and Sridhar Pathak of Allahabad, who became an influential Braj poet after publication of his long poem on the beauty of Kashmir in 1904.[97] In reality, the *chhayavaad* movement was then not only against the trite court poetry produced in a language like Braj and the didactic elements of poetry in Kharī Bolī; *chhayavaad* was a new world-making in poetry, where the individualism was displayed in personalized relation with the world. No wonder, as shown earlier in the chapter, the *chhayavaad* poets were as much concerned with the poetic "I" as with the idea of the world.

World versus *Vishva Sahitya* in Hindi

It is needless to repeat here that the world in the lyrics of *chhayavaad* poets was not seen by their critics as a desire for a new world; nor did these critics see it as a call for world humanism and world companionship. In fact, many thought that the *vishva* in these lyrics was an aspiration to find a place in the Hindi literary canon. One of the editions of *Sarasvati* includes a long Sanskrit poem composed in a form of dialogue between the poets, Nirala, and Varma. This resembles the dialogue between Krishna, and Arjuna from Bhagavad Gita, who are contemplating the mysterious ways of creating "*vishva sahitya*":

> In the desolate darkness, on a deserted mountain,
> > speechless with agony,
> beautiful Mahadevi of the broken heart-strings questioned
> > Surya [i.e., Nirala].
> Mahadevi spoke:
> Sir, by what efforts can I obtain great status
> and brilliant fame as a poet of Hindi?
> Having made Mira unequalled, they have degraded Valmiki and Lord Dvaipayana
> > as well. How, then, can I become glorious?
> Surya spoke . . .[98]

The mock-poem uses words such as "agony," "desolate," and "broken" to poke fun at the emotive world in *chhayavaad* lyrics. Note that Varma is identified as someone with broken heart-strings who is aiming to become a great Hindi poet and whose benchmark is the "unequalled" Mira, the female *bhakti* poet. As I will show in the next chapter, Varma's verses have often been interpreted as devotional in spirit (displaying Mira-like characteristics) in translation and in the original, though in actuality the two poets are very different. Significantly, the concept of *vishva sahitya* that is based on popularity is also being criticized in this mock-dialogue between Nirala and Varma.

Although readers and editors of *Sarasvati* did not appreciate the *vishva* in *chhayavaad* lyrics, they did recognize the importance of *vishva sahitya* as a concept. In fact, in some cases, as I will show later, what *vishva sahitya* means also matters to *chhayavaad* poets. For instance, in an essay published in the May 1921 edition of the *Sarasvati* magazine, Ramendra Kumar Sharma imagines literature as a field to have been born even before language, and *vishva sahitya* to have existed forever. He adds that the present task of people who affirm *vishva sahitya* is to gain knowledge and understand the *dharma* of *mānav jīvan* (human life). In another fascinating essay in the July 1921 edition, on "World Language,"[99] the author imagines a globalized world where people have invented a language that helps them communicate with each other despite their cultural differences. Manoharlal Srivastav, the author of "World Language," claims that if *vishva sahitya* did not exist, the concept of many languages would not have existed, and there would have been just one *"vishva bhasha"* (world language). Srivastav recognizes the importance of this "world language" in assisting the needs of travelers and business, but he considers *vishva sahitya* to be only possible because of the existence of different languages.

Similarly, Naveen Chandra, in the March 1921 edition of *Sarasvati*, writes that a literary text can only be called a *vishva sahitya* if it does not have the shadow of the poet's personality and that the literary text presents ideal and moral characters. In contrast, *chhayavaad* lyrics were seen to be an extension of the poet's life. Chandra's essay, titled "Trinity,"[100] identifies Valmiki, Tulsidas, and Homer as ideal examples of *vishva sahitya*, possibly because the three poets created epic heroes. The explications of *vishva sahitya* in *Sarasvati* are interesting and useful because, though these critics were unsympathetic toward the *chhayavaad* poets, who were speaking and creating a new humanism and world in their poetry, they acknowledged world consciousness and world spirit as the essence of *vishva sahitya* in their periodical. As shown in this chapter, for *chhayavaad* poets, the idea of world spirit and worldwide companionship formed the basis of the world in their lyrics. A more expansive work on *vishva sahitya* in Hindi was presented in 1924 by Padumalal-Punnalal Bakshi, who published *Vishva Sahitya*.[101] Bakshi had also edited *Sarasvati* in the past. The book includes several essays on the concept of *vishva sahitya*; it is certainly a more detailed work on the concept than Tagore's own writings on *vishva sahitya*.

Bakshi's book includes a preface by the editor Sri Dularelal. In it, Dularelal writes that these days there is no dearth of Hindi writers or even Hindi publishers, but both authors and publishers are more interested in making money rather than teaching something useful to the readers.[102] Dularelal adds that by writing this he does not mean to hurt anyone who is writing in Hindi, but he does want to highlight that economics should not govern the production of literature. It needs to be mentioned here that *chhayavaad* poets were very popular. Dularelal adds that today, India needs to connect with all the ethnicities of the world (*sansār*) to establish sympathy and support; he gives the example of Tagore doing this through his work. As if speaking the language of *chhayavaad* poems in prose, Dularelal suggests that the concepts of *"vishva-prem"* (world-love), *"vishva-sahitya,"* and *"vishva-parichaya"* (world-introduction) are not new.[103] Perhaps, referencing the First World War, Dularelal writes that sustained peace is needed for the growth of the entire *sansār* through *vishva-prem*. The most effective way to enact *vishva-prem* is through the construction of a *sahitya* that can be called *vishva sahitya*.[104] Comparing the present to a time when movement from one part of India to another was impossible, Dularelal remarks that today people are able to not only travel to Europe and America but also read news and literature of foreign countries. As a result, poets and authors are thinking about a *vishva sahitya* that rises beyond cultural and provincial differences.[105] Dularelal adds that Bakshi, who served as the editor of *Sarasvati* and also published work on different aspects of *vishva sahitya*, has brought out this book on *vishva sahitya* by collecting his earlier published essays. *Vishva Sahitya*, he informs his readers, is the only work available in Hindi on various aspects of *vishva sahitya*.[106]

Indeed, the essays by Bakshi touch on several topics related to *vishva sahitya*. For instance, in one of his essays, "The Development of *Sahitya*,"[107] Bakshi writes that *sahitya* is created when human beings communicate with the natural world; the feelings generated by the natural world constitute the beginning of *vishva sahitya*. The *vishva* in *chhayavaad* lyrics communicated with the natural world. Bakshi also suggests in another essay, "The Meeting of *Sahitya*,"[108] that *vishva sahitya* cannot be created without translation. He writes that literature from around the world has specificities that result from historical, cultural, religious, and linguistic nuances; consequently, translating those literatures becomes the only way to know those differences. At one point, Bakshi references Goethe and points out that he wanted to tie all the countries together in the string of world literature, adding that currently scholars opine that the German language has a lot of world literature. Unlike Tagore—who did not directly inform the connection of *vishva sahitya* and *vishva mānav* with translation but instead decided to translate "comparative literature" as "world literature"—Bakshi writes that without translation, *vishva sahitya* is not possible.[109] Moreover, Bakshi suggests that there should not just be the translation of literary texts, but a translation of historical and religious texts so that the culture and traditions of the various literary traditions can be better understood.

Bakshi concludes his long book on *vishva sahitya* by reminding his readers that those who are narrow-minded and petty, those who think that their literature is the only literature in the world, and those who cannot rise beyond a few authors such as Tulsidas, Matiram, and Bihari (all premodern Braj and Avadhi poets) will inadvertently give up the greatest gift that the world offered to them: *vishva sahitya*.[110] If Bakshi lists popular authors who are often seen as the icons in premodern Hindi to emphasize that these are the only authors one should read (very much reminding us of the Kipling-Tennyson debate in

Tagore's discussion of *vishva sahitya*), Nirala presents a different perspective in 1930. Lamenting that Hindi has not done anything for *vishva sahitya*, Nirala writes in "The Desire of Literature"[111] in 1930 that the wish of *vishva sahitya* has been fulfilled by various creators in the world, except the ones who write in Hindi, because the educated class either does not respect Hindi or does not know how to write in it. Nirala's remark suggests that Hindi was not even a recognized language in its immediate world in the early twentieth century.

Indeed, when *chhayavaad* lyrics emerged, Hindi was called Kharī Bolī in literary and non-literary circles. In fact, at the beginning of the twentieth century, various North Indian languages such as Urdu, Braj, Avadhi, Maithili, and Bhojpuri had robust poetic traditions, while what is now known as modern Hindi[112] and its poetry remained at the periphery. In this respect, the new world in the *chhayavaad* lyrics was momentous. Though the *chhayavaad* movement was short-lived, it changed the course of Hindi language at a time when Urdu's poetic idiom was highly sophisticated and in its full glory. With the arrival of the *chhayavaad* lyrics, Hindi suddenly became the language of poetry as it replaced the court poetry in Braj language, presented itself for the first time as a major viable rival to Urdu, and challenged the objective and descriptive poems of *Dvivedi*-style poetry. The subjective "I" in *chhayavaad* lyrics became the platform to speak of a new world, world companionship, and world humanism that was not interested in divine figures, but in ordinary human beings. It spoke of a *vishva* that was based on *vishva chetnā* (world consciousness). Critics of the *chhayavaad* poets in Hindi, however, identified those lyrics as abstruse, escapist, apolitical, and at best poor imitations of the British romantics and the recently awarded Nobel laureate Rabindranath Tagore. Even the word "*chhayavaad*" was initially used as a derogatory term, given to the poets who were imitating and translating a philosophy that was only a shadow, a "*chhaya*," of Tagore's Bengali lyrics. Certainly, *chhayavaad* poets looked at the *vishva* within their personalized lyrics in Hindi by creating a new world, *jagat*, and *sansār*. As illustrated in this chapter, the *vishva* in the *chhayavaad* lyrics was in conflict with the world-making of those lyrics in the original in their immediate world, *jagat*, and *sansār*. Equivalently, the *chhayavaad* movement, though not typically read or canonized as an offshoot of world modernism, was very much in line with Ezra Pound's philosophy of "make it new," but perhaps different from James Joyce's idea of the modernist aesthetic as an engagement with horse piss and rotten straw. The world in *chhayavaad* lyrics, however, is hardly canonized and anthologized as exhibiting modernist sensibilities that are opposite to the fragmentation and alienation of a modern individual.[113] If world literature still is an elliptical refraction of national literatures, and a mode of reading that gains in translation,[114] and untranslatability a theoretical fulcrum of comparative literature,[115] the world in the lyrics of *chhayavaad* poets has a caveat: the worldliness and world-making of the original, synchronically and diachronically, is as important as its translated version(s), if there is one, whether in single, comparative, or world literary debates.

4

(Woman) Author and the World

By investigating the tension between the *vishva* in Mahadevi Varma's *sahitya* and the world, *jagat*, and *sansār* around it, this chapter suggests strategies for reading women authors in world literature debates. While describing the significance of world-making of the *vishva* in *sahitya* for *ānand* or joy, Tagore mentions authors such as Kalidas, Tennyson, Kipling, and Vidyapati. None of these authors are women. Tagore knew that *vishva sahitya* could not be a mere replacement of one author by another, or one language with another; nevertheless, women authors are conspicuously absent from his delineation of *vishva sahitya* as a concept. Similarly, Bakshi (toward the end of his book *Vishva Sahitya*) suggests that narrow-minded people—who think that *their* literature is the only literature in the world, and who cannot go beyond Tulsidas, Matiram, and Bihari—will not realize the gift of *vishva sahitya*. Bakshi does not mention whether going beyond poets writing in Avadhi, and Braj languages (such as Tulsidas, Matiram, and Bihari) could also mean reading women authors in those languages or beyond. Additionally, none of the essays on the concept of *vishva sahitya*, addressed in the previous chapter, suggests reading women authors who could be compared with the given examples of authors such as Valmiki, Homer, or Tulsidas. Though the sixteenth-century woman poet-saint Mira is mentioned in the mock-poem on *vishva sahitya* as a touchstone for Varma to emulate, Varma is also made fun of for seeking suggestions from her male contemporary, Nirala, on how to become a Hindi poet. Equivalently, in her essay "Sahitya, Culture, and Governance,"[1] initially delivered as a speech to a state legislative assembly in India, Varma declares that Kalidas, Tulsidas, Shakespeare, Tolstoy, and Gorkhy are as much "ours as of the world."[2] She adds, as if echoing Tagore, that *sahitya* only creates unity, and students should be taught about *"vishvabandhutva"* (world-friendship) through literature or *sahitya*.

Oddly, the lone *chhayavaad* woman poet, who wrote "I-style" lyrics at a time when the literary scene in many places in India and elsewhere was not receptive to women, decides to not include any women authors in her speech about world-friendship in her formal address to the state legislative assembly of Uttar Pradesh in India. Her silence on the names of women authors is noteworthy when we consider that Varma is often recognized as an activist who worked very hard for educating women in North India, specifically in the state of Uttar Pradesh, and extensively wrote essays on discrimination against women in social and literary spheres. Varma belonged to a generation for whom writing was not only a form of self-expression but also a form of public address; authors were also writing for the nation.[3] Yet, the *vishva* in Varma's social and political essays, public addresses, and even "life-sketches"—a genre that she pioneered—hardly ever focuses on her subjectivity. For instance, in "life-sketches" that seem more like testimonial accounts, Varma often recalls and describes other people, not necessarily how she personally thinks and feels about them in first-person voice. It is as if Varma deliberately and carefully effaces her own gender, sexuality, personal life, and identity as a woman, not only in the *vishva* of her *sahitya* but also in any kind of world-making of that *sahitya* in world, *jagat*, and *sansār* by her, as seen in "*Sahitya*, Culture, and Governance."

The closest that readers come to Varma's first-person voice is in the *vishva* of her *chhayavaad* poetry. But the poetic "I" of the *chhayavaad* movement was separate from the "real self" of the poet, as indicated in the earlier chapter, even though readers and critics took it as the actual poet speaking. In Varma's context, her identity as the lone woman, writing in conservative North India in the 1920s[4] in the Hindi literary world, could only be accepted if the *vishva* in her poetry was mystical and spiritual. Consequently, the real poet, Mahadevi,[5] as she was/is often called and sometimes referred to herself, became an epitome of a woman writing poetry for the unknown beloved in *bhakti* or devotional traditions in modern Hindi. Though Varma defended her poetry as not being mystical,[6] the frequent address to an unknown listener in her verses, and the longing between the poetic "I" and "You," earned her comparisons with the woman poet-saint Mira, and she was accordingly given the title of "modern Mira."

The image of "modern Mira" was itself built over decades in Hindi magazines and periodicals that set Varma apart from other women writers and poets of her times. If the "modern Mira" title was irritating to Varma, the association with this canonized and reputed woman-poet-saint also shielded Varma from uncouth and vulgar speculations about her personal life and choices. The comparison with Mira becomes relevant when we consider that Varma had decided to not live with her husband and instead had gone to pursue her literary and educational aspirations. Since Varma's *vishva* in her lyrics was for the divine Krishna, just like Mira's, her position as a woman author presented very few obstacles to intellectual friendship with her male counterparts. In fact, it is said that Varma's "salon" had a sanitizing effect; there, even the most uncouth and rough "literary 'brothers' of Hindi letters were on their good behavior."[7]

Certainly, Varma's caution in treading a thin line between the poetic, the authorial, and the real self helped her to defy social norms of her time in a patriarchal setting.[8] Varma also created a permanent place for herself in the Hindi literary world at a time when women had few opportunities to become poets and thinkers. Yet, the world-making of the *vishva* in her lyrics as that of a woman waiting for her beloved, and the *vishva* in her essays, public addresses, and editorial work present a bifurcated Mahadevi Varma. In fact, as the chapter indicates that the world-making of the *vishva* in her lyrics, and the *vishva* in her prose work, have created different authors in the original Hindi and in translation, especially in English.

Over the past decade or so, Varma's prose work has found continuous new life in English translations, in contrast to her poetry.[9] Currently, a substantial body of her work in English translations exists. This may give English readers, whether in India or beyond, the impression that Varma is foremost a prose writer rather than a poet. For many Hindi readers, poetry remains Varma's first introduction in the original, though most of her prose work was published at the same time when she was writing "I-style" poetry. In some English translations, Varma has also become canonized—quite surprisingly, as an Indian feminist[10]— whereas her poetry is absent from anthologies that advertise themselves as focusing on Indian poetry, Indian writings, and even Indian women writings.[11] Moreover, the original verses of Varma have largely continued to be read, in translation and in the original, as mystical or extremely personal.[12] According to this interpretation, Varma's poetry might not have anything to do with the humanism, world-friendship, and world consciousness in a new world that *chhayavaad* as a movement stood for, as indicated in the earlier chapter.

The conundrum, then, is an eternal one: How to read[13] the *vishva* in the *sahitya* of an author in translation and in the original reflecting the text's immediate world, *jagat*, and *sansār*, in single, comparative, and world literary debates, if she is a woman, especially a woman who also writes poetry?[14] The chapter argues that the *vishva* in Varma's lyrics needs to be read against the grain. That is, the *vishva* in her lyrics needs to be put into conversation with the *vishva* created in all the *sahitya* by her, where the poetic "I" and "You" reflect the complexity of selfhood for a woman in India, rather than a figure that is mystical and religious. By reading the *vishva* in Varma's lyrics as mutually enforcing and endorsing the *vishva* in her other *sahitya* (prose and editorial work that often use pronouns such as "we"), comparatists can furnish the historical context of the world, *jagat*, and *sansār* for her various subjectivities in different genres. Such a reading assists in reinterpreting the *vishva* that her poems actually construct—one that is indicative of *chhayavaad*'s humanism and connected with ideas such as world consciousness, worldwide companionship, and feminism. In addition, by reading against the grain, the chapter challenges the world-making of Varma's *vishva* as that of modern Mira's, while highlighting the politics of world-making through literary canons in literary traditions and emphasizing as an antidote the need to read the worlds within texts "in relation"[15] to each other when the author is a woman.

World-making versus *Vishva*

Mahadevi Varma's journey toward becoming the "modern Mira" is important for the scholars to know, considering her status as a woman poet in the Hindi world of letters. Her journey of becoming a "modern Mira" is indicative of the enormous influence the material world, *jagat*, and *sansār* can put on the *vishva* of a woman author's *sahitya*, preferring a particular world-making that might not necessarily agree with what the author created in her literary texts. In 1930, *Sahitya Bhavan*, one of the leading new publishing houses of Allahabad, published Mahadevi Varma's first collection of poems, *Nihar*. After this publication, Varma's poems began to appear in major Hindi literary journals such as *Sarasvati*, *Madhuri*, and *Sudha*.[16] By then, Varma had already been published in the Hindi periodical *Chand*. Regardless, *Nihar* by itself was special. First, it was by the lone Hindi *chhayavaad* woman poet, who was writing poetry in "I-style." Second, the "Introduction" was by Harioudh, a famous Hindi writer, who not only appreciated Varma but also encouraged her to write verses on "*Bharatmata*" (mother India) that expressed India's current conditions. By doing this, Harioudh wrote, Varma could increase her popularity, as only those who can be mothers can truly experience with sensitivity the plight of mother India.[17] Though subtle, Harioudh's remarks suggest that the Hindi world of letters was trying to separate itself from Urdu, and that welcoming patriotic poetry in the "I-style" (written by Varma in the *chhayavaad* idiom) would help those lobbying to make Hindi the national language of India.

When *chhayavaad* was flourishing, a few critics had remarked that the *chhayavaad* poems were love poems whose inspirations were fake, and that they could not be equal to the *ghazals*, which at that time represented the epitome of expressing romantic love. An editorial published in 1928 in *Sarasvati* compared the *chhayavaad* poets to incomprehensible nightingales, who are given credit for singing something, though the subject of their songs is incomprehensible. Criticizing the language of the *chhayavaad* poets, the editorial points out that poetry in general is only successful if it is understood. Otherwise, it is just the song of a bird; and the birds (here meaning *chhayavaad* poets) should not expect to be published, as poems cannot be riddles. Comparing the *chhayavaad* poems to the Urdu love songs and *ghazals*, the editorial proclaims that these poems are inspired by the same "dagger that cuts across the heart"[18] of a young heart in love. But instead of the deep wound that produces a *ghazal*, *chhayavaad* poems are inspired by a gentle strumming in the heart. "Poet and Poetry,"[19] a much earlier essay published in July 1907 in *Sarasvati*, argues that Hindi authors and poets should read Urdu literature so that they can enrich Hindi. Mahavir Prasad Dvivedi, the editor of *Sarasvati*, encouraged authors to read Hali's Urdu verses, which challenged the poetic traditions of his time, as he believed this would result in breaking through the Braj and *riti* poetics.[20] Hence, by gently encouraging Varma to compose verses that address the plight of *Bharatmata*, Harioudh is world-making Varma as a prominent Hindi woman national poet, while encouraging her to create a specific kind of *vishva* in her *sahitya*.

Just a year after Varma's publication of *Nihar*, which had gathered significant critical acclaim, the editor of Allahabad press had compiled and published the first anthology of Hindi women poets, *Stri-Kavi-Kaumudi*.[21] The anthology was primarily intended for use in girls' schools, and it generated quite a bit of interest, not just in the Hindi intellectual circles and prestigious magazines such as *Chand* but also in Kolkata's literary journal *Vishal Bharat*.[22] Indeed, *Stri-Kavi-Kaumudi* presents itself as a unique and exhaustive work on women authors. It includes a critical essay on historical and literary developments of poetry by women authors from the *bhakti* tradition to *chhayavaad*. The editor of *Stri-Kavi-Kaumudi* takes pride in explaining that unlike other anthologies of Hindi poetry by Shivsingh Saroj or Mishrabandhu (which had either given brief introductions of women authors while mostly discussing male authors, or just given a short slim list of names of women authors while focusing on the works of male authors), *Stri-Kavi-Kaumudi* includes actual works by women authors as well as critical commentary on those works.[23] Further, in *Stri-Kavi-Kaumudi* the poems by women authors are also accompanied by the poet's biography and a glossary of difficult words.

While describing the selection process for the anthology, in the critical essay on women poetry Ramshankar Shukla writes that the anthology's editor chose poems that display the dominant themes in which their respective authors have shown most interest. The essay begins with Mira as the first prominent woman poet in Hindi, and concludes with a discussion on Mahadevi Varma's *chhayavaad* poems. The introductory essay discusses Varma enthusiastically and seems to suggest that Varma's high educational attainments in English, Sanskrit, and Hindi gave her the skills to write mature, mystical, and refined poems that were in a simple language but were nonetheless incredibly moving.[24] In the critical essay, Shukla identifies Varma as the youngest and the most prominent poet composing verses in the contemporary "I-style," who is interested in spiritual mysticism, and whose verses display a "heart that is full of anguish and pain."[25] As an example, Shukla asks readers to read her work "My Life's Introduction"[26] in the anthology.

The critical commentary that preceded Varma's poems indicates that almost all of Varma's verses illustrate separation and longing. These commentaries also reveal that the Hindi literary world was very hopeful that Varma, who at that time was just twenty-three years old, would become a successful Hindi poet. It was perhaps a coincidence that the anthology began with Mira's sketch and ended with Mahadevi Varma's photo. Taking this as a cue, along with the apparent similarities between Mahadevi Varma and Mirabai's poetic content, and some life choices such as not living with their respective spouses, readers began to perceive Varma as the "modern Mira." Schomer notes that by the time Varma's collection *Rashmi* came out, the idea of calling Mahadevi Varma the "modern Mira" was so familiar that her poetry had begun to be discussed in terms of its devotional elements—as representing a "*virahini*," or "a woman separated from her beloved," where the beloved was always the absent god.

This world-making of Varma as the "modern Mira" was furthered by the reviews and literary criticism in Hindi magazines. For instance, in a 1934 review, Ramvilas Sharma wrote that, like a true devotee who wants nothing but a connection with the god, Mahadevi Varma want to remain absorbed in separation[27] from her beloved. The image of a "mystical poetess in waiting" had only strengthened with time. An even more interesting correspondence that occurred in relation to Mahadevi Varma's iconization as the "modern Mira" in Hindi literary and public life was Gandhi's appropriation of the sixteenth-century poet Mira to represent the Indian nation and the national symbol of purity and devotion. The re-inscription of the premodern poet Mira on the national stage only fueled Mahadevi Varma's appropriation as "modern Mira" in the Hindi literary circle, which had not seen a prominent woman poet in the limelight and was lobbying to make Hindi the national language of India. By the 1930s, Varma had not only become a woman poet of importance who participated actively in *kavi-sammelans* (poetry-gatherings) and received several prizes, she also presided over a *kavi-sammelan* to which Gandhi himself was invited. In 1938 Varma was selected to write the Hindi *Sahitya Sammelan*'s (Hindi literary society's) new series on living modern Hindi poets.[28] The prestige of these awards and honors corresponded with the mass entrance of women into the national movement, meshing smoothly with Gandhi's appropriation of Mira as a symbol of purity and devotion and with Mahadevi Varma's image as the selfless and pure icon of femininity for Hindi literary society.

In reality, Varma's and Mira's poetic content and craft are very different, and an iconization of one as the other only leads to misreading in literary discourses. Born in Rajasthan in 1498, and betrothed to the prince of Mewar, Mira is often said to be a contemporary of Surdas. The first hagiography of Mira was written by Priyadas (1712 CE) in his commentary on Nabhadas's *Bhaktamala*. This account has provided the fodder for developing conjectures on her life. Very early in her life, Mira became a devotee of Krishna or Giridhar, whose references we find in almost all her verses. It is said that when she could not perform her wifely duties as a result of her devotion to the god, the Rana (it is unknown whether this was her father-in-law or her husband) tried to poison her, though she survived.[29] One does not know if Mira's reference to prosecution and poisoning in her verses is metaphorical or real, but she is "regarded as the exemplar of single-minded spiritual dedication, a theme constantly voiced in her *padas*."[30] Bear in mind that Mira's verses express her love *only for* Giridhar or Krishna. Further, her poems have been passed down orally. There is not one definite text; several versions exist in Gujarati, Rajasthani, and Braj, which have also been, no doubt, interpolated.

The major theme of Mira's poems is the outspoken love of a woman separated from her beloved. For instance, in one poem, the speaker identified as "Mira" describes the physical pain her eyes suffer because of not seeing Hari (or Krishna). The long separation between Hari and Mira has befuddled the usual concept of time and motion. For Mira, a night of separation from Hari feels as long as six months. This palpable suffering displayed in disillusionment with time and physical discomfort can only be cured through the sight of Hari, and thus, the poem ends with: "Mira's lord, when will you meet me, to remove sorrow and to bring joy?"[31] Another popular Mira poem depicts her dancing in frenzy because she has become a "slave girl" to her Narayana (Krishna). This blatant display of transgression from a woman causes people in the verse to call Mira mad, believing that she has destroyed her family and marriage. In fact, her husband, wishing to kill her, sends a poisoned cup that the "mad" Mira drinks. The intensity of her love is such that even poison cannot harm her. The verse ends on a triumphant note: "Mira has readily found her lord, the courtly Giridhar, the eternal one."[32]

In contrast to the presence or absence of the speaker and listener(s) in Mira's poems identified as Mira, Krishna or Giridhar, Varma's verses mostly deliberate about the identities of the speaker and the listener(s). For instance, Varma's lyric "Who Are You in My Heart?" contemplates the changes experienced by the speaker because the poetic "You." In the verse, the imperceptible "You" fills anguish with sweetness, overflows the thirsty eyes with tears, and paints golden dreams in the empty house of sleep. Each stanza consists of oxymoronic and paradoxical images: the one who had been imprisoned is imprisoned in victory, in the ocean of darkness the image of light is unwavering, and sweet fragrant camphor rains in flames. It ends with the refrain: "Who are you in my heart?" Unlike Mira's verses, where the beloved was an actual divine entity, Varma's poem displays an uncertainty about the tangible presence and identity of the other(s). The repeated question "Who are you in my heart?" echoes throughout the poem with no affirmative conclusion, only to end in a cryptic message:

> Today, has ecstatic creation gone
> to unite with the lover even in the destruction?
> Who are you in my heart?[33]

In Mira's verses, separation and union result from the absence and presence of Giridhar, the divine. While love, separation, joy, irreverence toward social norms, pain, and other emotions are staged in front of an audience in Mira's verses, there is no embodied being to witness the poignant pain of construction and deconstruction in Varma's poem. Thus, from the sheer comparative thematic point of view, both poets differ in their very conception of the referents that make their poems' *vishva* poetic. If Mira's verses are specifically about Giridhar, herself, and her conflict with a society that sees her as mad, Varma's poems are compressed into the *vishva* of just two words: "I" and "You."

The repercussions of world-making Mahadevi Varma as the "modern Mira" have been such that there is a clear-cut division in the ways her work has been translated and received in English. Translations and re-translations of Varma's prose into English along with commentaries on them have established her as a socially conscious and feminist author.[34] Owing to her image in the Hindi literary tradition as the "modern Mira," translators in English have perhaps preferred Varma's prose, which has seemed to them to be more modern and relevant to an (inter)national audience. Thus, for example, the iconic *Women Writing in India* does not introduce readers to Varma's poems, but to her prose—despite that Volume One of this anthology is otherwise heavily dominated by women's poetry. The editors, quite appropriately, suggest that a certain disservice has been done to Varma's writing by the mystique that has grown around her as modern Mira.[35] Her poetry, the editors add, is either addressed in devotional terms or Romantic agony, but never analyzed as displaying cultural renaissance and expressing feminist concerns. It is significant to note here that the editors of *Women Writing in India* place Varma's prose in Volume One (which spans from 600 BCE to early twentieth century), whereas many of Varma's contemporaries in languages other than Hindi appear in Volume Two (which is devoted solely to the twentieth century and includes more prose than poetry). It seems that even with all the editors' good intentions, the overpowering world-making of Varma's similarity to the sixteenth-century Mira, could not earn her a place with her fellow women contemporaries in 1991, when the two volumes were published. Despite being critical of Varma-Mira comparisons, unwittingly Varma gets placed by the editors in a volume that has less to do with present. This fact is especially important to note when we consider that Varma was active as an author and passed away in 1987, just a few years before *Women Writing in India* came out.

Though a few poems of Varma have appeared in translation into English in Sahitya Akademi's literary journal *Indian Literature*, and a few translators such as David Rubin, Sarah Green Houston, Anita Anantharam have translated Varma's poems, L. S. Sinha's *Selected Poems*,[36] published in 1987, is the only book solely dedicated to translations of Varma's poems from *Nihar, Neerja, Sandhya Geet*, and *Deepshikha*. The book includes a photograph of Varma with lines from one of her poems in longhand. These lines ironically suggest ways for readers to subvert the personal and devotional reading of her lyrics:

These tears are not water.
This pain is not sandalwood.[37]

L. S. Sinha states in the "Preface" that the purpose of translating Varma's poems is to emphasize her mystical and Mira-like qualities: "Those who have read and appreciated the poetry of Mahadevi Varma have invariably been impressed, even moved, by the beauty of her expression heightened by the tenderness of emotion of love."[38] Sinha connects Mahadevi Varma's image of the "modern Mira" with that of Tagore, remarking that the "one great poet whom"[39] Mahadevi Varma "resembles most, is surely Rabindranath Tagore."[40] Yet, sadly, whereas Tagore, "whose works were originally in Bengali, could reach out to a very large number of readers through his own English translation of *Gitanjali* and other poetic compositions,"[41] Mahadevi Varma, despite "her great popularity,"[42] hardly reached out beyond "the aesthetic sensibilities of non-Hindi speaking people even in her own country."[43] Sinha adds that the collection, a selection of Varma's poems, is an attempt in that direction.[44]

Furthering the image of the "modern Mira" pining for her absent divine beloved, Sinha writes that the major problem in translating Varma is the fact that an "intense devotion to the lord she is in love with, has naturally led her to borrowing images from temple worship, in a number of items associated with it."[45] Her poetry was "marked by a depth of emotion born out of an intense and abiding love for her lord."[46] Regarding the speaker and addressee in Varma's poems, Sinha explains that many regard Varma as being in love with a divine being, and others conjecture "this love as the ordinary eroticism of day-to-day life,"[47] but "as we read poems after poems of Mahadevi, it is difficult to accept this simplistic analysis."[48] Although at first glance the play between the poetic constructs "You" and "I" may seem simply to refer allegorically to a divine lover (Krishna), Varma uses language and the poetic scenario to complicate these notions. In fact, through her poems, she subtly subverts culturally accepted notion of a female subject in waiting.

Take, for example, the poem "That Cruel Mirror Broke."[49] Each stanza of the poem ends with the refrain, "that cruel mirror broke," and in the process contradicts or supports the sentiments expressed before. The poem has a recurrent theme of a poetic self, engaging in an internal dialogue. Except for the reference toward the end of the poem to adorning hair and eyes, all the stanzas remain mysteriously opaque about the gendered identity of the poetic speaker, who is looking in the "cold" mirror, musing over their reflection, and pondering the imaginary constructs "I" and "You" that just broke with the mirror. Indeed, the poem evokes a subtle play of subjectivities, complicated by a reflection in the mirror that is broken, where the speaker's reflection had scorned the persona looking at the mirror. Inside the speaker, affection and illusion (identified in the next line with tears and laughter) have played hide and seek. Since the mirror is now broken, the platform where the two could coexist is no longer possible. The mirror appears to be not only a mode where subjectivities are connected—as it draws "two outlines of us,"[50] or "to show union between the two"[51]—but also a stage where contradictory images unite, as in "day-night"[52] and "happiness-pain."[53] Now that the cruel mirror is broken, the speaker wonders in the present tense where "shall I look to adorn my hair,"[54] "to anoint fragrance on my ecstatic body,"[55] "wear the kohl of dreams on my eyelids,"[56] "with whom will I be thrilled,"[57] "with whom will I be angry,"[58] and "with which reflection shall I fill the darkness within!"[59] The poem ends on the same note as it had begun. After questioning the whereabouts of the "familiar self," which provided the place for this "You" to hide, where even attachments did not belong to the speaker:

That cruel mirror is broken![60]

While translating this verse from Hindi into English, David Rubin prefaces it as "an allegory of the realization of the individual's identity with Brahman, the One, the real of the real,"[61] where the act of breaking the mirror of "maya frees the poet, allowing her to see that all the dualities of earthly life are illusory—the individual and Brahman, human and divine, lover and beloved, worshipper and worshipped."[62]

Although it could be argued that the poem becomes an allegory for the realization of the poetic speaker's identity with the divine energy, there are other plausible explanations. The poetic speaker could be exiled from their beloved and is suffering, though we do not know the situation that led to that exile—or separation. In the poem, the poetic "I" suggests that the *vishva* (Varma uses this word) was created by tears and happiness. We are also not aware of whether the separation is voluntary because the poetic "I" and "You" together had once created a *sansār* (Varma's use of the word) of mistakes in order to be united. Further, there are no indications that would help us in locating the "You" of the poem. It could very well be a reflection, or a dialogue with multiple selves, because at one point the poetic "I" suggests that it is either "You" or darkness in the *vishva* (her use). In fact, the so called "absent lover" exists within the speaker. There are no referents that indicate that the beloved is male, or female, or even a separate entity at all. It is quite possible that the beloved is nothing but a part of the modernist poetic self, musing over the death of an old self (who had an anointed body and adorned hair). The next to the last stanza of the poem confirms this, suggesting that the poetic self has been separated or alienated from the "familiar self." The line "my bondage is your convenience"[63] literally undermines the importance of "You," shown through the semi-formal "*tum*" in the poem to the extremely informal yet endearing word "*terā*" (equivalent to "tú" in Spanish). The dramatic final line sums up the gist of the poem, confirming that the split between "I" and "You" is vast because the poetic "You" looks for happiness in the self, but the poetic "I" looks for pain.

Considering that Varma's poems continue to be discussed as spiritually infused, it is hard to disagree with Rubin, who is among a handful of translators who have translated Varma's poems. Regardless, we must recall that the tears and pain in her poems, as Varma herself mentioned in L. S. Sinha's book, are not indicative of water and sandalwood fragrance, ingredients used in temples for worshiping gods. Her poems can very well be read as a dialogue within the corporeal self. Indeed, in her essay "Modern Poet" or "Adhunik Kavi"[64] Varma describes the poet's work as that of an individual self who is deeply intertwined with the society as a whole. Further, Varma writes in another essay that women in modern society have not been able to develop an "individual, appropriate, and rational personality,"[65] but when they do develop such a personality, they are frowned upon and disrespected.[66] Recognizing the historical and literary significance of the poetic "I" and "You" in Varma's poems, and criticizing her clichéd image of "modern Mira" in world-making, Dudhanath Singh suggests that the poetic "I" and "You" in Varma's verses are unlimited. "Should we see,"[67] he adds, "Mahadevi in them—only Mahadevi—or a poetic world embedded in these pronouns constructed by Mahadevi via pronouns as a reflection of all the women in the world?"[68] Such a perspective is a rare departure from approaches like that of Karine Schomer, who sees Varma's poetic collection as transformative, helping the writer to untangle philosophical questions via art, where the journey toward self-discovery becomes a tool for understanding the personal and its connection with the universal.[69] Indeed, behind the personal and empathetic "I-style" poems of the *chhayavaad* poets is the history of a modern human being, speaking of a new humanism through a new world-making in the *vishva* of its lyrics.

Unlike the *bhakti* poets who wanted to speak with their individual gods, the poetic "I" of the *chhayavaad* lyrics is not looking for a god, but for a new relationship in the *vishva*, *jagat*, and *sansār* with respect to gender, politics, and social status. To reduce the *chhayavaad* poems to romantic lyrics, and Varma to a modern Mira, is to neglect and misread the poetic "I" of twentieth century Hindi literature. In fact, while contextualizing Varma's pronouns, Pant writes that Varma's poetic "I" is neither anguishing for an "unknown" medieval "You," nor is the "I" a feeble woman who coquettishly slips on the bank of a river to seek attention.[70] In fact, the relationship seen between the "I" and "You" in these lyrics heralds a new wave of world humanism (*vishva mānavtā*), and compassion. In one of her essays, Varma herself writes that she does not believe in worshiping; nor does she wish for any sort of divine place in her poems. Varma stresses the voice of the poetic speaker in one of her poems, titled "The Self was Not Lost":[71]

> You have neither experienced pain
> Nor have you been curious to seek!
> You could never forget yourself
> so you never lost your "self"
> and you never found *khuda*.[72]

Varma uses the word "*Khuda*" in this poem. Since the "self" could not be forgotten by the "You," *Khuda* (God) was never found. The *sufis* and the *bhakti* poets either annihilated the poetic "I" in order to reach God or saw the divine being within the poetic "I." The *vishva* in Varma's worldly poems refuse to surrender the poetic "I" to an unknown divine.

Varma's *Sahitya* and *Vishva*

Superficially speaking, the time span of Varma's poetic career can be summed up in two works: her first poetry collection *Nihar*, which greeted readers when the "I-style" poetry had become immensely popular and Pant had formally defended the *chhayavaad* movement, and *Deepshikha*, which marked the movement's conclusion. Between these two collections, Varma published three additional volumes of poetry, as well as countless essays and prose works that came out in various magazines and were later published in book versions in the 1940s and beyond. Even before Varma's first poetry collection came out in 1930, she began publishing in the mid-1920s, in *Chand*. Most historians argue that in the last decade of the nineteenth century, the "woman's question" had effectively disappeared from the mainstream public agenda in India.[73] However, between the 1880s and 1920s the woman's question was being carried forward *by* women in various periodicals that they were either spearheading as editors or contributing to as writers.[74] In Hindi, for instance, *Stree Darpan* had distinguished itself from magazines such as *Sarasvati*, *Chand*, and *Grihlakshmi* published from Allahabad. Unlike other women's periodicals in Hindi where often male editors had co-opted their wives as editors, *Stree Darpan* was launched by a woman independently in 1909.[75] As an editor of *Stree Darpan*, Rameshwari Nehru undertook the unusual task of not only cultivating women's minds but also trying to change the minds of men (who were prone to infantilizing women) through dialogue and interaction.[76] By the time Varma formally entered the Hindi poetic scene, the *chhayavaad* movement was at its peak, and she already had a living example of Rameshwari Nehru running a successful woman's Hindi periodical.

Certainly, Varma's political and social leaning in the world, *jagat*, and *sansār* can contextualize the *vishva* in her lyrics, and one of the ways in which they can be understood is by knowing a bit about the periodical. *Chand* was a progressive Hindi magazine, which began publishing from Allahabad in 1922. What was remarkable about *Chand* was that, though it specifically represented itself as a periodical that focused on women and their engagement with politics, social problems, unjust laws, domestic issues, and sexual equality, it did not alienate other readers. In fact, the inclusive readership of *Chand* is evident in the way readers are addressed in its iconic 1928 edition (titled *Hanged*)[77] which came out during Diwali, the festival of lights. The editor addresses the readers as "Dear Sisters, Mothers, Brothers, and the Elderly,"[78] and asks them to consider the special issue as a reminder of grim realities on a day of festivities. The special issue critiqued the British laws that were cited as a basis for hanging young revolutionaries who were fighting for freedom in India. *Chand* also regularly devoted sections to the topic of creating solidarity among women around the world. For instance, in its regular sections titled "World [*Vishva*] Clarinet"[79] and "World [*Vishva*] View,"[80] readers could easily find news and opinion pieces on women's movements taking place in various parts of southern India, and also in different parts of the world, such as Turkey. One of the editorial pieces titled "How and Why?"[81] in the 1930 edition states that the magazine has received hundreds of personal letters from women who are struggling in their domestic and work spheres; this struggle, the anonymous author remarks, is symptomatic of a bigger social problem. The author unequivocally suggests that men and women are equal.

Chand was not just a local Hindi periodical. The 1928 edition of the magazine contains a translation of Victor Hugo's work with the title "*Chhayanuvād*" (Shadow-speaking-after). In the 1930 edition of *Chand*, a *ghazal* titled "The Plea of Bismal,"[82] which criticized the British government, was published. Unlike *Sarasvati*, *Chand* was a pioneering magazine, as it paid attention to women readers as well. Though this was an age of political activism and social changes and progressive outlook on women's role in society, it was still unpopular for women to be actively involved in the literary fields and circles. In fact, for some time the rumor in Allahabad was that one of the men on the staff of *Chand* was writing poetry, as women poets could not be found and did not exist, and Varma was receiving the prize as a token.[83] Despite the rumors, misogyny, and sexism surrounding Varma, many of her early poems were published in *Chand*, and they have never been collected as a separate volume.

Varma later served as an editor of *Chand* in 1935, and she encouraged women to participate in intellectual and literary debates throughout her life. The magazine published several of Varma's feminist and political essays starting in 1935; these would later be collected and published together as one of the first feminist writings in Hindi in India, *The Links to Our Chains*,[84] in 1942, almost in tandem with her poetry collection *Deepshikha*. Varma's unique position as a poet, activist, writer, educator, and feminist can be appreciated by knowing that at a very young age she rebelled against her child marriage, decided to not live with her husband, wanted to study, and wrote works that would today qualify as subaltern literature. At one point in her life, she seriously considered converting to Buddhism after becoming frustrated and anguished by the plight of Hindu women. In fact, Varma decided to go to the Himalayas to be ordained by a Ceylonese priest, who would only talk to her behind a wooden frame to keep from being distracted by any sexual passion.[85] A thoroughly disappointed Varma returned to Allahabad to continue her MA in Sanskrit, which in itself was quite rare for women at that time. In 1932, a time when middle-class women were expected to marry and not have a profession of their own, Varma created a niche for herself by becoming not only the first female editor of a Hindi literary periodical but also an educator and principal at a women's college, Mahila Vidyapith College, in Allahabad.

Most of these activities were either volunteer or low-paying work. Despite this lack of monetary compensation, the college became central to Varma's aim of engaging more women in the literary world, which coincided with her editorship in *Chand*. The editing position gave her the unique opportunity to mold the new college in a way that encouraged formal education among women from economically depressed backgrounds, child widows, and young wives of the men jailed by the British, and to create a formal platform where women poets and writers could be published. As a result, among other things, by 1935, Varma had published a special issue of *Chand*, titled "Women-scholars."[86] The special issue was the first of its kind, wherein a total of 500 poems and articles by women were published under a female editorship. The cover page of the magazine carries a sketch by Varma of a woman with a lamp in her hand worshiping the moon, or *chand*, the title of the periodical. Varma would later create various iterations of this sketch (i.e., a woman with a lamp) for *Deepshikha*. The "Women-scholars" edition of *Chand* began with a poem by Rameshvari Devi Chakori, and it ended with Varma's verse.[87]

In between, the special issue included several other poems and intriguing essays that focused on topics such as different styles in women's literature, the responsibility of a woman-scholar, women's movements in Asia and India, divorce, women-scholars, and inter-caste marriages. This special issue of *Chand* also carried Varma's editorial essay "The Position of Women in Literature." In this essay, Varma surveys women's contributions to the field of Hindi literature in the first two decades of the twentieth century. She argues that women have restricted themselves to the genre of lyrics and short stories because of the social constraints placed on them, which prevented them from gaining experiences that could be translated into other genres such as drama, novels, and narrative poetry.[88] The essay was one of the most unique editorials of *Chand*, departing from all the others on two levels. Varma not only encouraged women to enter the world of literary criticism, but unlike authors in other periodicals (where the discussion on the uplifting of women was always addressed to men who were asked to think of solutions), Varma urged women to take the reins.[89] The special issue garnered so much attention that many editors of Hindi periodicals, as well as certain segments of English magazines, expressed their appreciation for it.[90] It needs to be kept in mind that Varma was also producing "I-style" poetry while doing all this work.

The *vishva* in Varma's lyrics can be contextualized by knowing that when *The Links to Our Chains* was published in 1942, Varma prefaced it by writing that she prefers writing essays to express her ideas, as the genre allows her not only to express herself but also to analyze the context and nature of her thoughts.[91] She remarks that some of her essays included in the volume might lead readers to perceive her as a radical—which would be true, because she is intolerant toward injustice.[92] As if to soften this earlier remark on being a radical, Varma immediately adds that she is devoted to those light-imparting elements of creativity in whose presence deformity fades into darkness. Continuing her "light" metaphor, Varma suggests that darkness is nothing but the absence of a *deepak* or lamp, an image she often uses in her "I-style" *chhayavaad* lyrics; she compares her current work to a small lamp capable of destroying darkness.[93]

Clearly, Varma's work for the Hindi periodical along with her activities as a scholar, educator, and activist are all important to consider when contextualizing her poetry, and vice versa. These other forms of work show that while Varma was composing her "I-style" lyrics in first-person voice—lyrics which are often read as disconnected with the real world—she was deeply involved in political, feminist, social, and literary activities and debates in Allahabad. If this involvement is recognized, the *vishva* in her lyrics becomes part of the *chhayavaad* that was actively engaged in humanism, world-making, and reconfiguring women's position in society, rather than pining for an absent unknown beloved. In short, reading the subjectivities in the *vishva* of Varma's *sahitya* in relation to each other emphasizes the unique characteristics of her lyrics in world, *jagat*, and *sansār*. As an example of connecting the poetic and prose *vishva* in her *sahitya*, consider how Varma uses the imagery of lamp and light in her verses as well as her feminist work, *The Links to Our Chains*.

Varma's last collection of poems, *Deepshikha*, includes a sketch of a woman draped in a *saree* with one hand on her forehead, suggesting that she is searching for something or someone, while holding a lit lamp or *deepak* in her other hand. This is similar to Varma's sketch for the feminist issue of *Chand*, which focused on "Women-scholars." The first poem from *Deepshikha* begins as follows:

Unwaveringly burn, my lamp
dissolve steadily![94]

The beginning of the poem is a reminder of Varma's several verses on the lamp earlier in her career, the special issue of *Chand*, and her thoughts on the death of Tagore. She pays homage to Tagore by writing that she will continue to burn the lamp that he has lit.

Varma's lamp is consistently self-consummating, while storms and cataclysmic floods sing its praise. In another poem of hers, "Sweetly Softly Burn, My Lamp,"[95] published in *Neerja*, the speaker asks to light the way of the beloved while fading slowly:

Pour out your abundant incense fragrance,
let your body become soft as wax.
As your life slowly melts away
give forth an infinite ocean of light.[96]

Similarly, in "Let Me Light All Unlit Lamps," published in *Deepshikha*, the speaker utters:

> Let me light all unlit lamps
> Darkness is enveloping, let me light the *ragini deepak*.⁹⁷

Sometimes we also encounter a poem such as "Wax-like Body Is Now Dissolved"⁹⁸ that begins as follows:

> A wax-like body has now melted, a lamp-like body has burnt
>
> Take a few colorful moments of separation
> Take a few remaining tears
> Take a few dry scattered dreams of flowers
> The breath has again gone to search
> for that loose unclear path.⁹⁹

The poem ends on an equally mysterious note:

> So tell me, what's the message?
> Is there more to burn for?
> Beyond this path of fire is there a place of sandalwood and moonlight?
> For one beckoning
> hundred times the breath has fluttered!
>
> A wax-like body has now melted, a lamp-like body has burnt.¹⁰⁰

In *Nihar*, Varma had written a verse on "Lamp":¹⁰¹

> After silencing the intense mind
> After putting all the fervor to sleep,
> Burn the breaths quietly
> hide the crying inside;
> where was a love so rare learnt?
> my enchanted little lamp!¹⁰²

In this lyric, the poetic "I" is communicating with the lamp, who has mastered the art of quietly burning and suffering. Certainly, the image of lamp is significant to Varma, who uses it not only to highlight the poetic speaker's ability to vanquish darkness and spread light, but also as a beacon of hope that is constantly self-consuming.

Thus, to understand Varma's *vishva* in her lyrics and completely do away with the "modern Mira" image, it is necessary to read the subjectivities Varma creates as mutually enforcing, endorsing, and in relation to each other. As mentioned before, Varma's literary work spans three important genres: lyric, essay, and "life-sketches." In all of these genres, Varma creates multiple different subjectivities.[103] Take, for instance, the following stanza:

> Who are you in my heart?
>
> Who, imperceptible, always
> fills my anguish with sweetness?
> Who, unknown, overflows
> like storm clouds in my thirsty eyes?[104]

The foregoing quote is from Varma's poem, "Who Are You in My Heart?" The poem has twelve stanzas comprising six quatrains and six three-lined verses. Each quatrain is followed by a three-lined stanza ending with the refrain, "Who are you in my heart?" which also happens to be the title of the poem. The four-lined and three-lined stanzas together form a small independent unit, like the couplets of a long *ghazal*. Unlike most *ghazals*, where couplets end with a "*radīf*" (the repeating word), Varma's poems, often classified as "*gītī kāvya*" (lyric poems), follow a different pattern. The lyric begins with a single line called "*tek*" (refrain) which sets the scene. This line is followed by couplets, quatrains, and so on called "*prasār*" (expansion) to elaborate on the "*tek*," with a possibility of ending with a "*samāpan*" (conclusion) that reiterates the "*tek*," which seldom subverts the main poetic idea embedded in it. The poem engages in a playful speculation on the disembodied identity of the nameless and genderless "You," who brings out a plethora of emotional responses rendered through the images in the genderless poetic speaker, "I."

In prose, Varma constructs her subjectivity as follows:

> Usually the poet's condition in the visible world is just like that of other individuals, in that a poet exists both at the individual and the collective level. In the former case she is complete as a unit, in the latter, her individual self [her own unit] is an intricate part of, and intertwined with, society as a whole [the external world]. Her inner world must develop in such a way that it will keep perfecting her individual life in harmony with her collective life.[105]

The previous prose cited is taken from "Modern Poet" or "Adhunik Kavi" published in *Deepshikha*. The excerpt is from a recent translation of the essay, where the translator, Francesca Orsini, has replaced all the masculine verbs and nouns with feminine ones, which makes sense to our feminist sensibilities. In Hindi, nouns referring mixed masculine and feminine groups are masculine, and verbs are always gendered. Since in the Hindi version Varma speaks about poets as a mixed group, she uses "*kavi*," and not "*kavitri*" (woman poet). In this essay, Varma makes references to her own poetic works and also presents a strong defense of the poetics of the *chhayavaad*. In "Modern Poet" or "Adhunik Kavi" Varma writes that in the early part of her poetic career she wrote poems with titles such as "The Helpless Woman," and "The Widow," which found publication in some magazines, along with the sketches that accompanied these poems. But when she arrived in Allahabad for formal education, she abandoned them and undertook a poetic direction where "individual sorrows took the shape of deep collective anguish,"[106] in which "the concrete form in front"[107] of her "hinted at a subtle consciousness and beyond."[108] Consequently, poems that specifically addressed the plight of an unfortunate woman offered a broader perspective on women's condition in society. In addition to that delicate balance between the individual and the collective, in the quoted section from the essay, Varma identifies two worlds (she uses the Hindi word "*jagat*")[109]—inner and outer—that are dependent on each other, common to both the poets and non-poets. She writes that the task of poets is to develop and balance the intellectual and emotional elements of these two worlds.

If the quoted excerpt from the essay is not personal and speaks in masculine plural terms and pronouns about the poets' world, the "life-sketches" display a different kind of subjectivity, where the "I" is freely used and contextualized in relation to other people in the world:

> There was not much time then to argue or discuss: the old man's granddaughter must be near death! Poor unfortunate soul! But I am no doctor or practitioner of indigenous medicine, I thought. And while it is customary for people to include poets at head-shaving and ear-piercing ceremonies [happy occasions], they have not yet begun to invite poets to preside over the final moments of a person's life.[110]

The quoted section is taken from Varma's "life-sketch," published in 1941, a year after her poetry collection *Deepshikha* came out. In this particular "life-sketch," Varma recalls the moment when, at the age of twenty-seven, she agreed to informally adopt an unwed eighteen-year-old woman and the woman's twenty-two-day-old son. In general, Varma's "life-sketches" present a range of characters who are social outcasts. She is unafraid to speak of the Dalits, child widows, and voiceless women who are caught in patriarchy.

In the preface to her "life-sketch," Varma writes that the characters presented in the eleven stories are taken from her life, and that these stories are being published in a collection not to put these individuals' wounds on display, but to generate empathy and pity for them. It is significant to note that though Varma calls this work a result of her *smriti* (memories), she also writes in the preface that her intention has been to present the characters, and since she is writing their stories her persona is bound to seep into the narratives, which the readers are asked to ignore. If the verse that I quoted is in first person, speculative, disembodied, abstract, and characterized by a play between the addressee (often indicated as "You" in the lyrics) and the personal pronoun possessive determiner "my," the essay is distant and in the third-person voice, indicating the different worlds poets inhabit and must balance, while the "life-sketch" returns to the pronoun "I," engaging with various "others" who are identifiable, embodied, and concrete in social, economic, and political realms. Immediately, Varma's curated subjectivities across genres are visible; and thus reading them "in relation" thicken the *vishva* in her lyrics.

In Varma's lyrics, the humanism of *chhayavaad* finds a new vigor because of her feminist ideals and grassroots-level activism. Varma herself writes that her sharp prose can supplement the subtle world that her poems elusively generate and suggest.[111] While her poetry highlights a play between the pronouns "I" and "You" that might seem grammatically idiosyncratic and untouched by the political chaos of Varma's time, her prose reflects directly on the sociopolitical situation. The themes that she addresses in her prose are politically charged; in contrast, her poems' themes are confined to the desire, destruction, longing, dialogue, and natural imagery between the "I" and "You." In her prose, Varma spoke directly about women's education, socio-literary reforms, national language, the role of the artist in a society, and other political questions. Unlike her poems, where the collective "we" is absent and the pronouns "I" and "You" are used, her prose helped her to contextualize the various voices of marginalized and oppressed people. It also helped her as a woman to establish solidarity. Indeed, Varma writes in defense of *chhayavaad* that the movement produced poems that alerted people to a collective consciousness underneath the subtle[112] feelings in the poems. The subtlety reflected in Varma's lyrics through "I" and "You" carries the collective consciousness of the marginalized, as addressed in her prose.

At a time when the authorial and poetic "I" often led to intrusive engagement, as literary critics offered speculations, gossip, and critiques about writers' private lives, perhaps a conscious distinction and separation among the various subjectivities in literary and non-literary world was a mode of survival for a woman intellectual. Though Pant, and Prasad used first-person voice in their verses and prose in Hindi, and in some of their lyrics the poetic "I" spoke in feminine verbs, for Varma to do this in her lyrics and other works was risky. Consequently, her lyrics in Hindi language, where verbs are gendered and plural is always in masculine, offer a unique case. Indeed, Rubin writes that the "I" had previously been of very little importance to Hindi literature, which was so strongly "devotional in the medieval period and later concerned, above all, with technical bravura in the succeeding era known as *ritikal* (1650–1850)."[113] The poets of these two schools remained anonymous, "expressing their individuality only in the success or failure of their seemingly endless treatment of familiar subjects,"[114] such as Radha-Krishna trysts or the description of a beautiful woman. In the *chhayavaad* tradition, however, even if the poet used the traditionally accepted tropes, they referred back to the poetic "I" in the poem. Further, Rubin adds that of all the four major *chhayavaad* poets, Mahadevi Varma is the only one who did not describe natural or historical events in her poems.

Apart from the social expectations she faced as a woman author in the world, Varma also had strict ideas about the various genres and their purposes. For instance, she distinguishes[115] between the English word "essay" and the *bhasha* word "*nibandh*," which has become its synonym in many modern Indian languages. According to Varma, essays are supposed to freely express thoughts, whereas a "*nibandh*" has a structure: an introduction, an explication of the introduction, followed by an argument, and a tightly knit conclusion. Even within her prose she recognizes two streams: one, where she is writing memoirs or sketches that allow her to be "*bhāvuk*" (emotional) as she is closer to the people she is writing about (something that we saw in her description of the eighteen-year-old woman she decides to adopt); second, in "*nibandh*" like "Modern Poet" or "Adhunik Kavi," where she only writes what can be argued objectively with logic. With respect to poetry, Varma points out[116] that she has a "*dishā*" (direction) and a deep faith in her "*aham*" (self) that stems from her belief in human beings, thus requiring a different kind of expression ("I-style") to do justice to what she calls her "*antarjagat*" (inner world). She highlights that this expression of the inner world belongs neither to a literary movement nor to an act of experimentation. In fact, it is her unwavering faith in humanity and human beings that comes out in an individualized and personalized poetic "I" that speaks the truth.[117]

Varma in the "Adhunik Kavi" writes that when *chhayavaad* was flourishing, the middle-class was experiencing a nationalist awakening that had a specific political goal. Since it was extremely difficult to change the institutions that curtailed the life of an individual in British India, the *chhayavaad* poets turned inward to speak of the individual who lived in a "lifeless culture and decrepit society."[118] Varma points out in the same essay that the *chhayavaad* poets were not some medieval saints who could drown their disappointments by chanting the name of Ram, a Hindu god; instead, they chose to speak of the subtle aspects of human nature that suffer because of unchangeable circumstances that are part of the real life. It is with this knowledge about the origins of the subtle, and its meaning for the *chhayavaad* poets, that the listener(s) and speaker of Varma's lyrics can be embodied within those lyrics' social milieu. Further, Varma very clearly mentions in the "Modern Poet" or "Adhunik Kavi" essay that she does not believe in the religious element of the poetry, or for that matter even in an abstract spiritualism. For her, all subtle feelings that could be qualified as "spiritual" carry an invisible truth in them; this truth arises from the knowledge of incompleteness of the visible by manifesting in universal brotherhood and humanism.[119]

Certainly, poets like Pant, Nirala, and Prasad used first person to write subjective lyrics for world-making—yet many of their poems, unlike Varma's, ended up having a referent noun. For instance, Nirala's verses such as "The Call of the Poor,"[120] "Widow,"[121] and "The Beggar,"[122] published in 1923, are each about a particular person. The pronouns can be contextualized because the poem titles inform the readers about them. In contrast, Pant's "She Is Laying in the Shadow of the Tree" reads as follows:

> Is she awake or asleep?
> Fainted or in a foolish dream?
> Woman or celestial nymph or *maya*?
> Or just a shadow of a tree?[123]

Here, the speaker is speculating about the identity of a "she," who could be a woman, dream, nymph, *maya*, or just a shadow of the tree. The title of the poem indicates that it is a feminine noun. Most of Varma's poems almost never establish the identity of the speaker or addressee in the title of the poems, as the "You" in most of her lyrics does not refer to a proper noun. Further, very few details are given in the *vishva* of the poem to establish the gender identity of "I" or "You." Thus, the concluding stanza of "I and You"[124] reads:

> You secretly come to tie me
> in petty constraints,
> Can you ever separate
> scorching heat from fire?[125]

Just before the quoted stanza, the poetic speaker in the poem indicates to the listener that the "I" and "You" are inseparable, like the sunlight from the sun, but are also separate, like the cloud is from the lightning. Ramchandra Shukla, a fierce critic of *chhayavaad*, had once remarked that in a true sense Varma was the definitive *chhayavaad* poet because her poems are without context and meaning, bordering on the mysticism of *bhakti* poets. Despite this criticism, which was aligned with his response toward *chhayavaad*, Shukla admired Varma's talent of weaving images and metaphors (as we can see in the previous examples) together in a lyric.

Certainly, world-making of the *vishva* in Varma's lyrics as devotional and personalized, not in touch with the social upheavals of their times, was consistent with the prevailing paradigm for assessing *chhayavaad* lyrics in general in the early twentieth century. The legacy of this way of analyzing Varma's poetry continued even close to the end of the century. For instance, while describing the nature of Varma's poems, David Rubin, who has translated some of Varma's poems into English, calls them strikingly original work that displays an "evolving representation of total subjectivity measured against the vastness of cosmic nature with nothing, as it were, intervening—no human social relationships, no human activities beyond those totally metaphorical ones involving weeping, walking the road, playing the vina, etc."[126] For Rubin, Varma's five volumes of poems spanning from 1930 to 1942 create an extraordinary extended epic self, where a "private universe of abstracted emotions becomes objectified and the impersonal cosmos is experienced on the most subjective level so that each in a sense defines and enhances the other."[127] The problem with looking at Varma's poems as an extension of a self, as Rubin does, is that this perspective reverts to ahistoricism and mysticism. If Shukla's comments on Varma's verses stem from his strict ideas about what *chhayavaad* was, and what a woman poet in the early twentieth century could be suggesting through the poetic "I," Rubin is reinforcing the dominant narratives about lyric in the Western world.

Conversely, Dudhanath Singh, a Hindi critic, believes that both the "I" and "You" pronouns in Varma's lyrics both refer to women.[128] When we consider this possibility, Varma's addressee as well as the speaker in her lyrics acquire a new dimension, and her poems become a call for women to break through the shackles of time and create a new world, no matter how bizarre and "mad" it may seem. For instance, the poem "Reply"[129] describes the unique play between the poetic constructs "I" and "You." It begins as follows:

In this teardrop
let the empire be washed away,
let blessings like rain
scatter this loneliness.[130]

The speaker presents to the listener various situations where desires can awaken a slumbering solitude and take away despair, or a mind that can be lost in the diminishing stars that can possibly give happiness to the speaker, or a complete outpouring of compassion on the scattered self by the listener(s). The poem is an address to the disembodied poetic "You" in the present tense, where the poetic "I" progressively negates the addressee's efforts to create joy for the poetic speaker, culminating in an ironic conclusion on the futility of these efforts, because nothing could ever stop this continuous play within the speaker. The addressee discovered the "You" in pain, and hence will always look for the pain in the "You":

But this will not end
the play of my breath
I found you in pain
I will look for pain in you.[131]

Indeed, the disembodied speaker and the addressee in the lyric seem abstract unless we contextualize this lyric in its immediate world (*jagat*, and *sansār*), where Varma was creating a *sahitya* that spoke of oppressive conditions for women, including patriarchy and caste and class discrimination. In this context, a cultural renaissance was taking place, and *chhayavaad* poets were imagining world companionship and world humanism. Certainly, all these things together are a reminder to the poetic "I" that a painful discovery of the self, who in the final stanza of the poem is identified through the verb "discover" as female, is inextricably tied to the other, "You."

Recently, Aamir Mufti suggested that the "I" in the twentieth century Urdu poet Faiz Ahmad Faiz's *ghazal* enacts in a literary-historical register the dilemmas and complexities of a "Muslim" selfhood in India;[132] and Faiz's famous lines "*pahli si mahabbat*"[133] (the love that was before) is pointing out the interiority in the poem with that of the external world, and the "relationship of the modern poet, located in the national-cultural space that is (late colonial) India, to that classical tradition."[134] In a similar vein, the speaker of Varma's poems (such as, say, "Desire"), like Faiz's poetic "I," wishes for a different relational world for the "I" and "You," no matter who they might be:

This mad love desires,
a unique new world![135]

Varma imagines a unique world or *sansār*, as used in the poem, where life glows by dying softly and tenderly, peace is in dying, and grief is a sweet stream of wine; where the unbound horizon meets its limits, the sky sleeps in the sea, desires are measured with life's sensations, and the innocent heart buys madness with mute pain.[136]

Varma wrote in the preface[137] to her *Rashmi* that what *sansār* usually refers to as pain in her poems is absent from her actual life because not only is she loved, cherished, and respected, but she also has everything material that is needed.[138] She adds that pain is the only poetics that can tie the entire *sansār* and humanity together. Happiness, she suggests, can only lead to the first step toward humanity. Pain, on the other hand, makes human beings experience "*vishva jīvan*" (world life) in their personal life, and *vishva vedna* (world pain) in their subjective pain, exactly in the same manner as a water droplet merges into the ocean—a situation that is *nirvana* for the poet.[139] Indeed, as Varma writes in the preface, poetry is in the inner and outer *sansār* of human beings that connects them to the world (she uses the word "*vishva*") and to imagination.[140]

Describing the split subjectivity in Varma's poems and prose as a strategy to keep the public and private separate at a particularly conservative time for women in northern India, Francesca Orsini remarks that this strategy gave Varma the chance to shield her private self and allowed her to play with the abstract, sexuality, desire, and even irony in poetry.[141] Strategically useful though the separation of subjectivities across genres may have been for *Mahadevi* in Hindi literary contexts in the early twentieth century, if *Varma* is to be included in the debates on *vishva sahitya*, whether in the original or in translation, in single, comparative or world literary debates, the *vishva* in her *sahitya* needs to be seen mutually enforcing, and endorsing that is reflecting her immediate world, *jagat*, and *sansār*. This will not only open the *vishva* in her poetry as expressing desire, feminist concerns, humanism, or social change, but also sew together Varma's split subjectivities that are neither ahistorical nor apolitical. Reading Varma against the grain, in the original and translation, not only takes us beyond the excellent, though limited, study of Varma's work that focuses on a development of the self as a poet[142] and frees Varma's *vishva* from the modern Mira comparisons, it also invites worldly relations within her texts that do justice to her position as an author in the world.

5

World in Translation, World in the Original

When Tagore translated the English term "comparative literature" as "*vishva sahitya,*" he did not consider fidelity to an original central for readers to experience joy or *ānand*. For him, the *vishva* in *sahitya* has immense potentiality to transcend contentious debates on translatability and untranslatability, faithfulness and unfaithfulness, and original and translation in *jagat*, and *sansār*. The myriad world-making of a *vishva* in a literary text guarantees that no aspect of a text could remain unrealized forever in a world that is eager to connect with the universal spirit. As a result, for Tagore, all the world-makings of a text become part of a shared history of the *vishva mānav* that only perpetuates *ānand* or joy. Clearly, in Tagore's view of *vishva sahitya*, the "original" is not exclusive to comparative literature, just as "translation" is not exclusive to world literature. The *vishva*, or universe, or world in a text, whether it is in the original or in translation, is whole by itself. This chapter tussles with the possibilities, and polemics of reading texts in the original, and in translation.

Idealistic and controversial as the translation of comparative literature as world literature might be, nowhere does this idea of the "whole" become more apparent than in literary canons that represent a nation-state, either for comparative literature or world literature discussions. With respect to a national literary canon, India offers more exceptions than rules. There is no Gujarati *Indian* literary canon or Tamil *Indian* literary tradition. Only two bodies of literary canons claim the nation-state of India in their names: Indian Writings in English and Indian Writings in English Translation. One is in the original and the other in translation. Unlike, say, Hindi literature, Bengali literature, Malayalam literature, or Tamil literature, these two categories—Indian Writings in English and Indian Literature in English Translation—carry the promise of an *Indian vishva* or universe for the world, *jagat*, and *sansār* in the original and in translation.

The dissolution of boundaries between what might be called an "original" and what is traditionally referred as "translation" in Indian Writings in English and Indian Literature in English Translation is also polemical. In *Imaginary Homelands*, referring to cosmopolitan authors like himself, Salman Rushdie writes that "having been borne across the world, we are translated men."[1] Rushdie goes on to suggest that while he was working on *Midnight's Children* in north London, the view from his window of the city was completely different from the one he was creating in his novel in English, in the original. He admits that what he was actually doing was creating a novel of memory and about memory in the Proustian style, so that the India he was producing was uniquely *his* India.[2] Equivalently, Sisir Kumar Das suggests that "a considerable quantity of writing in modern Indian languages is now available in English translation,"[3] and that "very little attempt has been made to view them as part of one literature that is Indian literature."[4]

If Rushdie is offering a version of *vishva*, universe, world of India in the original, Das is insisting on a version of *vishva* of *one* India in translation. Both versions of an Indian *vishva* are available through English. Certainly, claiming or disclaiming India in a particular language is not new. For nineteenth century orientalists, Indian literature was essentially defined as literature produced in a language such as Sanskrit.[5] In 1835, when T. B. Macaulay declared that "a single shelf of a good European library was worth the whole native literature of India and Arabia,"[6] he had assumed that literature in languages other than Arabic or Sanskrit did not exist in India. Ironically, the nineteenth century was the age of blossoming of prose in many Indian languages that Macaulay did not care for.

Correspondingly, in the late eighteenth century, Din Muhammad, a new migrant to the metropolis in Great Britain, "decided to articulate his own knowledge of India for a primary audience of Anglo-Irish merchants, soldiers, and administrators directly or indirectly associated with the East India Company and its territories on the Indian subcontinent."[7] Vinay Dharwadker writes that Din Muhammad positioned himself intricately on the British discourse on India that emanated from the society around him by placing his travels "thematically, structurally, and stylistically on a continuum with the genre of the travelogue that dominated that discourse in the eyes of the British reading public of the time,"[8] and by doing this, "he reoriented the form rhetorically in order to represent a distinctively 'Indian understanding of India.'"[9] Din Muhammad started a new discourse about India in the same language, generic configuration, and stylistic canon as English authors; on the other hand, however, he articulated his representation of an alternative Indian understanding of India explicitly as a counter-discourse to theirs.[10] Certainly, Din Muhammad's acute awareness of the literary discourses circulating on India by the British, his desire of world-making a counter-narrative of India as a new migrant, and his intention to situate his work with respect to Britain's other colony—Ireland—do not sound different from the aims of many postcolonial writers who are part of the canon of Indian Writings in English, or in the original. But not all scholars accept this version of the Indian *vishva* in English as the original.

Identifying postcolonial authors as cultural translators, Harish Trivedi[11] notes that Homi Bhabha[12] gives the most comprehensive, sophisticated, and influential formulation of the concept of cultural translation by taking the example of Rushdie's *Satanic Verses*. For Trivedi, in cultural translations it is the author who becomes a metaphorical translator, where any literal translation might be absent. In many cases, as Trivedi points out in that essay, the author is at a center, operating as a translator of the periphery. As a result, Trivedi remarks that the literary translation of a culture has ceased to be a priority in the metropole. Significant and noteworthy as Trivedi's comments are, cultural translations may not always be completely separated from literal translations, and they do not become *less original* for being one or the other. This is especially true when the authors happen to be bilingual or multilingual. In *Kanthapura*, Raja Rao,[13] a man educated in four languages, tries to give expression to his thoughts in his own idiom by freeing himself of syntactical prisons, interspersing the textual world with many languages, warning readers to not view him only as an Indian or Kannada author, and thus demanding constant active participation from readers to understand the polyglotism, heteroglossia, and neologistic intersections captured in the novel.

Similarly, Arundhati Roy in *The God of Small Things* stretches the limits of English language by creating a new Malayali Syrian world in her novel, which is set in Kerala. The question, then, is: Is there a difference between a *vishva* in translation and a *vishva* in the original? Do differences between the *vishva* in the original and the *vishva* in translation add any specific value to a text's position in literary traditions, especially if the text is a recipient of prestigious awards? As shown in earlier chapters, the world-making of the *vishva* in a text, whether in the original or in translation, is invariably pressured by the immediate and distant worlds, immediate and distant *jagat*, and *sansār*. In multilingual societies like India, where readers might be engaging with the *vishva*, universe, or world in a text in the original or in translation in their immediate and distant worlds (*jagat*, and *sansār*), often simultaneously, where do the originals end and translations begin?

In this chapter, I argue that the dividing line between a world in the original and a world in translation is not particularly productive in multilingual contexts. Rather, the inquiry could be about comparing the world-makings of the *vishva* in the original and translation in worlds, *jagat*, and *sansār*. This kind of scholarly examination is especially important because it is often assumed that world literature is only in translation, and comparative literature is only in the original. As a case study, this chapter analyzes *Chemmeen*, a Malayalam novel published in 1956 by Thakazhi Sivasankara Pillai, and *The God of Small Things*, published in 1997 by Arundhati Roy, in order to discuss the possibilities and pitfalls of a world in translation, a world in the original, in India and beyond.

Chemmeen's *Vishva* in India and Beyond

On the surface, Pillai's novel *Chemmeen* is a story of forbidden love set in a small fishing community in coastal Kerala in southern India. It has the makings of any great love story: two young star-crossed lovers hold different religious affiliations, the poverty-stricken fishing community can only survive and thrive if it follows age-old traditions and superstitions, and a wife's chastity in body and soul holds the key to the longevity of her husband's life in the unpredictable sea. Karuthamma, the lower-caste fisherwoman, is in love with the Muslim Pareekutty. Karuthamma's father, Chembankunju, exploits Pareekutty's affection by taking money from him to fulfill his lifelong dream of buying a boat and fishing net. In the process—like any true tragic lover—Pareekutty is ruined. Karuthamma, though in love with Pareekutty, is then married off to Palani, an able fisherman. He, of course, has no idea about Karuthamma's past. The narrative ends, as any great love story does, with the two dead lovers, Karuthamma and Pareekutty, locked in each other's embrace after a deadly storm. Close to the dead lovers lies Palani's big catch on the shore, which ended up taking Palani's life on the night the two lovers met for a tryst. The moral is simple: transgression of social, moral, economical, sexual, and religious norms ends in ruin and death. Even the sea goddess, Katalamma, conspires to punish those who fail to uphold the sanctity of traditional values and man-made laws.

Gripping and heart-wrenching as the novel is, it is the story around *Chemmeen*'s *vishva*, in world, *jagat*, and *sansār* that is useful for my task, especially in the context of reading literature in translation, and in the original in India and beyond. Written in less than eight days, Thakazhi Sivasankara Pillai's *Chemmeen* gained success that was previously unheard of for any Malayalam novel. There had already been *Indulekha*,[14] which was quite ahead of its time in portraying the life of a rich and educated upper-caste woman, but this novel did not put Malayalam literature on the literary map the way *Chemmeen* did. Pillai rightly said that everyone knew there was a language called Malayalam and that it had a literary tradition, but "it was with *Chemmeen* though that a Malayalam novel first found its place among many other languages of the world."[15] *Chemmeen* not only became a major representative of Indian literature abroad but even within India, it began speaking to different literary communities in distinct ways. For instance, the Hindi as well as Maithali poet and writer Nagarjun's *The Sons of Varuna*[16]—published in 1957, a year after *Chemmeen*—explores the lives of people in a small fishing community similar to the one in Pillai's novel. It is hard to confirm whether Nagarjun had actually read Pillai's novel, but he must have heard of it because of the awards and praise *Chemmeen* had gathered in India and beyond in the late 1950s.

Like Pillai's novel, *The Sons of Varuna* is about the lives of fisherfolks, though this novel is set in North India. The livelihood of fishing communities in Nagarjun's novel depends on the ponds that once belonged to the feudal lords. After the independence of India, these ponds were randomly assigned to people, often from the middle and upper-caste and class, who had political and cultural clout in the area. Nagarjun's narrative centers around Khurkhur and his family, whose lives are dependent on fishing from these ponds. At the heart of the text, the welfare of the community is more important for the characters than anything personal. This is where Nagarjun's novel differs from Pillai's *Chemmeen* and aligns with the ideology of the Progressive Writers' Movement (PWM), which focused on social institutions and protest movements as more important than individual desires and revolts. Though the romance between Madhuri and Mangal could remind readers of the protagonists in *Chemmeen*, the characters in Pillai's novel never cry out slogans or demand economic freedom from the shoremaster who decides on the price of the fish as well as the bride. In contrast, Nagarjun's characters shout *"inqalab zindabad"*[17] and phrases such as "fishers will win the battle, and will get equality. The ponds are ours!"[18]

Chemmeen's *vishva* as well as its world-making in world, *jagat*, and *sansār* is unique for two reasons. First, this novel was very different from Pillai's earlier works, as it broke away from the PWM. Second, it gathered enormous attention in Malayalam and beyond, receiving national and international awards and recognition. In fact, while describing the context that led to the birth of *Chemmeen* in Malayalam, Pillai states that *Chemmeen* was his first foray into writing a love story, very different from his earlier, more directly political works:

> At times, the novel *Chemmeen* that I was planning to write sounded almost like a threat. Many of my friends assumed that it would deal with the lives of fishermen; that it would be about the coalition of fisher folk, and would stir up unrest and revolution in their minds. It wasn't that all that I had written until then had to do with only the workers' union and unification of their forces; but that thread of thought was what bound them together. My friends, no matter how close they were to me, couldn't comprehend either the company I kept when not with them or my state of mind. . . . It was a chaotic literary environment. However, I continued to write. I couldn't but write . . . to disrupt everyone.[19]

It is important to note here that Pillai (or Thakazhi, as he is known in many parts of India) calls the *vishva* in his novel a threat. By the time Pillai published *Chemmeen*, the literary scene in India had changed. The Progressive Writers' Association, which had been instrumental in creating a literary movement spanning across various parts of the Indian subcontinent, was breaking apart. In many parts of India, the centers of the Progressive Writers' Association became a mouthpiece for the communist party. Authors who had once been an integral part of the association and the movement severed their ties. These authors were thoroughly disillusioned by the restraints that the PWA was placing on literature. The movement which had begun in 1936 with Hindi-Urdu author Munshi Premchand's address in Lucknow seemed now a site of narrow-mindedness, propagandist ideology, and provincialism.[20] The times were also different. When Premchand had delivered his address, India was under the British rule, the subcontinent was still undivided, the Bengal famine was awaiting another decade, Gandhi was alive, and the world had yet to witness the horrors of the Second World War, as well as the Partition.

Pillai himself had belonged to the PWA in Kerala. All his works before *Chemmeen* centered on social realism and focused on the evils of society; individual emotions and desires were not the center of his aesthetic inquiry in his *sahitya*. By the time Pillai wrote *Chemmeen*, his focus had changed. In fact, as seen in the section where Pillai talks about his novel, he equally emphasizes the novel's practical effects: he mentions that the novel "was one of those strange and happy quirks of destiny"[21] that changed his "ramshackle hovel"[22] into a "house,"[23] and, he writes, quite poignantly, "I acquired some paddy fields."[24] Thus, there were two direct incentives for creating a unique *vishva* in *Chemmeen*: one, to provide a fitting retort to the drumbeat of speculation around Pillai, as he was breaking away from the ideological burdens of the social realist tradition of the PWM; and two, to attain some commercial success so as to provide his dream house with wood and tiles and make it into a light and airy home.

In addition to that, *Chemmeen* was the first Malayalam fiction to receive the then-recently established Sahitya Akademi award. Sahitya Akademi is a semiautonomous body of letters in India, and it is described in the Indian Constitution as a national organization that participates actively in the development of Indian letters, fosters and coordinates literary activities in all the Indian languages, and promotes the cultural unity of the country through literary and translational endeavors. Though Sahitya Akademi came into existence in 1954 and became an autonomous organization in 1956, the need for an organization like this had been felt for decades. The proposal to establish a National Academy of letters in India had been under the consideration by the British government of the country long before independence. In 1944, the Government of India had accepted in principle a proposal of the Royal Asiatic Society of Bengal that a National Cultural trust should be set up to encourage cultural activities in all fields.[25] Every year since its inception in 1954, the Sahitya Akademi has awarded prizes to the most outstanding books of literary merit published in any of the twenty-four major Indian languages recognized by the Akademi. Having received the Sahitya Akademi award for best work in Malayalam in 1957, *Chemmeen* was immediately translated into many foreign and Indian languages. It was first translated into Czech,[26] into Hindi by Bharati Vidyarthi in 1959, and into Tamil by Sundara Ramaswamy in 1962; the same year, Narayana Menon also translated it into English.[27]

The *vishva* in *Chemmeen* reached other languages of the world when the novel became UNESCO's 1962 Indian selection for their series of representative works, part of a program launched in 1948 "to encourage translation, publication and the distribution of texts significant from the literary and cultural point of view, in spite of being little known beyond national boundaries or beyond the frame of their linguistic origin."[28] After the two world wars, the newly formed United Nations created UNESCO in the fourth decade of the twentieth century, with the main goal of promoting international collaboration in science and culture through education. In 1948, UNESCO started a unique project of translating literary works from many world languages into English and French, forming UNESCO's Collection of Representative Works. The goal of the UNESCO Collection of Representative Works[29]—summed up aptly in the words of critic, translator, and poet Édouard Joseph Marc Maunick—was to connect people with their and other people's history and cultural traditions so that there could be a confirmation of their existence in the world as well as a consolidation of their place in the universe. The program aimed, in the words of the poet, to educate people about their own histories of the past and the present, as well as the organic connection of their regional histories and literary traditions with those of humanity.[30]

By 1991, UNESCO's Collection of Representative Works: Indian series had translated and published 101 Indian texts into various languages, such as Hungarian, German, Spanish, and French.[31] Though the program formally came to an end in 2005 due to a lack of direct financial support, the collection "remains a reference for publishers looking for opportunities for new editions of reference works."[32] *Chemmeen* became part of UNESCO's Indian series in 1962, and this recognition facilitated the translation of the novel into Russian, Spanish, Arabic, Japanese, Vietnamese, Sinhala, and Chinese, making it into a work with a global presence. The translation of the novel's title into various languages reveals *Chemmeen*'s status in the respective publishers' eyes.[33] The French version, for instance, published in 1965 and commissioned soon after the novel became a UNESCO "representative work," has the untranslated Malayalam title *Chemmeen* followed with a subtitle, "Un Amour Indien: Roman."[34] Curiously, the French translation found a new life in Pondicherry, in India, which was once a French colony. The Indian French edition (reprinted in 1999) introduces the novel's original title, *Chemmeen*, with the subtitle *Un Amour Indien*.[35] The Spanish translation completely does away with the main title, calling the novel *Muralla de redes*.[36] Bharati Vidyarthi, who so far is the only translator of the novel into Hindi, translated the Malayalam title as *Machuare*,[37] meaning "fishermen," without providing a concrete reason for her choice; Vidyarthi published this translation in 1959, long before the English translation was made by Menon. The novel was translated from Malayalam. Vidyarthi could have translated the title as "*Jhīnge*" (Shrimp), closer to "*Chemmeen*." But perhaps in North India, far away from the sea, very few would be interested in a book titled "Shrimp." Certainly, the title *Machuare* piques curiosity and promises intriguing stories of a fishing community; it is also in harmony with Nagarjun's novel, which in contrast spoke to the ideologies of the PWM.

The Bengali translation of the novel, published in 1965, is called *Chingri*,³⁸ the Bengali word for "shrimp/prawn." "Chingri" or shrimp is a delicacy in Bengali cuisine and a household name for the fish-eating Bengalis living on the banks of the Ganges; it is definitely not the stretch that the equivalent term would have been for Hindi speakers. Additionally, the subtitles, absent in the Malayalam version, are fascinating in the novel's afterlives in various languages in *jagat*, and *sansār*. *Chemmeen*'s Hindi translation, *Machuare*, is followed with a parenthesis: "a novel from (the) Malayalam language." The most recent edition of the Hindi translation now bears the subtitle "a Malayalam novel" or "Malayalam novel." Recent editions of the Hindi translation of *Chemmeen* no longer carry the information previously given on other Hindi translations from Malayalam published by the Sahitya Akademi. They also continue to lack either a "Translator's Note" or any information on the translator of *Chemmeen*. The Bengali versions, however, do include the translated introduction from Menon's English *Chemmeen*. The older English editions of Menon's translation of the novel kept the Malayalam title (*Chemmeen*) with no subtitles or extra information in parentheses. However, the recent translation of *Chemmeen* by Anita Nair, published in 2011 by HarperCollins Publishers with the cover image of a still from the Malayalam movie *Chemmeen* (produced in 1965), carries a declarative statement (virtually a subtitle) just below the title: "The Enduring Classic."

If the Hindi version is world-making the uniqueness of the novel's *vishva* to the Hindi-speaking community in the country of origin as a "novel from the Malayalam language," and recently as just "a Malayalam novel," the French public would have been more drawn to a broader subcontinental subtitle—"an Indian love story"—instead of "a Malayalam novel." The recent French translation of the novel from India builds on the familiarity and regionality of the Malayalam original title, and adds a pan-Indian dimension, with *Chemmeen: Un Amour Indien*. The geographical specificity of the novel, perhaps, is not of much relevance to Spanish or French readers. Also, it is important to note here that both the French, and Spanish translations were done in 1965 from Menon's English version; there is some ambiguity about the Bengali version.³⁹ Thus, via English, *Chemmeen* becomes in effect an "Indian" novel, both within and outside India—not always, or even primarily, as a representative of a *bhasha* Indian tradition. Further, *Chemmeen*'s translation into English has made the novel a part of the Indian Literature in English Translation. There have not been any recent editions or new translations of *Chemmeen* in Spanish. However, the French edition has found a new life in the Indian world, *jagat*, and *sansār*; and the Bengali edition also maintains a healthy life, with the most recent editions produced in 2015. The 1959 Hindi translation of the novel has had new editions re-issued almost every decade, and the subtitle continues to grant the translated *vishva* in *Chemmeen* the identity of a Malayalam novel in the Hindi world, *jagat*, and *sansār*.

Commenting on the translation of Malayalam literature in an interview given to the bilingual journal of Sahitya Akademi, *Indian Literature*, Pillai mentions that very few Malayalam books have made their way into other languages. He particularly chooses Bengali and remarks, "Only very few Malayalam books have been published in Bengali. True, they have Tagore and Saratchandra Chatterji. They don't care about translating works from other languages. Malayalam swallows everything from other languages. It is good. I don't want to blame them."[40] In this same interview, given just after receiving the 1984 Jnanpith Award (the highest literary award in India, given annually in recognition of the best creative literary writing in any of the twenty-two languages recognized in the Indian Constitution), Pillai observes that the situation in Hindi is a bit different, as the reading public is interested in reading works from other languages, whereas Bengalis are preoccupied with their Tagores and Saratchandras.[41] Ironically, in "Society as Hero," Pillai writes that *Chemmeen*'s world can only be understood by people such as Bengalis who live close to the sea.[42]

Pillai's thoughts about Malayalam translations into Bengali are validated by Meenakshi Mukherjee, who claims that the alleged literary superiority of Bengali literature did not favor translation into Bengali from Indian languages for a long time, though Bengali language has been very receptive to translations from European literature.[43] Moreover, whatever translations took place were mostly "officially undertaken projects, sponsored by the Sahitya Akademi or the National Book Trust,"[44] which in a way do not indicate a literary or commercial interest. As can be seen, the questions of translation, and the original, and how the *vishva* in one literary tradition relates with/to the other, are not easy to measure in terms of just cultural and literal translations, especially when the *vishva* in a text becomes representative of a canon. The Malayalam *Chemmeen*'s *vishva* with respect to Spanish, and French worlds, *jagat*, and *sansār* is very different from the Indian world-making of its *vishva* in translations in Hindi, Bengali, French, and English. In the next few pages, I examine the dynamics among various translations and world-makings of *Chemmeen* by doing a close reading of the texts to analyze the translational history of the novel and the agency of characters in the *vishvas* of the translations.

To Compare, to World

Chemmeen makes extensive use of Malayali fisherfolk's dialect. The fisherfolk's dialect is lost in all translations, whether into neighborly languages or into far-flung languages. Dialect is not the only aspect of the novel's distinctive language. Comparing translations of *Chemmeen* in Hindi, Tamil, and English, Raji Narasimhan argues that a good translation of the novel will focus on the femininity in the text. Narasimhan describes the "pre-historic divisions of roles [that have] been imbued with gender properties by the fisher folk. . . . The fisher-wife is called upon to pray for her fisher-husband's safe return from the sea. . . . Around and from the ideology condensed in this figuration, the feminine character and overall femininity of *Chemmeen* are built."[45] According to Narasimhan, the femininity of *Chemmeen* does not spring from the love affair between the fisherwoman Karuthamma and the Muslim Pareekutty, but from the tension between Karuthamma, who is at the brink of her sexual awakening, and her mother Chakki, who has to "domesticate" her daughter's sexuality. Thus, according to Narasimhan, "The translating language . . . must bend to the emotional inflections of the two major female characters, as the Malayalam does."[46] One might assume that at the end of Narasimhan's article, the translations of *Chemmeen* in languages such as Hindi, and Tamil would read better than the translation done in English, especially when scholars such as Meenakshi Mukherjee have argued that the translation of text from "Hindi to Bangla or from Marathi to Kannada"[47] is a "far more natural and satisfactory activity"[48] compared to the same novels "rendered into English, where negotiating semantic and cultural hurdles to achieve equivalence of meaning tends to be relatively uphill task."[49]

In *Chemmeen*'s case, Narasimhan dismisses all translations as not reaching the ideal.[50] She describes the Hindi translation as a "passive rendering"[51] that does not get close to the "springs of warmth in the original."[52] She adds that the Tamil version of the novel suffers despite being close to Malayalam because the translator, Sundara Ramaswamy, identifies too closely with the characters and renders the theme of femininity too sentimentally and is thus out of balance. On the other hand, Narasimhan writes that the English translation by Menon gets to the heart of things without being sentimental,[53] but it does not induce one to "reread the original."[54] Despite praising Menon over Hindi, and Tamil translators, Narasimhan remains ambivalent, and reluctantly declares toward the end of the essay that "English has claimed him [Menon]. He has claimed it too."[55] It is true that Hindi, Tamil, and even English, for that matter, cannot capture the untranslatable fisherfolk's Malayali dialect, nor the tone, timbre, and pitch of the voice that Narasimhan recognizes as necessary for this text to demonstrate its otherness in the translated versions. I want to elaborate here that Karuthamma's sexual awareness and femininity, which Narasimhan thinks of as the essence of the novel in Malayalam, does find its place to varying degrees in the *vishva* of several translations of *Chemmeen*: Vidyarthi's Hindi version, Menon's English version, and Nair's recent English version. I specifically want to show this through comparisons because I do not understand Malayalam, and for me the *vishva* in Hindi, Bengali, and English *Chemmeens* would be, as Trivedi say, a cultural translation, even though the original *Chemmeen* is not in English like Rushdie's novels.

I compare sections from the three translations of *Chemmeen* by Vidyarthi, Menon, and Nair (from Malayalam into Hindi and English, respectively) to assess the agency given to Karuthamma. I examine the novel's final chapter, where the lovers are about to unite, while Palani is at the sea fighting the storm and catching a shark. I selected this section because Karuthamma's character reaches a new height in it. She gathers courage and recognizes herself as someone other than a defeated and disappointed woman. Though initially she links her fortune with the ability to be Pareekutty's lover and Palani's wife, she immediately takes action to change her life. She even initiates sexual contact with the Muslim Pareekutty. However, the three translators considered here—two in English and one in Hindi—give different degrees of agency to Karuthamma. These distinctions indicate different world-makings of the *vishva* in the original and translations.

Here is the passage as it appears in Nair's translation, published in 2011, from Malayalam into English (Narasimhan does not take into account this translation):

> She moved into his outstretched arms and laid herself against his chest. She raised her face to his. He whispered into her ears, "My Karuthamma!"
> "What, my dearest?"
> His hands moved over those buttocks that once he, a Muslim, and the riff-raff of the shore had ogled at.
> Parkeekutty asked, "Karuthamma!"
> Once again in a trance-like state she responded, "What?"

"Who am I to you?"

She cupped his face between her palms and with half-closed eyelids whispered, "Who are you to me? Why, you are my pot of gold!"

Once again they were one. In rapture, she whispered sweet nothings into his ears. She wasn't able to break or move away from that embrace.[56]

Here is the same scene in Menon's translation from Malayalam into English, published in 1962:

> She entered his extended arms and her body became one with his. Their faces met. He whispered in her ears.
> "My Karuthamma!"
> "Yes!"
> He stroked her all over and his hands slowly moved to where he and the rude young boatmen of the seafront used to stare.
> "Karuthamma!"
> Again she answered him obediently in that semiconscious state of ecstasy.
> "Yes—"
> "What am I to you?"
> She took his face in both her hands and looking at him with half-closed eyes, she said, "Everything. My pot of gold."
> Again they became one. And in that state he whispered gently in her ears.
> She could not break herself away from that embrace.[57]

The Hindi translation from Malayalam by Vidyarthi, published in 1959, if rendered literally, translates as follows:

> She entered the space between Pari's outstretched arms and laid herself against
> his chest. Their lips met. Pari whispered in her ears, "My Karuthamma!"
> "Yes!"
> Pari started stroking Karuthamma's back with his hands. Pari called out
>   her name
> again, "Karuthamma!"
> "Yes!"—from a trance-like state Karuthamma responded again.
> "Who am I to you?"
> She cupped Pari's face in her palms, and while looking at him with half-closed
>   eyes Karuthamma said, "You?" My treasure trove!"
> They again became one. In that joyful state she kept saying sweet nothings in
>   Pari's ears.
> She did not have the power to break away from that intimate embrace.[58]

In Vidyarthi's and Menon's versions, Pareekutty's religious affiliation has been completely cut out from this scene, perhaps to keep the text secular in the post-independent Nehruvian India of the 1960s. Nair, on the other hand, is not shy about Pareekutty's Muslim identity. She also identifies Pareekutty's hands moving over Karuthamma's buttocks, which Menon more modestly describes as "where he and the rude young boatmen of the seafront used to stare." The Hindi version chastely renders Pareekutty's hands moving over Karuthamma's buttocks as a "back rub." But the Hindi translation compensates for that loss by suggesting that the lovers kissed, something that neither Nair nor Menon mention. Further, in the quoted section, Karuthamma utters "sweet nothings" in Pareekutty's ears. Both Nair and Vidyarthi have kept this unchanged; unfortunately, Menon's version takes the agency away from Karuthamma and gives it to Pareekutty. Clearly, through the comparative analysis of the various world-makings of the *vishva* in *Chemmeen*, Karuthamma's and Pareekutty's levels of agency as a fisherfolk woman and a Muslim man in their immediate world, *jagat*, and *sansār* can be critiqued, even if the reader does not know the world or *vishva* in the original in Malayalam.

Additionally, Karuthamma's agency, an important force in the novel, is at times missing in the famous movie *Chemmeen*, produced in 1965 in Malayalam, which may now be the most common way that Pillai reaches the contemporary Malayali audience in the original, or even in translation. Indeed, a still from the movie *Chemmeen* is displayed on the book jacket of Nair's translated version. Sanju Thomas writes that the book cover of *Chemmeen* translated by Nair glorifies the Malayalam movie more than the actual novel. For instance, she suggests that there is no mention of the novel receiving any literary award, but the success of the film is shared.[59] The movie gives agency to Pareekutty and also establishes his immediate community. It directly indicates Pareekutty's Muslim identity by showing his father and other men from his community wearing beards and *dhotis*. The English, Hindi, and Bengali versions of the novel, on the other hand, do not give much information on Pareekutty's kith and kin. In these versions, Pareekutty's outfit is described in passing in a sentence or two right in the beginning of the text, and there is no description of his family members. The celluloid, however, offers the possibility of establishing a distinct religious and ethnic identity for the characters in Pareekutty's life through outfits and dialogues. Further, in the novel versions, Pareekutty is passive and more than willing to sacrifice himself for Karuthamma. In contrast, in the movie, it is Pareekutty who suggests that Chembankunju, Karuthamma's father, visit him in the night in order to take dried fish from his shack—a suggestion that is absent from the Hindi, English, and Bengali *vishvas* of *Chemmeen*.

The movie *Chemmeen* won the National Films Awards (then known as the President's Gold Medal Award), which was established in 1953 to honor excellence in films and arts in various Indian languages on the national stage. *Chemmeen* was the first Malayalam movie to receive the national award for the best film in India in 1965. Before *Chemmeen*, Marathi, Bengali, and Hindi films had received this award. With *Chemmeen* receiving the award in 1965, the Indian national award for best film category included a Dravidian-language feature film for the first time; a film in another Dravidian language, Kannada, would later receive the award in 1970. This award and recognition of a Malayalam movie is significant because in the 1950s and 1960s there were massive protests in southern India against Hindi, which was being projected as the national language of India and also as a replacement of English.[60]

The film *Chemmeen* itself involved an array of people from across linguistic traditions. It was directed by legendary Malayali director Ramu Kariat, and its famous musical score was written by Salil Chowdhury, who composed songs in Malayalam, Hindi, and Bengali. These now-classic songs were sung by Manna Dey and Yesudas (among others), who frequently sang songs in many Indian languages. The movie was edited by Hrishikesh Mukherjee, who had directed many Hindi films that were famous for their social messages. Though this was a time when literary texts were frequently adapted into movies and did not depend on being adapted into movies for their survival, the movie *Chemmeen* rekindled an interest in the novel. M. T. Ansari writes that though the novel *Chemmeen* was quite popular, not many were familiar with the novel before the movie was produced.[61] Today, as Ansari writes, it is hard for scholars to have their first reading of the novel perhaps in the original. This is because of the inter-semiotic translation, as seen here in the translation of a Malayalam novel into a Malayalam movie. Due to the film's popularity, most people, including literary scholars, are likely to imagine the novel's characters—Palani, Karuthamma, Pareekutty, and Chembankunju—as the Malayali actors who played these roles.[62]

To return to the comparative translations of the novel and movie, both English versions of the novel and the Hindi one, as examined in this chapter, attribute different kinds of agency to Karuthamma. However, many scenes that could give Karuthamma agency are missing from the movie *Chemmeen*.[63] The movie, though, still establishes a recurrent theme of resistance through the romance between fisherwoman Karuthamma and Muslim Pareekutty. For instance, there is a distinct moment in the Menon version of the novel as well as the Malayalam movie when Palani asks Karuthamma if she loves Pareekutty. Unlike the novel, where Karuthamma replies in the past tense (suggesting that at one point she did love Pareekutty, but not anymore), the movie gives a different dimension. Karuthamma, in the movie, responds in the present.[64] The shift makes Palani's death more realistic, since his wife broke the sacred laws of the shores, and it presents the affection between the fisherwoman Karuthamma and the Muslim Pareekutty as a continued act of resistance in modern India. This resistance has also become a major theme in many Indian films such as *Bombay*, produced in 1995, which has been dubbed into many Indian languages and beyond.

Although the forbidden love between the Malayali Muslim Pareekutty and Malayali fisherwoman Karuthamma is a major addition to a genre of films produced in India that portray inter-religious transgressions through inter-semiotic translations, the movie is silent on the issue of religious conversion. The three translated versions of the novel that I compared include an important paragraph where, after being slandered by the fisherwomen, Karuthamma's mother Chakki declares to the world that the family would convert to Islam or Christianity if the shoremaster punished them for buying boats and nets, a privilege reserved only for the upper-caste in the fisherfolk community. Though nowhere in the literal translations of the novel it is clearly indicated that Karuthamma is a Hindu, the idea of converting to Islam definitely suggests that Chakki is willing to marry Karuthamma to Pareekutty, if the need arises. For instance, when Chakki faces slander from women on the shore for not arranging a marriage for her daughter, and for buying boats and nets, they remind her that the "Shore Master knows how to deal with scum who have no respect for traditions!"[65] Chakki replies, "What can he do to us? We'll become Muslims if need be or convert to another religion. . . . What will the Shore Master do then?"[66] However, there is no guarantee that Chakki and her family will escape her caste status, and become equal to the shoremaster, if they convert to Islam or Christianity. This is specifically important because converting to Christianity has been a political issue in Kerala. *The God of Small Things* highlights this contentious issue through characters like Velutha who are regarded as caste Christians, even though they converted to Christianity to escape the caste atrocities prevalent in Brahmanical Hinduism.

Nevertheless, this omission of a passage on conversion (to escape religious and caste atrocities) from the movie is noteworthy,[67] especially when, over half a century after the novel's publication, the Malayalis "might have seen the movie [translation] first and then read the novel"⁶⁸ in the original, or perhaps not even that. Nair, the most recent translator of the novel into English, writes that the first time she heard the idea of translating the novel Malayalam *Chemmeen*, she was reminded of a song from the movie version:

> From somewhere the strains of a song wafted in my head. The desolate Parekutty singing his heart out on a moon-drenched seashore. The restless Karuthamma standing with her bosom heaving, wanting to escape everything and run to Parekutty's side. The glean in Chembankunju's eye when he spots Palani for the first time. Scenes from the film *Chemmeen* played out in my head. . . . Was the chitchat turning into something of consequence? Was that how it happened? Was that how I took on *Chemmeen*?⁶⁹

Anita Nair's recollection of the song from the movie *Chemmeen* gives another dimension to the world-making of *Chemmeen*'s *vishva* in world, *jagat*, and *sansār*, where the original is no longer the first or only point of experience, even for those who understand Malayalam, and the translation inherits in itself a history of the changing literary cultures. Not only is there an uneven distribution of the *vishva* in *Chemmeen* in various languages/literatures, in various media; there is also a clear division in the portrayal of an individual as well as a community's collective agency across these different versions. To complicate matters more, a song from the movie *Chemmeen* surprisingly emerges in Arundhati Roy's *The God of Small Things*. Roy not only gives the original song in Malayalam in roman script and its translation for the English world, but she also orients the readers about *Chemmeen*, something that she does not necessarily do with other literary texts that enter her narrative.

World-making of Small Things

Just as Anita Nair was reminded of songs from the movie *Chemmeen* while she was deciding to translate the novel from Malayalam into English, Arundhati Roy brings the songs from the movie *Chemmeen* into her novel, *The God of Small Things*, during a crucial moment in the novel, where Ammu is about to do something that brings her close to Karuthamma's fate. In the beginning of the novel, Roy writes that "when Ammu listened to songs that she loved on the radio, something stirred inside her."⁷⁰ What stirred inside Ammu, according to the narrator, was something like a liquid ache. On such days, "she walked out of the world like a witch,"⁷¹ and she "temporarily set aside the morality of motherhood and divorcee-hood."[72] On days when Ammu dressed up and sat next to the river listening to her radio, "everyone was a little wary of her,"[73] and they agree that it was best to "just Let Her Be."[74] Indeed, the song blasting on Ammu's radio suggests a remarkable moment in which the *vishvas* in two novels, one in Malayalam and the other in English, become infused with each other.

Chemmeen's appearance in *The God of Small Things* points out moments where language becomes inadequate for speaking about the brutality, cruelty, and uneven power dynamics that exist in society when it comes to a "woman that they [members of society] had already damned,"[75] who "had little to lose, and could therefore be dangerous."[76] The references to *Chemmeen* appear not just when society views Ammu as nurturing an "Unsafe Edge,"[77] a cross between the "infinite tenderness of motherhood and the reckless rage of a suicide bomber,"[78] but also in the poignant scene where the twins, Estha and Rahel, wonder whether their mother, Ammu, is having an "aftermare." Indeed, these moments in the novel affirm that the movie and the novel *Chemmeen* are important for understanding the *vishva*, the world of the god of loss, in *The God of Small Things*. The direct reference to *Chemmeen* takes place when "Ammu groped for her tangerine transistor, and switched it on. It played a song from a film called *Chemmeen*,"[79] which was, as the narrator tells the reader, a story of a poor girl forced to marry a fisherman from a neighboring beach. When the fisherman discovers that his wife had a lover before him, he decides to go into the sea, where he gets caught in a whirlpool and is washed up on the beach. The lovers are also found dead on the beach as they had made a suicide pact. In the end, everyone dies, including the shark. The sea claims all.[80]

The narrator's summary of *Chemmeen* foreshadows what is going to transpire in the *vishva* in *The God of Small Things* and threatens the intimate moment and world that Estha and Rahel share with their mother, Ammu. Just like Karuthamma, who did not think about her daughter when she decided to meet Pareekutty, Ammu, too, forgets about her children in her intimate moments with Velutha. Indeed, just after a dream in which she identifies Velutha (a Dalit Christian, who belongs to a community of people that converted to Christianity to escape the low-caste status in Brahmanic caste order) as the one-armed god of loss, Ammu switches on the radio, which plays the song from the movie. The twins and Ammu hum the song from the movie *Chemmeen* together. Regardless of the vivid dream that portends Velutha's dismemberment and disfiguration by the police, and the playing of the Malayalam song from the tragic *Chemmeen* in the backdrop, Ammu decides to meet Velutha. Just as the wife of the fisherman on the shore "went astray,"[81] as translated by Roy in the *Chemmeen* song, Ammu decides to continue her affair with Velutha, even though she knows that it will not end well and that it is nothing but madness. Her "Unsafe Edge"[82] that borders madness, which as Ammu fears runs in her family, is not, then, just a problem with the Ipe genes; it is symptomatic of a malady in Malayali society that touches all classes, castes, and religions, as evident through the reference to *Chemmeen*.

When *The God of Small Things* was published, it took the literary and commercial English world by a storm, in India and beyond. The novel launched Roy into the material world, *jagat*, and *sansār* in unprecedented ways. To understand the remarkable moment in which the novel appeared, Julie Mullaney notes, one must first analyze its status and achievement as Roy's first novel, and then the scale and breadth of the critical reception of the text. Mullaney writes:

> When it [*The God of Small Things*] appeared in Britain in April 1997 (after its launch in Delhi), the novel was duly praised by critics such as Michael Gorra, Shirley Chew, Ian Jack, and a diverse gathering of fellow novelists like John Updike, Salman Rushdie, Ali Smith, and Meera Syal. . . . It was perhaps of little surprise then that the novel won the Booker Prize in October 1997, passing at the post contributions by Jim Crace, Bernard MacLaverty, Madeleine St. John, Tim Parks and the other newcomer Mick Jackson. It featured heavily on authors and critics lists for "Book of the Year" including that of Shusha Guppy who heralded the arrival of an "authentic new voice."[83]

Roy became known to those interested in Indian Writings in English even before she received the Booker Prize. Unlike most places in the world, *jagat*, and *sansār*, where Roy's first novel was celebrated as a modern classic, in India "Roy's ongoing engagement with the matrix of private and public history and mores led to a mix of controversy and praise."[84] Critics like Sunil Seth and Supriya Chaudhuri and authors like Kamala Das, Anita Desai, and Amitav Ghosh welcomed the novel.[85] Left-wing Indian critics and Marxists, however, took issue with Roy's representation of the communist leader, E. M. S. Namboodiripad. In the novel, Namboodiripad is portrayed as Comrade Pillai, who refuses to help Velutha, a Dalit, which eventually leads to his death.

In India, the novel also generated controversy with respect to its treatment of love, sex, and abuse. For instance, unable to understand the difference between child abuse and sexual pleasure between two consenting same-sex adults, S. P. Swain wonders about the reason behind the pedophile Orangedrink Lemondrink Man's encounter with the young child, Estha. For Swain, what the Orangedrink Lemondrink Man does to Estha is either "solitary pleasure"[86] or "sadistic pleasure,"[87] not child abuse by a pedophile. In addition, Swain writes, "All said, one wonders how the Booker Committee could decide to honor such an erotic book as *The God of Small Things* with the prestigious Booker Award."[88] Swain's ignorance about child abuse has roots in the Indian penal system, which until 2012 employed Section 377 to punish homosexuality as well as child abuse. Homosexuality is no longer a crime in India, and there are special laws that protect children from sexual abuse. To complicate matters further, however, in the world in the novel, the History House (often called the Heart of Darkness, an allusion to Joseph Conrad's novel) is where Roy's narrator conflates homosexuality and child abuse. The narrator suggests that the Ayemenem's own Kurtz, Kari Saipu, had "shot himself through the head ten years ago, when his young lover's parents had taken the boy away from him and sent him to school."[89] Roy does not indicate what the boy's age was, but it is very clear that Saipu and his young lover were in a same-sex relationship.

Leila Neti argues that Roy's novel falters "in its capacity to imagine love or pleasure in ways that are not already scripted as arising within, even if as a challenge to, the normative terms of heterosexuality. It is not simply that the text ignores the possibility of queerness."[90] Neti continues that "in two separate representations of homosexual acts, the characters are pathologized, one as a child molester and the other as a queer colonizer in an ambiguously consensual affair with a lover much younger than himself."[91] For Neti, "Roy's text arguably reviles and vilifies homosexuality even as it overtly critiques the demonization of non-normative heterosexuality." [92]

It was not only Estha's abuse, Kari Saipu's homosexuality, Ammu's forbidden relationship with Velutha, or the twins' incest that generated controversy around the world, *jagat*, and *sansār* of Roy's *The God of Small Things*, but also the fact that the *vishva* in the novel somehow became representative of India. Roy received the Booker Prize the year India celebrated its fifty years of independence. Consequently, wittingly or unwittingly, for the global world, her novel does become the *vishva* of the new India, like *Chemmeen* half a century ago. Certainly, the world-making of *The God of Small Things* in India has been more complicated than, say, in the United States and United Kingdom, where the text has been hailed as an example of the finest "Indian literature," and where "Indian literature" often gets reduced to writings done in English by Indian authors or diasporic and immigrant authors. In that respect, the world-makings of *The God of Small Things*, and *Chemmeen* have been quite similar in India. Within India, the world-makings of the two novels vary in different literary traditions, where they are not necessarily identified as offering a world or *vishva* of India. Outside of India, however, both of the novels came to be perceived as representatives of India, both in translation and in the original.

Commenting on *The God of Small Things* winning the Booker Prize, Roy told her interviewer, Kathy Arlyn Sokol, that she did not believe in prizes or "best books." According to her, this was a roll of the dice; the process of choosing books for prizes always is. Prizes are a way for the publishing industry to tell readers, "read this one"[93] or "read that one."[94] It is significant to note that Roy mentioned in the same interview that she initially expected her book to be read by 3,000–8,000 people if it were to become successful. She did not plan on publishing or releasing the book beyond India. The number makes sense, considering that not everyone in India reads in English, and sometimes the number of readers of other Indian languages surpasses the number of English readers. One can gather from the interview that Roy did not write her book with a particular global audience in mind. In fact, she describes her experience of being catapulted onto the world stage as follows:

> The fact that you can kind of tunnel through the world in this way is wonderful, but also very frightening. It's a combination of being very exhilarated and very fatigued; more fatiguing than exhilarating because basically the pressure is on from the world to turn me into an institution. And I'm not an institution, I am a person—disorganized, inefficient, and kind of private.[95]

Roy's insistence on her personhood and suggestion that she should not be treated as an institution reflects on what she thinks about literature. In the same interview, Roy goes on to mention the "democratization" of literature. According to her, the "big dudes" of literature whose work would cause people to go crazy is no more going to work because so many people are writing today. She adds, "There are so many books and writings from other places now rather than from just what has been perceived to be the center of the universe, Europe and America. People from other places are going to start telling their stories."[96]

In fact, Arundhati Roy calls Malayalam, the language of Estha and Rahel as well of Roy, an alien mother that has the extraordinary ability to be equally unmotherly toward those who wish to belong to her, and toward those who wish to separate from her. As if fusing cultural and literal translations, and eliding any differences between the original and translation, Roy writes that though *The God of Small Things* was written in English, she "imagined it in English as well as Malayalam."[97] In fact, she writes that "the landscapes and languages colliding in the seven-year-old twins' Esthappen and Rahel's heads"[98] metamorphosed "into a thing of its own."⁹⁹ In a 2018 lecture, Roy gives an example of this collision between languages when Estha and Rahel's mother, "Ammu, scolds the twins and tells them that if they ever disobey her in public she will send them somewhere where they learn to 'jolly well behave'—it's the well that jumps out at them."¹⁰⁰ And quite rightly, because

> The deep, moss-lined well that you find in the compounds of many homes in Kerala, with a pulley and a bucket and a rope, the well children are sternly warned to stay away from until they are big enough to draw water. What could a Jolly Well possibly be? A well with happy people in it. But people in a well? They'd have to be dead, of course. So, in Estha's and Rahel's imagination, a Jolly Well becomes a well full of laughing dead people, into which children are sent to learn to behave. The whole novel is constructed around people, young and old, English-knowing and Malayalam-knowing, all grappling, wrestling, dancing, and rejoicing in language.¹⁰¹

This strange concoction of joy and pain of languages and cultures as evident in Estha and Rahel's imagination is the reality of an author living in a multilingual context, where no language can be taken for granted. The language of the writer, as Roy puts it, "has to be made. It has to be cooked. Slow-cooked,"¹⁰² with multiple meanings and layers.

Further, this slow-cooking does not happen in a vacuum, especially in a country whose identity as a nation-state was a colonial idea, a British idea, and where, according to Roy, "English has continued, guiltily, unofficially, and by default, to consolidate its base"¹⁰³ because writing and speaking in English "is a practical solution to the circumstances created"¹⁰⁴ by British imperialism. In such a context, languages merge, infuse, differ, and sometimes consume each other, while the author engages in world-making in the text. Indeed, Geetha Ganapathy-Doré writes that the "Malayali peculiarities of English are translated by Arundhati Roy in the form of eccentric spelling,"¹⁰⁵ using "punctuation to highlight the lengthening of vowels,"¹⁰⁶ and that specific features like the "agglutinating tendency of the Malayali speakers which results in wrong accentuation"¹⁰⁷ are "faithfully transcribed not with a view to sitting in judgement over their deviation from standard English but to make the style realistic (Stoppit, mo-stunfortunate, Thang God, Prer NUN sea ayshun)."¹⁰⁸ Besides this hands-on play with the Malayalam and English languages, the novel engages in a different kind of translation where Malayali literary as well as cultural references are translated for the readers within India and beyond, just as the case was with *Chemmeen*.

India in the Original, India in Translation

In his essay "Society as Hero," Pillai reminds his readers that *Chemmeen* is not just a love story, but a narrative that transcribes, translates, and informs readers about the beliefs and superstitions of the specific people on the sea-coast of Kerala. Pillai describes the significance of the sea to his readers by educating them about the intimate connection that people in this fishing community feel with the sea:

> The people there, as they rise from their sleep in the early morning and rub their eyes, the first thing that they look at, every day, is the vast expanse of the sea—the mystery that is called the sea.... Seeing the sea for a lifetime from birth to death must have some influence over the human soul, and there is the idea of the Goddess of sea, Katalamma ... I do not think people of the plains as in Uttar Pradesh are able to understand the magnitude of the idea of Katalamma, the Sea-Goddess, the Mother-Goddess. But they may have other things which we lack. Kerala has a peculiarity. There is nothing like a wide meadow in Kerala but in Tamil Nadu you find the expansive meadows. Likewise, we have the sea, the concept of Katalamma, and from that concept was born the story of *Chemmeen* (The Shrimp). And that happens to be apparently a love story. The aspect of love in *Chemmeen* is in fact only a peg to hang several things, like the philosophy of the fisherfolk of Kerala and the secrets of Kerala, which I really wanted to depict through a love story.[109]

In the foregoing extract, readers can see that Pillai is confident that people from different states of India cannot understand the significance of the sea, which he thinks is paramount for understanding the *vishva* in *Chemmeen*. To him, residents of Tamil Nadu, which is linguistically and culturally closer to Kerala than Uttar Pradesh, might not be able to grasp the gravity of the sea that his readers encounter in *Chemmeen*. For Pillai the story in *Chemmeen* is deeply connected with its geography. In the passage quoted earlier, it can also be seen that Pillai does not consider the universal element as an important aspect of *Chemmeen*'s particular success in English or any other Indian language. In fact, Pillai thinks that the Tamil, and Hindi versions of *Chemmeen* are bound to not make a mark because people from North India or even from parts of South India cannot understand a culture where the influence of the sea on the human soul is ever-present.

If Pillai is thinking here mostly about the inability to understand and translate cultures with dissimilar geographical conditions, Meenakshi Mukherjee adds a different dimension to the idea of reading literature in translation.[110] Mukherjee writes that the advantage of Indian novels written in English is that they can reach a wider audience, both at home and abroad. Theoretically speaking, Indian novels translated into English should have the same trajectory. But that is not usually the case. According to Mukherjee, this is because either they are not translated well or else the choice to translate a particular author's work is "faulty." Further, she points out that if a vernacular text's popularity is rooted in a regional dialect, the very reason that made it popular can become a cause for its untranslatability.[111] At the same time, she adds, "it is difficult to decide beforehand what is translatable and what is not."[112] Commenting specifically about Pillai's *Chemmeen*, Mukherjee writes, "What could be more local and particular than *Chemmeen*? Yet the reader of the English version is moved by what appears to be universal human tragedy,"[113] even though the Malayali fisherfolk's dialect is lost in Menon's 1962 translation.

The unavoidable neglect of the unique dialect in *Chemmeen* is not just visible in its first English translation. The Hindi version, too, has no "Translator's Note" on the difficulty of translating the unique Malayali dialect into Hindi. Nair's 2011 version addresses the challenge, but Nair expresses her initial apprehension that she was not sure if she had the ability to comprehend the nuances of Malayalam. The very first sentence, which Nair translates as "That father of mine talks of buying a boat and nets,"[114] was an obstacle for her, as it was written in the fisherfolk's dialect. In fact, Pillai writes that the dialect used in *Chemmeen* was one that he had heard,[115] not necessarily spoken, since he was nine. Indeed, just to compare the difficulties for the translators, take a look at how Menon translates this: "You know, my father is going to buy a fishing boat and a net, which will be our own."[116] Vidyarthi translates the original in Hindi[117] that could be translated as "Bappa is going to buy a boat and a net." We can see that the three versions differ from each other while translating the fisherfolk dialect, and also impact the meaning of the opening sentence of the novel. If Nair's version tells us that Karuthamma's dad, Chembankunju, is talking about buying a boat and nets, Menon's version is confident that Karuthamma's father is going to buy a boat and a net that will be theirs. In Hindi, Karuthamma's father is going to buy a boat and just a net, whether it will be Karuthamma's or not is not addressed. Considering that *Chemmeen* could also be interpreted as a novel about Chembankunju's greed and ambition, it is important to specify who desires owning what, and how much, and how many.

To further the issue of the world in the original, world in translation, and world-making, commenting on the Hindi translation of Roy's *The God of Small*

Things, Narasimhan writes that the novel is simply a wrong book to translate because the original language is overpowering.[118] Roy's *The God of Small Things* was translated into Hindi by Nilabh as *Māmūlī Chīzoṅ Kā Devtā*[119] and published by Rajkamal publishers in 2004. Though the Hindi translation lacks a "Translator's Note," a short blurb inside the book jacket states that Nilabh is a poet and translator who has worked with the BBC and has translated six books of poems and dozens of classical plays. There is no information on the languages that Nilabh has translated from and into. The back of the book jacket of the Hindi translation displays endorsements by famous Hindi authors such as Nirmal Varma, and Krishna Sobti. On the other hand, the translation of *The God of Small Things* into Malayalam raised different issues.

The Malayalam translation of the novel came out in 2011. The translation of the novel was done by Priya A. S., who has also translated Jaishree Misra's work into English from Malayalam. Roy mentions in a news article titled "Estha, Rahel Now Speak Malayalam" (published just after the launch of the Malayalam edition of *The God of Small Things*) that it should not be forgotten that this is a political novel, especially focused on the politics of caste.[120] Roy adds that she is a little upset that though the novel is widely read in Kerala, its political content has been overlooked. The article quotes Roy's remarks at the inaugural ceremony of the launch of the Malayalam translation of *The God of Small Things*: "There have been translations in several languages, including Estonian. But no other translation is as important to me as this. For, it is the language of Estha, Rahel, Ammu and Velutha, the novel's central characters."[121] However, the translation acquires a new light when Sanju Thomas, who has done a comparative study between the Malayalam and English versions of the novel, writes:

> According to the translator, the book is one of sorrows, and every other concern in the book—environment, revolution, party, caste, religion—is secondary. She [Priya A. S.] is disappointed that the Malayali did not understand the sorrow of Ammu that got translated into love and sex. She also feels that the Malayali failed to sympathise with the incest between the siblings. Priya explains that for Rahel it is a never-subsiding wail of reunion and for Estha it is the search for his long-lost mother. Priya thus declares her goal in getting into the translation: to make the Malayali see the sorrow in the work and make him/her appreciate the book.[122]

The Malayalam translator is moved by the sorrow in the novel, whereas the author reminds readers to keep the caste politics in mind. Thomas concludes that though the Malayalam translation is mostly successful, it fails when the translator appears overwhelmed by the author's success and when she is unable to distance herself from Ammu. It is, however, noteworthy that the translator, after listening to Roy in Malayalam, decided to translate the novel into the Kottayam dialect of Malayalam, which is spoken by Syrian Christians. The Hindi version makes no such attempts to translate *The God of Small Things* into particular dialects of Hindi. In fact, Estha and Rahel address Ammu in formal "you" Hindi, which seems awkward if a reader (like me) was familiar first with the original in English, and not with the Hindi translation.

As evinced through a comparative cultural and historical analysis of world-makings of the *vishva* in *Chemmeen* and *The God of Small Things* in world, *jagat*, and *sansār*, what makes a text Indian Literature in English Translation is as bizarre as what makes a text represent Indian Writings in English. Most of the time it is a stroke of luck because it is dependent on the vagaries of awards such as Sahitya Akademi or Booker Prize. Moreover, the act of reading a text that gets represented as Indian Writings in English, or Indian Literature in English Translation, whether in the original or translation, is fraught with worldly complexities. The original Malayalam *vishva* in *Chemmeen* in Kottayam dialect throws off even the contemporary Malayalam translator, Nair, who is reminded of the movie *Chemmeen* rather than the Malayalam novel. Though the *vishva* in Roy's English *The God of Small Things* gets translated into the Kottayam dialect in Malayalam, Roy laments that the original *vishva* in her novel that speaks of politics and caste is often not highlighted in Kerala. In contrast, when Santha Rama Rau, an Indian author and journalist, wrote the "Introduction" to Menon's *Chemmeen* in 1962, she remarked that in a multilingual and diverse country like India, the only way to reach a national audience is to write in English, so as to gain access to people who are educated and who could buy a book to read.[123] Rau gives the example of Rabindranath Tagore as someone who was able to capture the literary imagination of people both in Bengali and English, in India and beyond. However, she reminds readers that not all Indian authors have the same good fortune Tagore had; thus, translations are a necessary evil. Moreover, Rau adds that the concept of a "best-seller" in India is "strange" and "wonderful."[124]

There is, however, a problem when it comes to "strange" and "wonderful" best sellers in India—the label of "India," which Arundhati Roy calls a British idea. If Roy calls India a British idea, in "Indianness in Indian Literature," Pillai writes[125] that there is something called the Indianness of Indian literature, although it is quite possible that the distinct nature of Hindi, Tamil, or Malayalam literatures might call their Indianness into question. He mentions that there is an Indian way of living life. To elaborate on this point, Pillai recounts an anecdote at a conference where writers from Pakistan, Bangladesh, India, and some East European countries had gathered in Riga, Latvia. At the end of the conference, Pillai and other representatives of various countries were required to jointly issue a communiqué. He recalls that a harmless statement created much ado about nothing. The sentence had simply "stated that India, Pakistan, and Bangladesh once formed a single nation."[126] Pillai writes:

> The delegate from Pakistan was annoyed at this. He shouted that it was a wrong statement. He asserted that India and Pakistan had fought all through history, and that the two countries had never been one. I too shouted something at him. Some Southeast-Asian friends intervened. The Bangladeshi delegates, however, remained shrewdly reticent. The Pakistani delegate, a poet named Faiz Ahmad Faiz (an altogether strange name to me, although some of my North Indian friends seemed to know him quite well) refused to give in. The communiqué being inevitable, we settled on a less categorical statement that, in history, India and Pakistan had shared a common ground of experience. It appeared to me that the Pakistani poet was very adamant on this point because he desired a peaceful life back home. I, for my part, insisted mainly because of my Indianness—or lack of it.[127]

Pillai adds that his concept of Indianness is how a villager thinks, regardless of the language. He writes that perhaps there could be this difference: that the villager may not think of his/her culture in terms of an awareness of his/her Indianness.[128] He adds that "Indianness is not a life-style, nor a mere vision. It is an instrument a people fashion out with utmost refinement and efficiency in order to maintain a rhythmic balance of their individualistic, social and cultural existence."[129] Interestingly, Pillai does not recognize the most important political poet Faiz Ahmad Faiz, whose *ghazals* are famous in North India, who was part of the Progressive Writers' Association just like Pillai, and who is quite a household name among the well-read public in India and beyond. Pillai finds out from others that the poet is Faiz and has great repute, suggesting that what might count as the world or *vishva* in India in the original, and world or *vishva* in India in translation for one author may not for another within that very world, *jagat*, and *sansār*, even if that author is canonized and bestowed with prestigious awards.

Coda

World Literature and India

To a casual observer, world literature promises access to all the literatures of the world, whereas comparative literature offers only the possibility of comparisons between two or more literary texts. This line of thought hinges on a monochromatic definition of national and regional literatures, brought together in a multi-nodal conversation among literary traditions, and an application of a theoretical paradigm that magically breaks down a literary text into its atoms. The modus operandi of such an approach relies on comparisons that illustrate what is present and what is absent, what is translatable and what is untranslatable, what is theorized and what is untheorized, who is the self and who is the other in the globe. A binarized engagement of this sort only leads to narrow and unproductive definitions of comparative literature, and world literature in the world. By going beyond the hegemony of English in India, by centering the discussions of world literature on the Indic concept of "world," by analyzing world-makings of literary texts in the original, and in translation, and by utilizing *vishva sahitya* from the Global South, I have argued that the scholarly discourses on world literature can be radically altered. In short, world literature can be oriented toward a comparative literature, and comparative literature toward a world literature that is open to the poetics of a world in translation, and in the original.

At the risk of repeating Tagore: comparative literature is nothing but another name for *vishva sahitya* or world literature in India. To emphasize this, let me give a brief overview of the scholarly arguments on comparative literature, and world literature in India and beyond to highlight the significance of the differences in "being" in various worlds, *vishva, jagat,* and *sansār* at specific locations in time. Almost seven decades ago, Buddhadeva Bose set up the first department of comparative literature in India at Jadavpur University, Kolkata. This remained the only full-fledged department of comparative literature in India until two decades ago. Bose remarked in one of his early essays on comparative literature in India that although American universities make a distinction between world literature, and comparative literature, it cannot be denied that the two overlap in intention (if not in scope).[1] It is noteworthy that in this essay, Bose presents the distinction between comparative literature, and world literature as an *American* concern. In doing so, he suggests that what is considered world literature in the United States might qualify as comparative literature (or vice versa) in a multilingual country like India, where the concept of a national language-literature department, such as Indian literature,[2] is contentious.

More recently, Ipsita Chanda, who teaches at the Department of Comparative Literature in Jadavpur University, has argued that world literature's modus operandi is similar to postcolonial theory. Chanda recognizes both world literature, and postcolonial theory as inventions of the Anglo-American academic world, which focuses mostly on texts in English (she neglects to mention Francophone postcolonial studies, etc.). Chanda challenges David Damrosch's definition of world literature as comprising the literary texts that circulate beyond their countries of origin, either in translation or in the original language. By that definition, Chanda argues, for an average multilingual Indian, "every literature written in the language of her immediate neighbour easily enters the category of World Literature."[3] Chanda adds that for comparatists like herself, who do not work within the Euro-American academy, "world literature" is a baffling concept because it does not provide anything new, "except the impulse that brought Comparative Literature itself: the desire to understand the 'being' of difference."[4] Bose and Chanda, both comparatists, claim that the idea of national literature, which has remained the foundation for doing comparative literary work in many parts of the world, does not work well in multilingual societies like India. Further, they both suggest that translation is a way of knowing the *being of difference* in India.

Bose also writes that when critics of the newly established Comparative Literature department at Jadavpur University in Kolkata expressed reservations about reading literature in translation in the 1950s, he defended his department's pedagogical decision:

> Now the question of translation has been gone into so thoroughly in recent times... that it is unnecessary for the present writer to say a single thing about it. Yet it is well worth repeating that to take the extreme-purist viewpoint would be to commit oneself to the absurd position that since one doesn't have the time to learn Sanskrit, Chinese, Spanish, Russian and Norwegian, one must forbear from knowing the minds of Kalidasa, Li-Po, Cervantes, Dostoevsky and Ibsen. And even the extreme-purist often reads his *Mahābhārata* or his *Bible* in translation,

and has respect for men like Matthew Arnold, Andre Gide, Yeats, Shaw and Thomas Mann, who have written authentically on Tolstoy, Dostoevsky, Tagore and Ibsen without knowing a single word of Russian or Bengali or Norwegian. The knowledge of languages is important, but it has no direct bearing on literary understanding. Tolstoy thought *King Lear* insufferable, though he had read it in German, French and English, whereas Ezra Pound, without being a Chinese scholar, has done more for the diffusion of Chinese literature in the Occident, than any other single person except Arthur Waley. It is not only a question of how many, but of *how much* of any foreign language one can learn.[5]

Certainly, Bose is here affirming the value of reading in translation by suggesting that it is admirable to read in as many original languages as possible, but it is absurd to not read literature in translation because it is possible to understand literary texts in translation. Bose's views on translation and guilt-free reading and teaching of literature in translation in a comparative literature department certainly stem from his multilingual context in India, and also from his pedagogical and philosophical belief that comparative literature, and translation cannot be separate from each other. Hence, for Bose, the simple definition of world literature as literature in translation is simply another name for comparative literature in India. However, the list of authors, languages, and texts that he provides in the previous quoted text indicates a specific type of literary canon that is representative of comparative literature in the 1950s: a canon composed mainly of white male authors who wrote mostly in major and hegemonic languages.

Chanda, on the other hand, while championing the cause of comparative literature and discussing the impotency of world literature in the Indian context in 2013, does not discuss the modes in which multilingual Indians are reading each other's literatures. She does not address the complications that ensue from that process of translation, even though being in translation might just be a way of life in India. Certainly, not all Indians speak or read all of the twenty-four (or more) languages used in this nation. Pillai, addressed in the manuscript, does not read Faiz. By conflating the current definitions of world literature, and postcolonial theory, Chanda views both frameworks as located somewhere outside her window; to use the title of her essay, she sees them as working in and with only English.

Though Chanda does not engage with the polemics of translation, and originals, and she simplifies multilingualism in India, her critique of postcolonial theory is important because some of the most incisive critiques of world literature have "emerged from within the field of postcolonial studies."[6] For instance, Baidik Bhattacharya argues that world literature is a legacy of "British imperial encounters with its colonies,"[7] and that it would make sense if "Anglophone postcolonial writing" were seen "as world literature"[8] because it offers "the most productive site to negotiate with the vestiges of colonial history."[9] Bhattacharya claims that the "Anglophone territories are schizophrenic, with divided loyalties and multiple traditions" that make them perfect for anchoring a "search for a postcolonial literary history of world literature."[10] If for Chanda world literature is as baffling a concept as hybridity (coined by Bhabha),[11] for Bhattacharya, the world literature paradigm as traditionally conceived is dead.[12]

To return to the Anglo-American academy, where I am housed, Pheng Cheah has recently claimed that the literatures of the postcolonial South offer an important modality to world literature. Cheah calls the "encounter between cosmopolitanism and world literature: postcoloniality,"[13] which is addressed through his discussions of mostly Anglophone novels. For Cheah, then, the tension between cosmopolitanism and globalization, the world and the globe, is most acute in postcoloniality "because far from holding a world together, capitalist globalization incorporates peoples outside the European world-system by violently destroying their worlds."[14] Considering Bose's thoughts on translation, and comparative literature, and Chanda's views on postcolonial theory, and world literature, we might as well pause and reflect on Bhattacharya's "Anglophone postcolonial writing," and Cheah's "postcoloniality." Where in Bhattacharya or Cheah's proclamations do we really find a desire to reorient toward something that, to use Mufti's recent book title, will forget English in postcolonial studies or world literature literary domains?

I argue that the idea of moving beyond English needs to be critically connected with the insignificant position generally given to translation studies within literary studies, and specifically with respect to comparative literature. The lack of reference as well as trust in translation studies is visible in various frameworks within comparative literature as a discipline. André Lefevere writes that "since the inception of Comparative Literature as an academic discipline, both the production of translations and the study of those productions have been relegated to a position close to the sidelines of its field."[15]

While doing comparative work on Tagore, Pant, Varma, Pillai, and Roy, I have tried *not* to ignore translation. Through the course of the chapters, I highlight that translations are the path to understand diverse concepts of the word "world" that encourage us to go beyond a monolingual standardized globe. The comparative analysis of world-makings of various literary texts in this book also shows that it is truly hard to stay away from translations when doing comparative or world literary work, either for monograph or in a class. Indeed, as Lefevere points out, much of "what we teach in classrooms, as well as the vast majority of texts perceived as literature outside of our classrooms, appears in some form of translation."[16] He further remarks that readers of literature are very often and increasingly "exposed to literature in its translation for comic strips, film and television."[17] Lefevere adds that "both inside the classroom and outside of it, what we call 'literature' in our day and age is an amalgam of all this, combined with the printed texts of the originals."[18] This shadow presence of translation in pedagogical as well as research-focused activities reflects a bigger issue: the translator's invisibility, about which Lawrence Venuti has written,[19] and I have tried to address this by contextualizing translations in their immediate worlds.

Contextualizing, and analyzing the world-making of translations is central to discussions on world literature because for Emily Apter, among others, untranslatability, and translatability have become a source of both joy and pain, hope and hopelessness. Like Walter Benjamin, who is often discussed when conceptualizing these terms, Apter does not explicitly define "untranslatability," or even "translatability" for that matter, in her *Against World Literature*. Nevertheless, she states the central aim of her work as unfolding the problematics of "an approach to literary comparatism that recognizes the importance of non-translation, mistranslation, incomparability, and untranslatability."[20] Thus, by negating translation, comparisons, and translatability, Apter uses untranslatability as an "epistemological fulcrum for rethinking philosophical concepts and discourses of the humanities."[21] She proposes that both translation studies and world literature falsely extend the promise of worldly criticism, as both are unable "to rework literary history through planetary cartographies and temporalities despite their recourse to world-systems theory."[22] Further, Apter accuses scholars of both translation studies and world literature studies of ignoring their respective fields' internal theoretical problems.

Although Apter's *Against World Literature* claims to rescue comparative literature and languages from world literature by pointing out untranslatables, it does not include many case-sensitive or site-specific literary examples, and apart from some second-hand discussion of Arabic, nothing outside the zone of Western European languages. She concludes her book by saying: "I have tried to wean World Literature from its comfort zone—its ready promotion of identifying over differing and its curiously impassive treatment of 'world' and anemic planetary politics—by pressing on what a world is, philosophically, theologically and politically."[23] The near-total absence of literary texts in her book takes us away from the "literature" in world literature. Ending her book with an apocalyptic vision of "thanotropic projections of how a planet dies,"[24] Apter leaves us with an image of the planet dying because of untranslatable abstractions. Apter's thoughts on translation studies and world literature sharply contrast with Susan Bassnett's recent observations that the "problematics of defining comparative and world literature (including whether there is any methodological distinction to be made between these terms) have never prioritized the role of translation in the local or global circulation of texts."[25] Indeed, Lawrence Venuti has pointed out that "by smearing translatability as dubious,"[26] Apter has given unnecessary attention to untranslatability in a way that only hinders them from investigating the actual process as well as the politics of translation.[27] My book refrains from making any absolute claims about untranslatability, and translatability, because it is rooted in the close analysis of the *vishva* or universe in *sahitya* that allows numerous and even conflicting world-makings of that text in the world, *jagat*, and *sansār*. Moreover, my book does not differentiate between world literature, and comparative literature.

Recently, J. Hillis Miller asked about the differences that follow if one reads, teaches, or writes "about a given piece of literature in the context of comparative literature or, alternatively, in the context of world literature?"[28] In order to answer that question, he decides to read the image of tears in poems, specifically in John Keats's poem "Ode to a Nightingale." Miller writes: "I want to identify what actually happens when I read the word 'tears' in Keats's lines with either of the two contexts in mind: world literature or Eurocentric comparative literature."[29] He writes that his comparisons of the tears in Keats's poems with other poems are accidental, borne out of personal circumstances, whereas when he wants to read Keats's poem in the context of world literature about tears, his "first response is a sense of inadequacy."[30] This is mainly because Miller can "more or less read European tears poems in the original, with some help from translation,"[31] and though he "can find URLs on the Internet for tears poems in Urdu and Arabic,"[32] he knows "neither of those languages,"[33] nor does he "know any of the other dozens of non-European languages necessary to study or teach world literature, assuming the same scholarly assumptions of language competence are made for world literature as those we take for granted, or at least pretend to take for granted, for comparative literature."[34] For Miller, comparisons are then products of comfort and familiarity. World literature, on the other hand, gestures toward an inadequacy of the self, or seeks to know the difference in "being," as Chanda had remarked about comparative literature. It is this difference in "being" that I have shown in the preceding chapters by not distinguishing between "to world" and "to compare"—terms often used to differentiate between the disciplinary philosophies of comparative and world literature.

Djelal Kadir, while expanding on the ideas of "to compare" and "to world" as verbs in the context of comparative literature, and world literature, wrote a few years ago that when the word "world" in world literature is taken as a verb, then globalization is not a boundless sweep, but a bounded circumscription.[35] After all, comparative world literature does not mean comparing all the literatures of the planet, the non-globalized world, or the globalized world. Indeed, a world can be a product of globalization or not, but the globe is bound by the forces of globalization.[36] This is not to say that terms such as "world-making" or "world" are apolitical, unworldly, monolingual, or unidimensional gestures in a literary tradition. In fact, they are going to vary depending on one's vantage point; hence, there can never be *one* world literature, just as there cannot be *one* comparative literature. I have argued in this book that world-making is politically charged and multilingually rich, as it demands comparisons not only of different worlds but also of assessments and measurements of the scale of those comparisons through different perceptions in time and space. This means that world literature "is invariably a product of our optic and grasp,"[37] and comparatists "by virtue of their skills are engaged in the process of worlding."[38]

To compare is also, then, to world, meaning to actively engage in the process of imagining a worldview. It is in this worldview that my book is interested, where world literature is not an abstract ideal, or the sum total of all the literatures of the world, or an assembly of the best and shiniest products in one language. Rather, world literature is the multiple interpretations of the *world*, as elaborated through *vishva sahitya*, that can be gauged through the comparative processes of world-making mapped through literary texts in the original and in translations. My intention of giving primacy to both the *vishva*, universe, or world of/in translations, and originals in this book is critical for developing a vocabulary to speak of translations that will help in mitigating what Revathi Krishnaswamy has called a "world lit without a world lit crit,"[39] which was echoed years ago by Sarah Lawall.[40] In this book, then, I have sought to read, compare, and teach a world without failing both the original, and the translation.

In a way, the approach I have used—being aware about the politics of the original and translation in its immediate world—also questions traditional models for studies in English and comparative literature that do not sufficiently account for translation and multilingualism. Each of my chapters shows how texts in the original or in translation do not always circulate from a homogenized metropolitan center to a marginalized periphery; thus, they move beyond Franco Moretti's and Pascal Casanova's scholarship on the "world" in world literature. The processes of analyzing cultural histories of texts through world-making become even more intriguing when we consider the various words available to literary authors for the word "world" in Indian languages. As I have argued, *jag, jagat, vishva, sansār*, or *lok*, to use a few words for "world" in some Indian languages, indicate a complex web of connections of human beings with different aspects of the world, and those relations cannot simply be reduced to just products of global capitalism. Sometimes world-making that is done by the authors themselves stems from a desire to bring about a change in the immediate literary world. Thus, Pillai creates the *vishva* or universe in *Chemmeen* not only to break away from Progressive Writers' Movement but also to build a *pakka* (permanent) home for his family in the world, *jagat*, and *sansār*. Roy hopes that the translation of her *The God of Small Things* from English into Malayalam will encourage discussions on class, and politics that are often ignored when her novel is read in the original in Kerala. These acts of world-making—creating and remaking worlds—reflect a desire for a material world, *jagat*, and *sansār*, which may not necessarily mean a desire for the globalized metropolis, but rather for a re-ordering and reconfiguration of the *now* in the author's specific location through the *vishva*, world, or universe in their texts and *sahitya*.

The intention to create new worlds, or to remake the world, is not new in the context of the Global South. In fact, the intention and desire for a new world stem from different reasons as well. For instance, Mariano Siskind writes that in the early twentieth century, discourses on cosmopolitan aesthetics in Latin America were pregnant with a desire for the world in their epistemological structure. This desire for the world, and their opening of and to the world, helped Latin American writers and thinkers to transcend—and to some extent, even escape—nationalist cultural formations.[41] The *chhayavaad* poets, writing in Hindi, were creating new worlds in their immediate literary world through their subjective lyrics. They, however, were not escaping national-cultural formations like the Latin American writers, but they were also speaking of *vishva chetnā* (world consciousness) and *vishva sahitya*. The *chhayavaad* poets wanted to reconceptualize their immediate literary, and cultural environment with the desire for the world. In that respect, the emphasis on the world, universe, or *vishva* in *sahitya* by Tagore, or the desire for a new world, *jagat*, and *sansār*, is not expressed with the goal to be included in the literary canon at one of the cosmopolitan centers or universities, or to be translated into English, or to receive an international award. For Tagore, Pant, Varma, Pillai, Roy as well as for other thinkers, and translators addressed in this book, the desire for the world thus culminates in the concept of *vishva sahitya*, whose English translation is not world literature in English, but a worldly comparative literature that is open to the poetics of different worlds, *vishva*, *jagat*, and *sansār* in translation and in the original.

Notes

Introduction

1 See Pheng Cheah, *What Is a World? On Postcolonial Literature as World Literature*; Debjani Ganguly, *This Thing Called the World: The Contemporary Novel as Global Form*; Baidik Bhattacharya, *Postcolonial Writing in the Era of World Literature: Texts, Territories, Globalizations*.
2 Stefan Helgesson and Pieter Vermeulen, "Introduction: World Literature in the Making," in *Institutions of World Literature*, 1–20.
3 Helgesson and Vermeulen, "Introduction," 7.
4 Helgesson and Vermeulen, "Introduction," 7.
5 See Aamir Mufti's preface to *Forget English!: Orientalisms and World Literatures*.
6 Djelal Kadir, "To World, To Globalize: Comparative Literature's Crossroads," *Comparative Literature Studies*, 1–9; Djelal Kadir, "To Compare, To World: Two Verbs, One Discipline," *The Comparatist*, 4–11; Harish Trivedi, "Translation and World Literature: The Indian Context," in *Translation and World Literature*, 15–28.
7 David Damrosch, *What Is World Literature?*
8 See Mufti, *Forget English!* See also Bhattacharya, *Postcolonial Writing in the Era of World Literature*.
9 See A. R. Biswas, "East and West in Poetics," in *Critique of Poetics*, 464–532. Biswas suggests that the word "*sahitya*" has had three meanings in the past: *sahitya* as *kavya* (poetry), *sahitya* as literature in general (where *kavya* happens to be a part of it), and *sahitya* as the science of poetics. Biswas argues that the word "*sahitya*" comes from "*sahit*," meaning together. Unlike in Sanskrit poetics, where "*alankār*" has been a field of study, in modern Indian languages, it is *sahitya* that is the focus of study. See also M. Srinivasachariar, *History of Classical Sanskrit Literature*, 709. Srinivasachariar argues that there have been more than thirty treatises named with the word "*sahitya*," and that the word is derived from *sahit*, meaning "the quality of that which is attended with good." For more discussion on *sahitya*, see also Ranjan Ghosh, "The Ethics of Reading Sahitya," in *Thinking Literature across Continents*, 207–31; K. Krishnamoorthy, "The Meaning of 'Sahitya': A Study in Semantics," *Indian Literature*, 65–70; and Rosinka Chaudhuri, "The World Turn'd Upside Down," 145–71. See also Sujata S. Mody, *The Making of Modern Hindi: Literary*

Authority in Colonial North India. Specifically, in her chapter on "Prescriptive Prose," Mody speaks about the development of the concept of *sahitya* in modern Hindi. See also, Subramanian Shankar, "Literatures of the World: An Inquiry," 1405–13. In this essay, Shankar elaborates on the Tamil word "Ilakkiyam" for literature, which bears a close resemblance to the shared experience that is possible through *sahitya*.

10 For more on the "location" of world literature, see Francesca Orsini and Laetitia Zecchini, "The Locations of (World) Literature: Perspectives from Africa and South Asia," 1–12. For the concept of "*duniyā*," see Fatima Burney, "Locating the World in Metaphysical Poetry," 149–68.

Chapter 1

1. For more, see N. Krishnaswamy and Lalitha Krishnaswamy, *The Story of English in India*.
2. Many scholars have claimed that the word "*bhasha*," which simply means "language," is better than the word "vernacular." This is mainly because in a multilingual postcolonial context such as India, "vernacular" often refers to that which is not English. Further, the etymological history of "vernacular" as being the dialect of the ordinary folks that lacks a long literary tradition is inaccurate.
3. Samaj means "society" or "community" in many Indian languages. I will not italicize or transliterate it with diacritical marks as it is fairly a common word in the context of the Brahmo Society/Samaj.
4. The word "*sahitya*" can loosely be translated as "literature." I discuss this term in Tagore's context later in the chapter. For more on the history of the word "*sahitya*," see the note on *sahitya* in the Introduction. I will not transliterate *sahitya* with diacritical marks, as it is a fairly common word.
5. *Vishva mānav* can be translated as "universal/world human/man." The word "*vishva*" can be translated as "world" or "universe," and "*mānav*" can be translated as "human" or "man." I will explain the significance of the word "*vishva*" in the later part of the chapter. I will use the gender-neutral word "human" for *mānav*, because that is what Tagore meant when he spoke of *vishva-mānav*. Further, I will use *mānav* instead of *mānab* in order to maintain consistency with the usage of "v" in "*vishva sahitya*."
6. Rabindranath Tagore, "Visva Sahitya," in *Rabindranath Tagore in the 21st Century*, 277–88. I selected this translation of Tagore's essay because it is very well annotated. I will use "Visva Sahitya" when speaking of the title of this essay, as Rijula Das and Makarand Paranjape use that spelling in their English translation.

When discussing the idea of world literature espoused by Tagore, I will use *vishva sahitya*. For the essay in Bengali, see https://tagoreweb.in/Essays/sahityo-51/bishwa sahityo-1942.

7   To understand Tagore's relationship with politics and nationalism, see Debjani Sengupta, "The Relevance of Rabindranath Tagore's Politics on His 158th Birth Anniversary," *The Wire*, May 7, 2019, https://thewire.in/history/rabindranath-tagore-politics.

8   See Sabyasachi Bhattacharya, *Rabindranath Tagore: An Interpretation*, 90.

9   Bhattacharya, *Rabindranath Tagore: An Interpretation*, 92.

10 See Rabindranath Tagore, "Bengali National Literature," in Das and Chaudhuri, *Rabindranath Tagore: Selected Writing on Literature and Language*, 179–93.

11 "Swadeshi Samaj" can roughly be translated as "The Society/Community of Our Union/Country/Homeland." Tagore gave this lecture after the British announced that Bengal would be partitioned in 1905. In it, Tagore proposed a reorganization of rural Bengal to combat the divisive religious politics of the British. See Bhattacharya, *Rabindranath Tagore: An Interpretation*, 92.

12 In the past, Tagore's "Vishva Sahitya" has also been translated as "Universal Literature." See Rabindranath Tagore, "Universal Literature," in *Angel of Surplus*, 94–104; Rabindranath Tagore, "World Literature," in *Rabindranath Tagore, Selected Writings on Literature and Language*, 138–50; and Supriya Chaudhuri, "Singular Universals: Rabindranath Tagore on World Literature and Literature in the World," in *Tagore: The World as His Nest*, 74–88.

13 Tagore, "Visva Sahitya," 286. I will use "Bengali" when referring to the Bangla language. Both the terms are correct.

14 Sisir Kumar Das and Sukanta Chaudhuri note in *Rabindranath Tagore: Selected Writing on Literature and Language* that the essay shows no awareness by Tagore on the discipline of comparative literature. See "Notes" in *Rabindranath Tagore: Selected Writing on Literature and Language*, 376.

15 Matthew Arnold, "On the Modern Element in Literature," in *Essays by Matthew Arnold*, 453–72. In this lecture, Arnold declares, "Everywhere there is connexion, everywhere there is illustration: no single event, no single literature, is adequately comprehended except in its relation to other events, to other literatures" (456). It is noteworthy that in this lecture, which remained unpublished for a long time, Arnold quotes the chancellor of Cambridge, who had a few days before Arnold said, "We must compare." Arnold thinks of comparisons as a way to establish connections, and also as tools to assess and correct any mistakes.

16 Arnold, "Modern Element," 456.

17 Arnold, "Modern Element," 456.

18 उपमा कालिदासस्य भारवेरर्थगौरवम्।
 दण्डिनः पदलालित्यं माघे सन्ति त्रयो गुणाः ॥
 "Simile is Kalidas' forte, Bharavi—density of meaning; Dandi—simplicity and Magha possesses all three qualities!" (https://samskrtam.wordpress.com/2005/09/09/)
19 N. E. Vishwanatha Iyer, *Anuvād: Bhashayai Samasyaāi*, 86.
20 See "Sakuntala," in *Rabindra Rachanabali*, vol. 3, 723–33.
21 Both the spellings are correct. Shakuntala is more common.
22 Rabindranath Tagore, "Sakuntala: Its Inner Meaning," trans. Jadunath Sarkar, in *Sakuntala*, xiii–xxix. To compare English versions of Tagore's Bengali essay, see "Shakuntala," in *Selected Writing on Literature and Language*, 237–51. The translation is done by Sukanta Chaudhuri. Like the Bengali original, this translation does not begin with a quatrain by Goethe. Though 1920s translation does.
23 Tagore, "Sakuntala: Its Inner Meaning," xix.
24 Tagore, "Sakuntala: Its Inner Meaning," xviii.
25 Arnold, "Modern Element," 457.
26 For more on this, see Volume 1 of Lisa Block de Behar et al., eds., *Comparative Literature: Sharing Knowledges for Preserving Cultural Diversity*, 7.
27 Rabindranath Tagore, "Vishva Sahitya," in *Sahitya*, trans. Vanshidhar Vidyalankar, 46–64.
28 Tagore, "Vishva Sahitya," 62.
29 The "b" in "bishya" will be replaced with "v" in Hindi for "vishva." Bengali does not have the sound "v." Both Hindi and Bengali as well as many Indian languages have many common words. Often these words acquire a slight change in their phonetics.
30 Tagore, "Visva Sahitya," 277.
31 Tagore, "Visva Sahitya," 286.
32 Tagore, "Visva Sahitya," 286.
33 Tagore, "Visva Sahitya," 286.
34 Tagore, "Visva Sahitya," 286.
35 Tagore, "Visva Sahitya," 286.
36 Tagore, "Visva Sahitya," 286.
37 Tagore, "Visva Sahitya," 286.
38 Partha Chatterjee, *Lineages of Political Society: Studies in Postcolonial Democracy*, 104.
39 Chatterjee, *Lineages*, 104.
40 Though Tagore uses the word "*vishva-mānav*," loosely translated as "universe/universal man," Tagore implies the gender-neutral term "human beings." As indicated before, I will use "universal human being," though the translators, Rijula Das and Makarand Paranjape, use "universal man."

41 Tagore, "Visva Sahitya," 286.
42 Tagore, "Visva Sahitya," 286.
43 Tagore, "Visva Sahitya," 286.
44 Tagore, "Visva Sahitya," 286.
45 Tagore, "Visva Sahitya," 286.
46 Tagore, "Visva Sahitya," 286.
47 Tagore, "Visva Sahitya," 287.
48 Tagore, "Visva Sahitya," 288.
49 Tagore, "Visva Sahitya," 288.
50 Tagore, "Visva Sahitya," 288.
51 Tagore, "Visva Sahitya," 288.
52 *Samsara* and *sansār* are two spellings of the same word. I will use the latter.
53 Tagore, "Visva Sahitya," 288.
54 Both the spellings are correct, as mentioned before. The translators use the latter; I use the former.
55 Tagore, "Visva Sahitya," 287.
56 Tagore, "Visva Sahitya," 288.
57 Often we assume that world literature simplifies the "local," or the "regional," as it travels on the back of the global capitalism to global centers. This could not be further from the truth. As I show at various moments in this book, the "home," when contextualized adequately, presents an equally complex picture of a world.
58 Rabindranath Tagore, *Gora*, trans. W. Pearson, 402.
59 See Gayatri Spivak, "Resident Alien," in *Relocating Postcolonialism*, 46–65.
60 Tagore, *Gora*, 406.
61 David Kopf, *The Brahmo Samaj and the Shaping of the Modern Indian Mind*, 294.
62 Kopf, *Brahmo Samaj*, 298.
63 Kopf, *Brahmo Samaj*, 298.
64 Tagore, "Bengali National Literature," 185.
65 See Rabindranath Tagore, *Nationalism*.
66 See Tagore, *Nationalism*, 117–54.
67 Tagore, *Nationalism*, 131.
68 Tagore, *Nationalism*, 131.
69 Tagore, *Nationalism*, 131.
70 Tagore, *Nationalism*, 133.
71 I am using "v" instead of "w" in *svadesh* to maintain consistency.
72 See Tagore, "Bengali National Literature," 177. The lecture was delivered at the Bengal Academy of Literature in 1895 and was also published in *Sahitya* in 1907.
73 The translator Swapan Chakravorty has not italicized the word.
74 Tagore, "Bengali National Literature," 181.

75 Johann Wolfgang von Goethe, *Conversation with Eckermann*, trans. John Oxenford, 174–5. The book does not provide any details about the translator.
76 See John Pizer, *The Idea of World Literature.*
77 Krishna Dutta and Andrew Robinson, eds., *Rabindranath Tagore: An Anthology*, 92.
78 Dutta and Robinson, *Rabindranath Tagore: An Anthology*, 92.
79 See Thomas Silberstein, "Tagore and Germany," 90–2.
80 Silberstein, "Tagore and Germany," 90.
81 Silberstein, "Tagore and Germany," 90.
82 Sujit Kumar Mandal, "Translation as Reception."
83 Mandal, "Translation as Reception," 34.
84 See Raja Ram Mohan Roy, *Translations of Several Principal Books, Passages and Texts of the Vedas, and Some Controversial Works on Brahmunical Theology: With an Introductory Memoir*, vi.
85 The title can be translated as "Discussion on translation."
86 Rabindranath Tagore, "Bhūmikā," in *Anubād-Charcha*, 1–11.
87 Susan Bassnett and Harish Trivedi, "Introduction," in *Post-colonial Translation: Theory and Practice*, 1–18.
88 Subhas Dasgupta, "Tagore's Concept of Translation: A Critical Study," 132–44.
89 Dasgupta, "Tagore's Concept of Translation," 137.
90 Rabindranath Tagore, *Selected Letters of Rabindranath Tagore*, 80.
91 Before *Gitanjali*, Tagore had done translations, but not of his own work in a formal sense. There is, however, ample evidence to prove that he was always immersed in the process of translation. While reminiscing about his childhood education in *My Reminiscences*, Tagore writes about his teacher Gyan Babu, who translated and paraphrased Kalidas for him and also assigned him the task of translating *Macbeth* as punishment when Tagore could not keep himself focused on coursework. Tagore writes about his teacher:

> "When he found he could not secure my attention for the school course, he gave up the attempt as hopeless and went on a different tack. He took me through Kalidas's *Birth of the War-god*, translating it to me as we went on. He also read *Macbeth* to me, first explaining the text in Bengali, and then confining me to the school room till I had rendered the day's reading into Bengali verse. In this way he got me to translate the whole play. I was fortunate enough to lose this translation and so am relieved to that extent of the burden of my *karma*."

See Rabindranath Tagore, *My Reminiscences*, 111.
Parts of Tagore's translations of *Macbeth* have in fact survived, and they are now accessible in *Malupati*. See Mandal, "Translation as Reception." Any scholar of comparative literature or student of foreign language knows that translation is

perhaps the most intimate and essential way of knowing the world of language and literature.

92 See Subha Chakraborty Dasgupta, "Texts on Translation and Translational Norms in Bengal," 162–75.
93 Dasgupta, "Texts on Translation," 164.
94 Dasgupta, "Texts on Translation."
95 Tagore, "Literary Creation," in Das and Chaudhuri, *Rabindranath Tagore: Selected Writings*, 151–63.
96 Tagore, "Literary Creation, 152.
97 See Tagore, "Bengali National Literature."
98 Dasgupta, "Texts on Translation," 165.
99 Tagore, "Literary Creation," 152.
100 Tagore, "Literary Creation," 152.
101 Dasgupta, "Texts on Translation," 165. This open-ended process of translation is very different from Emily Apter's idea of translatability and untranslatability. See Emily Apter, *Against World Literature: On the Politics of Untranslatability*.
102 Dasgupta, "Texts on Translation," 166.
103 Sayantan Dasgupta and Chandra Mohan, "About CLAI," Comparative Literature Association of India, accessed February 9, 2020, http://www.clai.in/index.html. *Vishwa-Sahitya* and *Weltliteratur* are not italicized.
104 This remains true even if some scholars write that Tagore was not aware of the academic debates about the discipline of comparative literature.
105 For more on this, see Amiya Dev, *The Idea of Comparative Literature in India*. See also Amiya Dev, "Comparative Indian Literature," *Yearbook of Comparative and General Literature*, 114–17.
106 In the 1970s, Sujit Mukherjee published several works in which he proposed writing a new historiography of Indian literature that emphasized translation. In some of his works, he also suggested that translation could be used to recover and discover Indian literature. For more, see Sujit Mukherjee, *Toward a Literary History of India*. See also Mukherjee, *Translation as Discovery: And Other Essays on Indian Literature in English Translation*.
107 V. K. Gokak, *The Concept of Indian Literature*.
108 Gurbhagat Singh, *Differential Multilogue: Comparative Literature and National Literatures*. See Amiya Dev's rejoinder to this: Amiya Dev, "Comparative Literature in India," *CLCWeb: Comparative Literature and Culture*.
109 Rabindranath Tagore, *Letters from Abroad*, 38.
110 Tagore, *Letters from Abroad*, 39.
111 "Educational Ideas," Visva-Bharati, accessed February 9, 2020, http://www.visvabharati.ac.in/EDUCATIONAL_IDEAS.html.

Chapter 2

1. See Galin Tihanov, "The Location of World Literature," 468–81. Tihanov argues that a discussion of world literature as a construct involves engagement with language, time, space, and self-reflexivity.
2. Rabindranath Tagore, *The Essential Tagore*, eds. Fakrul Alam and Radha Chakravarty.
3. Martin Puchner, Suzanne Conklin Akbari, Wiebke Denecke, Barbara Fuchs, Caroline Levine, Pericles Lewis, and Emily R. Wilson, eds., *The Norton Anthology of World Literature*, Volume E.
4. Michael Collins, "Introduction," in *Empire, Nationalism, and the Postcolonial World*, 1–23.
5. For more on this, see Collins's *Empire, Nationalism, and the Postcolonial World*, where he argues that though Said's arguments about the self and the other are useful, they are also incredibly restrictive and flattening. In the Introduction, Collins also argues that the subaltern studies and postcolonial historiography have also not done justice to Tagore's work, either placing him in an elite-subaltern dichotomy or an imperial-national dichotomy.
6. Mukherjee, *Translation as Discovery*, 105.
7. Tagore, *Gitanjali*, 1910. (https://tagoreweb.in/Verses/gitanjali-62/amar-matha-noto-kore-3079). The original lines are: "আমার মাথা নত করে দাও হে তোমার/চরণধূলার তলে।/সকল অহংকার হে আমার/ ডুবাও চোখের জলে।"
8. Tagore, *Gitimalya*, 1914. (https://tagoreweb.in/Verses/gitimalya-63/amare-tumi-oshesh-korechho-3388). The original lines are: আমারে তুমি অশেষ করেছ / এমনি লীলা তব।/ফুরায়ে ফেলে আবার ভরেছ/ জীবন নব নব।"
9. Rabindranath Tagore, *Gitanjali: Song Offerings*, 1.
10. Rabindranath Tagore, *Gitanjali*, trans. William Radice.
11. See Radice, "*Gitanjali* Reborn," in *Gitanjali*, xii.
12. See Radice, "*Gitanjali* Reborn," xi–xiii.
13. Radice, "*Gitanjali* Reborn," xii.
14. See Tagore's letter dated October 11, 1913, to Charles Andrews in *Selected Letters of Rabindranath Tagore*, 127–8. Dutta and Robinson note in their commentary that Tagore's Nobel Prize was not based on the diverse body of work he had crafted in Bengali. The poet was well aware of this, and hence he was not sure about the sincerity of the praise that the Nobel Prize bestowed upon him.
15. For full script, see Tagore, "The Nobel Prize Acceptance Speech," in *The English Writings of Rabindranath Tagore*, 1–9.
16. See Shymal Kumar Sarkar, "Tagore and Translation," 66–85. The letter is quoted and translated by Shyamal Kumar Sarkar. See page 80. The letter is now preserved at the Ravindra Bhavana Archives in Shantiniketan.

17 The original letter, dated May 6, 1913, was translated and published by Indira Devi herself as "Genesis of English *Gitanjali*," 3–4.
18 "Genesis of English *Gitanjali*," 3–4.
19 "Genesis of English *Gitanjali*," 3–4.
20 "Genesis of English *Gitanjali*," 3–4.
21 "Genesis of English *Gitanjali*," 3–4.
22 "Genesis of English *Gitanjali*," 3–4.
23 Naresh Guha, "Discovery of a Modern Indian Poet," 58–73. See page 58.
24 Guha, "Discovery of a Modern Indian Poet," 58.
25 See Ezra Pound, "Tagore's Poems," 92–4. See page 93.
26 The *chhayavaad* poets, addressed in the next chapter, also speak of world fellowship.
27 Pound, "Tagore's Poems," 94.
28 Ezra Pound, *The Selected Letters of Ezra Pound*, 10.
29 W. B. Yeats, "Introduction," in *Gitanjali*, vii.
30 Yeats, "Introduction," viii.
31 Yeats, "Introduction," xiii.
32 Yeats, "Introduction," xiii.
33 Yeats, "Introduction," xiii.
34 Yeats, "Introduction," xiii.
35 Yeats, "Introduction," xiv.
36 Yeats, "Introduction," xv.
37 William Jones, "Preface," accessed February 11, 2020, http://www.columbia.edu/itc/mealac/pritchett/00litlinks/shakuntala_jones/00_preface.htm.
38 I say this because for most orientalists, anything other than Sanskrit or Arabic was considered a dialect, even when there were rich literary traditions in that language.
39 See Yeats, "The Return of the Stars." Quoted in Elizabeth Heine's work. See the following note.
40 Quoted in Elizabeth Heine, "W. B. Yeats: Poet and Astrologer," 60–75. See page 72.
41 Yeats, "Introduction," xx. The east-west binary is clearly visible.
42 See Vijay C. Mishra, "Two Truths Are Told: Tagore's Kabir," 80–90.
43 For the original, see Kabir, in *Kabir Granthavali*, ed. Parasnath Tiwari, 9. बालम, आवो हमारे गेह रे ।/तुम बिन दुखिया देह रे ।/सब कोई कहै तुम्हारी नारी, मोकों लगत लाज रे ।/दिल से नहीं लगाया, तब लग कैसा सनेह रे ।/अन्न न भावै नींद न आवै, गृह-बन धरै न धीर रे ।/कामिन को है बालम प्यारा, ज्यों प्यासे को नीर रे ।/है कोई ऐसा पर-उपकारी, पिवासों कहै सुनाय रे ।/अब तो बेहाल कबीर भयो है, बिन देखे जिव जाय रे ॥
44 Mishra, "Two Truths are Told," 82.
45 Mishra, "Two Truths are Told," 84.
46 Kabir, *Songs of Kabir*, trans. Rabindranath Tagore, 82–3.

47 I am going to use "v" instead of "b" when speaking of *jīvan devtā* to maintain consistency with my prior usage of "v" instead of "b" in *vishva*, *mānav*, and so on.
48 Hiranmay Banerjee, *The Humanism of Tagore: Special Lectures*, 32.
49 Banerjee, *The Humanism of Tagore*, 34–5.
50 Tagore, "Introduction to the Bengali Language," in *Rabindranath Tagore: Selected Writings on Literature and Language*, 343–5.
51 Tagore, *Selected Writings on Literature and Language*, 153.
52 Tagore, *Selected Writings on Literature and Language*, 153.
53 Tagore, *Selected Writings on Literature and Language*, 153.
54 Sisir Kumar Das, "Introduction," in *The English Writings of Rabindranath Tagore*, 1:12.
55 Roby Datta, "Preface," in *Echoes from East and West*, ix.
56 Sujit Mukherjee, *Translation as Recovery*, 115.
57 See Das, "Introduction," vol. 1, 1–21.
58 Quoted in Mukherjee, *Translation as Recovery*, 115.
59 This interest reached its full glory in several volumes of prose-poems that Tagore produced toward the end of his career. See, for instance, *Lipika* and *Punascha*.
60 Tagore, *Gitanjali*, 19.
61 https://www.tagoreweb.in/Verses/gitanjali-62/aji-shrabon-ghano-gohon-mohe-3096.
62 Ezra Pound, "Rabindranath Tagore," *Fortnightly Review* LXXXXIX (March 1913), accessed February 11, 2020, https://fortnightlyreview.co.uk/2013/04/rabindranath-tagore/.
63 The original lines are: "শ্রাবণ-ঘন-গহন-মোহে / গোপন তব চরণ ফেলে।"
64 This is the quoted line: "নিলাজ নীল আকাশ ঢাকি।"
65 This is the quoted line: "পথিকহীন পথের 'পরে।"
66 Tagore, *Gitanjali*, 2.
67 https://www.tagoreweb.in/Verses/gitanjali-62/tumi-kemon-kore-gan-koro-3100.
68 Mukherjee, *Translation as Discovery*, 5.
69 Mukherjee, *Translation as Discovery*, 5.
70 Buddhadeva Bose, "Tagore in Translation," *Yearbook of Comparative and General Literature*, 15–25. See page 23.
71 Bose, "Tagore in Translation."
72 He wrote copiously to his friends that his translations were not excellent; in that respect, his views aligned with those of his critics. But he continued to translate.
73 Tagore, *Selected Letters*, 90.
74 Tagore, *Selected Letters*, 90.
75 Tagore, *Selected Letters*, 93–4.
76 Tagore, *Selected Letters*, 93–4.
77 English became one of the official languages of India in the 1960s. Technically speaking, it was still not an Indian language when Tagore translated his *Gitanjali*

into English. However, various creative works (as well as bilingual editions) in the nineteenth century suggest that English had long since become an Indian language.
78 Tagore, *Selected Letters*, 419.
79 Tagore acknowledges doing a translation in a letter written to Mr. Rattray. See *Selected Letters of Rabindranath Tagore*, 520.
80 For more on this, see Bose, "Tagore in Translation."
81 The letter was written in 1913 from Illinois. It is quoted in Shyamal Kumar Sarkar, "Tagore on Translation," 74.
82 "The Nobel Prize in Literature 1913," accessed February 11, 2020, https://www.nobelprize.org/prizes/literature/1913/summary/.
83 See Tagore, *Selected Writings on Literature and Language*, 331–4.
84 Tagore, *Selected Writings on Literature and Language*, 333
85 Tagore, *Selected Writings on Literature and Language*, 333
86 Tagore, *Selected Writings on Literature and Language*, 333
87 Tagore, *Selected Writings on Literature and Language*, 333
88 Paniker Ayyappa, "The Impact of Tagore and his Works on Kerala Life and Literature," in *Rabindranath Tagore in Perspective*, 181.
89 Karine Schomer, *Mahadevi Varma and the Chhayavad Age of Modern Hindi Poetry*, 24.
90 Mukherjee, *Translation as Recovery*, 118.
91 Mukherjee, *Translation as Recovery*, 118.
92 See Ketaki Kushari Dyson, *In Your Blossoming Flower-garden: Rabindranath Tagore and Victoria Ocampo*.
93 Dyson, *In Your Blossoming Flower-garden*, 66.
94 Paz delivered the lecture "The Manuscript of Tagore" at Delhi University in 1967.
95 Octavio Paz, "Los manuscritos de Rabindranath Tagore," in *El signo y el garabato*, 146–9.
96 Howard Young, "The Invention of an Andalusian Tagore," *Comparative Literature*, 42–52.
97 Young, "The Invention of an Andalusian Tagore," 42.
98 Dyson, *In Your Blossoming Flower-garden*, 417.
99 Dyson, *In Your Blossoming Flower-garden*, 395–7.
100 Dyson, *In Your Blossoming Flower-garden*, 463.
101 Young, "The Invention of an Andalusian Tagore," 42.
102 Young, "The Invention of an Andalusian Tagore," 43.
103 Young, "The Invention of an Andalusian Tagore," 43.
104 Young, "The Invention of an Andalusian Tagore," 44.
105 Young, "The Invention of an Andalusian Tagore," 44.

106 Young, "The Invention of an Andalusian Tagore," 44.
107 Rabindranath Tagore, *Dear Mr. Tagore: Ninety-five Letters Written to Rabindranath Tagore from Europe and America, 1912-1941*, 37–8.
108 Rabindranath Tagore, "Prologo," in *Gitanjalí: poemas místicos*, trans. Pedro Requena Legarreta, i–xiii.
109 Tagore, "Prologo," x.
110 Rabindranath Tagore, *Ofrenda lírica, gitanjali, poemas.* trans. Juan Ramón Jiménez and Zenobia Camprubí de Jiménez, 19.
111 Tagore, *Gitanjalí: poemas místicos*, 5.
112 Tagore, *Gitanjalí: poemas místicos*, 2.
113 Tagore, *Gitanjalí: poemas místicos*, 6.
114 Aamir R. Mufti, *Forget English!*
115 For more on this, see Nabaneeta Dev Sen, "The Reception of Rabindranath Tagore in England, France, Germany, and the United States."
116 Victoria Ocampo, "Tagore on the Banks of the River Plate: West Meets East," in *Tagore Centenary Volume*, 27–47. See page 37.
117 Rabindranath Tagore, "East to West," *The Atlantic Monthly*, 732.
118 Cecilia Meireles, "Tagore in Brazil," in *Rabindranath Tagore: A Centenary Volume 1861-1961*, 334–8.
119 Meireles, "Tagore in Brazil," 335.
120 Dorothy Figueira, "Comparative Literature: Can This Marriage Be Saved?," 420–35.

Chapter 3

1 Rough translation: "shadowism." "*Vaad*" in Hindi roughly means "-ism" in English.
2 I give here the dates of the poets because I want to remind readers that these poets were writing at a time when modernism was at its peak in Anglo-American literary traditions. I also want to remind readers that some of these poets were contemporaries of Tagore, though they primarily wrote in Hindi. This chapter focuses mainly on four poets: Jaishankar Prasad (1890–1937), Suryakant Tripathi Nirala (1896–1961), Sumitranandan Pant (1900–77), and Mahadevi Varma (1907–87).
3 See David Rubin, "Introduction," in *Of Love and War: A Chayavad Anthology*, xii–xxxvii. Rubin claims that the *chhayavaad* lyrics are marked by what people in the West might call Romantic tendencies, symbolism, and mysticism. He adds that the *chhayavaad* lyrics seems to be influenced by a variety of sources such as the Upanishads, French symbolists, English romantics, Tagore, and so on. As it

can be gauged, the tendency is to *not* see *chhayavaad* lyrics displaying modernist tendencies, or to argue that *chhayavaad* lyrics express a modernist sensibility that is different from the fragmented and alienated individualism of Anglo-American modernism.

4 See Sumitranandan Pant, "Pravesh," in *Pallav*, 1–54. For Nirala's retort, see Suryakant Tripathi Nirala, "Pantji Aur Pallav," in *Nirala Rachanavali*, Vol. 5, 164–208. The essay was first published in a five-part series from Lucknow in the periodical *Madhuri*. The first and second parts appeared in the September and December 1927 editions. The subsequent sequels appeared in the April, May, and July 1928 editions.
5 See Gayatri Chakravorty Spivak, "The Politics of Translation," in *Outside in the Teaching Machine*, 179–200. See also Apter, *Against World Literature*.
6 See Jahan Ramazani, *The Hybrid Muse: Postcolonial Poetry in English*. Ramazani argues that "since poetry mediates experience through a language of exceptional figural and formal density, it is a less transparent medium by which to recuperate the history, politics, and sociology of postcolonial societies" (4). See also Julie Meisami, *Structure and Meaning in Medieval Arabic and Persian Lyric Poetry*. Meisami claims that the absence of reliable translations of poetry, and the general absence of poetry from academic and scholarly discussions, has led to a steady decline in the study of poetry. She takes the example of medieval Arabo-Persian poetry to support this argument.
7 See Stephen Owen, "The Anxiety of Global Influence: What Is World Poetry?" 28–32. Owen argues that world poetry is that which is admired by an international reader (championing what the poetry might be if it had not been lost in translation) and by readers at home (who are happy to know how much it is appreciated internationally, in translation). In addition, Robert Frost famously remarked, "I like to say, guardedly, that I could define poetry this way: it is that which gets lost out of both prose and verse in translation." The remark is often misquoted as claiming that poetry is "what gets lost in translation." See Robert Frost, *Conversations on the Craft of Poetry*, 7.
8 David Damrosch, "World Literature in a Postcanonical, Hypercanonical Age," in *Comparative Literature in an Age of Globalization*, 43–53.
9 Or, "मैं-शैली."
10 Sumitranandan Pant, *Chhayavaad: Punarmūlyāṅkan*.
11 Pant uses the phrase "Vishva Bodh Kī Saṅgati" in his discussion.
12 Pant's Hindi phrase is "Vishva Shaktiyōṅ Kī Prasṭha Bhūmi."
13 Pant, *Chhayavaad: Punarmūlyāṅkan*, 53.
14 Pant, *Chhayavaad: Punarmūlyāṅkan*, 57.
15 See Devraj's criticism, discussed later in this chapter.

16 See her essay on modern poet discussed later in this chapter.
17 Pant, *Chhayavaad: Punarmūlyāṅkan*, 59.
18 Pant, *Chhayavaad: Punarmūlyāṅkan*, 59.
19 *Jag* and *Jagat* have the same connotation when it comes to the word "world." Both are ephemeral and a result of *maya*.
20 The original title is "Vishva Vyāptī."
21 The original title is "Vishva Chavi."
22 The original title is "Vishva Veṇu."
23 The original title is "Jīvan-Yān."
24 See Pant, *Pallav*, 63. The original lines are: "स्पृहा के विश्व, हृदय के हास !"
25 See Pant, *Pallav*, 63. Original lines: "फूल, तुम कहाँ रहे अब फूल ?"
26 See Pant, *Pallav*, 65. Original lines: "अहे विश्व! हे विश्व-व्यथित-मन!/ किधर बह रहा है यह जीवन?"
27 See Pant, *Pallav*, 50. Original lines: "विश्व वेणु के-से झंकार/हम जग के सुख-दुखमय गान/पहुँचाते अनंत के द्वार!"
28 The original title is "Caha."
29 See Varma, *Nihar*, 14. Original lines: "चाहता है यह पागल प्यार,/अनोखा एक नया संसार!"
30 The original title is "Prashna."
31 See, Mahadevi Varma, *Rashmi*, 74–5. Original lines: "क्या कहीं अस्तित्व है झंकार का?"
32 See Varma, *Rashmi*, 75. Original lines: "विश्व में वह कौन सीमाहीन है?/हो न जिसका खोज सीमा से मिला!/क्यों रहोगे क्षुद्र प्राणों में नहीं,/ क्या तुम्हीं सर्वेश एक महान हो?"
33 The original title is "Vishva Chhavi."
34 See Pant, *Pallav*, 84. Original lines: "मुस्कुराते गुलाब के फूल!/कहाँ पाया मेरा बचपन?"
35 See Pant, *Pallav*, 84. Original lines: "विश्व-छवि से गुलाब के फूल/करुणा है यह परिवर्तन!"
36 The original title is "Mere Haṅste Adhar Nahiṅ Jag."
37 Original lines are: "मेरे बन्धन आज नहीं प्रिय,/संसृति की कड़ियाँ देखो !/मेरे गीले पलक छुओ मत/मुरझायी कलियाँ देखो!" See Mahadevi Varma, *Neerja*, 37–8.
38 Original: "मुझमें हो तो आज तुम्हीं 'मैं'/बन दुख की घड़ियाँ देखो!/मेरे गीले पलक छुओ मत/बिखरी पंखुरियाँ देखो!" See Varma, *Neerja*, 38.
39 The title in Hindi is Adhivās. See Nirala, "Adhivās," in *Nirala Rachanavali*, Vol. 1, 35–6.
40 See *Nirala Rachanavali*, Vol. 1, 35. The original text is "कहाँ -- /मेरा अधिवास कहाँ?"
41 See *Nirala Rachanavali*, Vol. 1, 35. The original lines are: "मैंने "मैं"- शैली अपनायी/देखा दुखी एक निज भाई।/दुख की छाया पड़ी हृदय में मेरे,/झट उमड़ वेदना आयी।"
42 Suryakant Nirala, "Toṛatī Pathar," in *Nirala Rachanavali*, Vol. 1, 323–4. The poem was first published in *Sudhā*, 1937.
43 Original: "मैं तोड़ती पत्थर।"
44 The original lines are: "तुम हो कौन और मैं क्या हूँ?/इसमें क्या है धरा, सुनो,/मानस जलधि रहे चिर चुम्बित/मेरे क्षितिज! उदार बनो।" See Jaishankar Prasad, *Lahar*, https://www.hindi-kavita.com/HindiLeharJaishankarPrasad.php.

45 Schomer, *Mahadevi Varma*, 44–5.
46 Varma, *Neerja*, "Dhīre Dhīre Utar Kṣhitij," 3.
47 Varma, *Neerja*, "Laya Kaun Saṅdes Naya Ghan?," 91.
48 *Meghdutam* and *Meghadut* are the same.
49 Suryakant Nirala, "Jūhī Kī Kalī," in *Nirala Rachanavali*, Vol. 1, 31.
50 Schomer, *Mahadevi Varma*, 30–1.
51 Schomer, *Mahadevi Varma*, 30–1.
52 Schomer, *Mahadevi Varma*, 30–1.
53 Schomer, *Mahadevi Varma*, 32.
54 Sumitranandan Pant, "Anubhūti," in *Kalā Aur Būḍhaā Chānd*, https://www.hindi-kavita.com/HindiKalaAurBoorhaChandPant.php#Chand13.
55 See "Mānav," in *Gunjan*, 35–6.
56 See *The Literatures of India: An Introduction*. The book is a collection of essays on various aspects of Indian literature. The section "The Lyric Poem" has five essays that touch on various traditions of lyric poetry in India. The writers specifically focus on Sanskrit, Bengali, Kannada, Tamil, and Urdu.
57 Virginia Jackson and Yopie Prins, "General Introduction," in *The Lyric Theory Reader*, 1–9. See page 3.
58 Yopie and Prins, "General Introduction," 4.
59 Yopie and Prins, "General Introduction," 6.
60 Namvar Singh, *Chhayavaad*, 11.
61 The original title is "Hindi Meiṅ Chhayavaad."
62 In earlier chapters, I have noted the usage of the word "*chhaya*" for "translation" in the context of discussions about *vishva sahitya*.
63 For more on the development of the public literary culture in Hindi, see Francesca Orsini, *The Hindi Public Sphere*. See also Vasudha Dalmia, *The Nationalization of Hindu Traditions: Bharatendu Harischandra and Nineteenth Century Banaras*.
64 Nirala wrote this in his essay "Khaṛī Bolī Ke Kavi Aur Kavitā" (Khaṛī Bolī's Poets and Their Poetry). It was published in the literary magazine *Madhuri* in August 1929. See *Nirala Rachanavali*, Vol. 5, 300–11.
65 See Alok Rai, *Hindi Nationalism*. The book focuses on the conflict between Hindi and Urdu and the various social, political, and economic factors that exacerbate this conflict.
66 See "Hindustan Kī Rāshtra Bhasha Aur Hindi," *Sarasvati* 3 (March 1916).
67 See "Adhunik Hindi Kavitā," *Sarasvati* 6 (June 1916).
68 "Panch Parmeshvar" or "Five Divine Beings." This is a famous Hindi story in which Premchand emphasizes that justice is above all relationships.
69 Schomer, *Mahadevi Varma*, 95.
70 Schomer, *Mahadevi Varma*, 95.

71 Schomer, *Mahadevi Varma*, 98.
72 Ramchandra Shukla, *Hindi Sahitya Kā Itihās*.
73 Kharī Bolī means "standard speech." Many argued that it was different from the Braj, Bhojpuri, Avadhi, and Persian languages that were in use in North India at that time. Whether Kharī Bolī is Urdu or Hindustani in *Devanagari*, or Urdu is Kharī Bolī or Hindustani in *Nastaliq*, are political questions that are beyond the scope of this chapter. One could say Kharī Bolī is Urdu and/or Hindustani, though it leans toward Sanskrit in its borrowing for vocabulary, whereas Urdu uses Arabic words when it comes to loan-words and technical terms. That being said, Hindi and Urdu share a large pool of common vocabulary, and in colloquial speech it is hard to pinpoint where Urdu begins and Hindi ends. Also note that "*bolī*" is different from "*bhasha*," the word for "language" in many Indian languages. Braj is often called Braj bhasha, whereas Kharī is mostly a *bolī* (a local idiom, dialect, or Saussurean parole).
74 Mahadevi Varma, *Path Ke Sāthī*, 12.
75 Schomer, *Mahadevi Varma*, 25.
76 "Kavi Rahasya" is the original title.
77 The original title is "Vishva Vyāptī."
78 "Siyāhī Ka Būnd" in Hindi.
79 Schomer, *Mahadevi Varma*, 97.
80 N. K. Devraj, *Chhayavaad Kā Patan*, 3.
81 Devraj, *Chhayavaad Kā Patan*, 15.
82 Devraj, *Chhayavaad Kā Patan*, 15.
83 The title in Hindi is "Vigyāpan."
84 Pant uses the word "Pravesh."
85 Pant, *Pallav*, 9.
86 Orsini, *Hindi Public Sphere*, 3.
87 The original title is "Mere Bachapan Ke Din."
88 Mahadevi Varma, "My Childhood Days," trans. Anita Anantharam, in *Mahadevi Varma: Political Essays on Women, Culture, and Nation*, 37.
89 The title is "Adhunik Kavi" in Hindi. For a recent translation of this essay, see Mahadevi Varma, "Introduction to *Adhunik Kavi* 'From My Point of View,'" trans. Francesca Orsini, in Anantharam, *Mahadevi Varma: Political Essays*, 89–116. I will use Orsini's translation, but refer the essay as "Modern Poet."
90 Mahadevi Varma, *Deepshikha*.
91 Varma, "Introduction to *Adhunik Kavi* 'From My Point of View,'" 96.
92 Varma, "Introduction to *Adhunik Kavi* 'From My Point of View,'" 96.
93 Varma, "Introduction to *Adhunik Kavi* 'From My Point of View,'" 96.
94 Varma, "Introduction to *Adhunik Kavi* 'From My Point of View,'" 96.
95 Varma, "Introduction to *Adhunik Kavi* 'From My Point of View,'" 97.

96 Schomer, *Mahadevi Varma*, 17.
97 Hans Theodor Gaeffke, *Hindi Literature in the Twentieth Century*, 12.
98 Quoted in Schomer, *Mahadevi Varma*, 99.
99 The original title is "Vishva Bhasha."
100 The original title is "Trīmurtī."
101 Padumalal-Punnalal Bakshi, *Vishva Sahitya*.
102 *Chhayavaad* poets were producing something unique for their readers. The *chhayavaad* poets were also very popular. It is not clear whether Dularelal "approved" of the *chhayavaad* poems.
103 Sri Dularelal, "Sampādkīye Vaktavya," in *Vishva Sahitya*, 5.
104 Dularelal, "Sampādkīye Vaktavya," 6.
105 Dularelal, "Sampādkīye Vaktavya," 6.
106 This is perhaps accurate because other works on *vishva sahitya* available in Hindi are often anthologies or essays on various literary traditions. Bakshi's piece is absolutely focused on the concept of *vishva sahitya*.
107 The original title is "Sahitya Kā Vikās."
108 The original title is "Sahitya Kā Sammilan."
109 Dularelal, "Sampādkīye Vaktavya," 70.
110 Dularelal, "Sampādkīye Vaktavya," 240.
111 The original is "Sahitya Kī Ākaṅsha."
112 The modern period in Hindi literature is roughly divided into phases, and Mahavir Prasad Dvivedi represents the second phase. The years between 1893 and 1918 are named after him and called the *Dvivedi Yug* (era). The *Dvivedi Yug* was preceded by the *Bharatendu Yug* (1868–93) and followed by *Chhayavaad* (1918–42). This is a rough estimate of timelines.
113 See the note on David Rubin at the beginning of this chapter.
114 See Damrosch, *What Is World Literature?* 281.
115 See Apter, *Against World Literature*, 3.

Chapter 4

1 Mahadevi Varma, "Sahitya, Sanskriti Aur Shāsan," in *Mere Priya Sambhāshaṇa*, 42–6.
2 See Varma, "Sahitya, Sanskriti Aur Shāsan," 46.
3 For more on this, see Francesca Orsini, "The Reticent Autobiographer: Mahadevi Varma's Writings," in *Telling Lives in India: Biography, Autobiography, and Life History*, 54–82.
4 Orsini, "The Reticent Autobiographer: Mahadevi Varma's Writings," 55.

5 Other male *chhayavaad* poets are not generally addressed by their first names. I will therefore use Varma, not Mahadevi.
6 For instance, see her essay on Mahadevi Varma, "Introduction to *Adhunik Kavi* 'From My Point of View.'"
7 Schomer, *Mahadevi Varma*, 257.
8 Orsini, "The Reticent Autobiographer: Mahadevi Varma's Writings," 54.
9 One could argue that this trend might have to do with the fact that poetry is often dismissed as hard to translate or lost in translation. See the previous chapter.
10 See Mahadevi Varma, "The Art of Living," trans. Chandra Agarwal, in *The Penguin New Writings in India*, 96–100. In this translation, Agarwal has replaced Varma's "Hindu" in the original with "Indian" in translation, wherever Varma uses "Hindu woman" in the essay. Also, see the "Introduction" in this book by Aditya Behl and David Nicholls, ix–xi.
11 See, for instance, *The Oxford Anthology of Modern Indian Poetry*. See also *The Vintage Book of Modern Indian Literature*. Also, Varma's poems do not feature in *The Penguin New Writings in India*. Moreover, the monumental two-volume anthology *Women Writings in India* (which includes English translations of women's writings in India from 600 BCE to the present) does not include Varma's poems. See *Women Writing in India*.
12 There are several scholarly books on Varma's poetry, especially in Hindi, that compare her poetry with Mira's. The argument in this chapter is to not further Varma's "modern Mira" image, however, interested readers can read Ramchandra Shukla or Raghuvir Prasad Singh's work. Also, *Mahadevi Varma Abhinandan Granth* has many essays that suggest and emphasize the "modern Mira" image.
13 See "Introduction," in *Women Writing in India*, Vol. 1, 1–40.
14 See Sandra M. Gilbert and Susan Gubar, "Gender, Creativity, and the Woman Poet," in *The Lyric Theory Reader*, 522–9.
15 For more on reading texts "in relation," see Debra A. Castillo, "Gender and Sexuality in World Literature," in *The Routledge Companion to World Literature*, 404–12.
16 Schomer, *Mahadevi Varma*, 240–1.
17 See "Parichay" in *Nihar*.
18 See the 1928 issue of *Sarasvati*.
19 The original title is "Kavi Aur Kavitā."
20 Ramvilas Sharma, *Mahavir Prasad Dvivedi Aur Hindi Navjagaran*, 330. In his 1907 Hindi translation of John Stuart Mill's *Liberty* (titled *Svādhīnta*), Dvivedi makes an interesting comparison among Hindi, Bengali, and Marathi languages. He laments in the "Introduction" (where he also describes his translation strategies) that Hindi lacks good literature, and even lacks the level

of consciousness that could make it a national language. Dvivedi also claims that all languages of India should grow and that translation is an important way of increasing readership. *Svādhīnta*'s function is exactly to enrich Hindi with literature of the world. See Mahavir Prasad Dvivedi, *Svādhīnta*.
21 See *Stri-Kavi-Kaumudi*, ed., Mishra, Jyotiprasad "Nirmal" Mishra.
22 Schomer, *Mahadevi Varma*, 240–1.
23 See Mishra, "Vaktavya," in *Stri-Kavi-Kaumudi*, 11–18.
24 Schomer, *Mahadevi Varma*, 240–1.
25 For original, see Ramshankar Shukla's essay in *Stri-Kavi-Kaumundi*, 40. The phrase is reminiscent of the editorial comments that I discussed earlier from the 1928 *Sarasvati* edition on Hindi and Urdu love poems.
26 The original title is "Mera Jeevan Parichay."
27 Schomer, *Mahadevi Varma*, 241.
28 Schomer, *Mahadevi Varma*, 243–51.
29 For more, see Rupert Snell, *The Hindi Classical Tradition: A Braj Bhāṣā Reader*.
30 Snell, *Hindi Classical Tradition*, 39. Snell writes that a *pad* can be a couplet, a foot, a line, or verse that is intended for devotional singing.
31 Snell, *Hindi Classical Tradition*, 106, 107. Translation is by Snell.
32 Snell, *Hindi Classical Tradition*, 105. Translation is by Snell.
33 Mahadevi Varma, "Who Are You in My Heart?," in *Mahadevi Varma*, trans. Sarah Houston Green, 28.
34 Various translations of Varma's essays and other prose work have a robust life in English. See Mahadevi Varma, *A Pilgrimage to the Himalayas, and Other Silhouettes from Memory*, trans. Radhika Prasad Srivastava and Margaret B. Lillian; Varma, *Sketches from My Past*; and Mahadevi Varma, *Links in the Chain*.
35 *Women Writing in India*, 461.
36 Mahadevi Varma, *Selected Poems*, trans. L. S. Sinha.
37 The verse is from "Ashru Yeh Panī Nahī Haiṅ." The original verse is "अश्रु यह पानी नहीं है, /यह व्यथा चंदन नहीं है!" For the full verse in Hindi, see Varma, *Agnirekha*, https://www.hindi-kavita.com/HindiAgnirekhaMahadeviVerma.php#Agni18.
38 L. S. Sinha, "Preface," in *Selected Poems*, 5.
39 Sinha, "Preface," 5.
40 Sinha, "Preface," 5.
41 Sinha, "Preface," 5.
42 Sinha, "Preface," 5.
43 Sinha, "Preface," 5.
44 Sinha, "Preface," 5.
45 Sinha, "Preface," 22.
46 Sinha, "Preface," 16.

47 Sinha, "Preface," 16.
48 Sinha, "Preface," 16.
49 I am working with my translation as I analyze this poem in this paragraph. For the original in Hindi, see Varma, "Tūt Gayā Vah Darpaṇa Nirmam," in *Neerja*, 64–5. The poem has been translated by L. S. Sinha as well as David Rubin. See Sinha, *Selected Poems*, 54–5. See also for comparison, David Rubin's translation in his *Of Love and War: A Chayavad Anthology*, 96–7.
50 The original line in Hindi is "अपने दो आकार बनाने."
51 The original line in Hindi is "दोनों का अभिसार दिखाने."
52 The original line in Hindi is "कैसे निशि-दिन."
53 The original line in Hindi is "कैसे सुख-दुख."
54 The original line is "किसमें देख सँवारुँ कुंतल."
55 The original line is "अंगराग पुलकों का मल मल."
56 The original line is "स्वप्नों से आँजूँ पलकें चल"
57 The original line is "किस पर रीझूँ किस से रूठूँ.
58 Check the previous note.
59 The original is "भर लूँ किस छवि से अंतरतम !"
60 The original is "टूट गया वह दर्पण निर्मम! !"
61 Rubin, *Of Love and War*, 96.
62 Rubin, *Of Love and War*, 96.
63 The line in Hindi is "मेरा बंधन तेरा साधन." The verse was revised by Varma; and she added new lines that were absent in the original *Neerja*. For the updated version in Hindi, see Mahadevi Varma, *Adhunik Kavi*, 63.
64 Varma, "Introduction to *Adhunik Kavi* 'From My Point of View,'" 89–116.
65 Mahadevi Varma, "The Links in Our Chain," trans. Shobna Nijhawan, in Anantharam, *Mahadevi Varma: Political Essays*, 71–9. See, 76.
66 Varma, "The Links in Our Chain," 76.
67 Dudhanatha Singh, *Mahadevi*, 60.
68 Singh, *Mahadevi*, 60.
69 Schomer, *Mahadevi Varma*.
70 See Pant, Chhayavaad: Punarmūlyāṅkan.
71 Hindi, like many Indian languages, does not have the concept of capital letters. I did not capitalize the "k" in "khuda" in order keep in line with the rest of the poetic sentiment. For original, see Mahadevi Varma, "Khudī Na Gayī," in *Pratham Āyām*, https://www.hindi-kavita.com/HindiPrathamAayamMahadeviVerma.php#Aayam16.
72 The original lines by Varma are as follows: "तुमने न वियोग की पीर सही नहीं खोजने आकुल प्राण चला !/ तुम आपको भूल सके न कभी जो खुदी न गई तो खुदा न मिला !"
73 See *Women Writing in India*, 2:167.
74 See *Women Writing in India*, 2:167.

75 See Kamlesh Mohan, "Image of Women in *Stree Darpan* (1909-1928)," *Proceedings of the Indian History Congress*, 762–70.
76 Mohan, "Image of Women in *Stree Darpan* (1909-1928)," 763.
77 The original title is *Fānsī*.
78 See Nareshchandra Chaturvedi, *Chānd Fānsī Aṅk*.
79 The original title is "Vishva Vīṇā."
80 The original title is "Vishva Darshan."
81 The original title is "Kyoṅ Aur Kaise?"
82 The original title is "Farīyāde Bismal."
83 Schomer, *Mahadevi Varma*, 183.
84 I am translating the title as *Links to Our Chains*. For original, see Mahadevi Varma, *Shrāṅkhalā Kī Kaṛiyāṅ*. The book is also available in English translation as *Links in the Chains*.
85 Varma, *A Pilgrimage to the Himalayas, and Other Silhouettes from Memory*, 10.
86 The original title is "Vidushi."
87 Nirala had written an essay on Chakori's poems in 1934.
88 Schomer, *Mahadevi Varma*, 226.
89 Schomer, *Mahadevi Varma*, 227.
90 Schomer, *Mahadevi Varma*, 227.
91 See Varma, *Shrāṅkhalā Kī Kaṛiyāṅ*, 5.
92 See Varma, *Shrāṅkhalā Kī Kaṛiyāṅ*, 5.
93 See Varma, *Shrāṅkhalā Kī Kaṛiyāṅ*, 5.
94 See Mahadevi Varma, "Dīp Mere Jal Akampit," in *Deepshikha*. https://www.hindi-kavita.com/HindiDeepshikhaMahadeviVerma.php#Deep1. The original lines are: "दीप मेरे जल अकम्पित,/चुल अचंचल!"
95 For original, see Mahadevi Varma, "Madhur Madhur Mere Dīpak Jal," in *Neerja*, 30.
96 Schomer, *Mahadevi Varma*, 279. Schomer's translation.
97 For original, see "Sab Bhujhe Dīpak Jalaṅ Lūṅ," in *Deepshikha*, https://www.hindi-kavita.com/HindiDeepshikhaMahadeviVerma.php#Deep5. The original lines are "सब बुझे दीपक जला लूं/घिर रहा तम आज दीपक रागिनी जगा लूं."
98 See Varma, "Mōm-Sā Tan Ghul Chukā," in *Deepshikha*. https://www.hindi-kavita.com/HindiDeepshikhaMahadeviVerma.php#Deep22.
99 See Varma, *Deepshikha*, https://www.hindi-kavita.com/HindiDeepshikhaMahadeviVerma.php#Deep22. The original lines are: "मोम सा तन घुल चुका अब दीप सा तन जल चुका है।/विरह के रंगीन क्षण ले,/अश्रु के कुछ शेष कण ले,/ वरुनियों में उलझ बिखरे स्वप्न के सूखे सुमन ले,/ खोजने फिर शिथिल पग,/निश्वास-दूत निकल चुका है!"
100 For original, see Varma, *Deepshikha*, https://www.hindi-kavita.com/HindiDeepshikhaMahadeviVerma.php#Deep22. The original lines are: "अब कहो सन्देश है क्या?/और ज्वाल विशेष है क्या?/अग्नि-पथ के पार चन्दन-चांदनी का देश है क्या?/एक इंगित के लिये/शत बार प्राण मचल चुका है!"

101 See Varma, "Dīp," in *Nihar*, 89–90.
102 The original lines are "मूक कर के मानस का ताप/सुलाकर वह सारा उन्माद,/जलाना प्राणों को चुपचाप/छिपाये रोता अन्तर्नाद;/कहाँ सीखी यह अद्भुत प्रीति?/मुग्ध हे मेरे छोटे दीप!"
103 Orsini argues in her "The Reticent Autobiographer: Mahadevi Varma's Writings" that Varma's different articulations of subjectivity should be viewed separately and were part of her artistic strategy.
104 Varma, "Who Are You in My Heart?," 27.
105 Varma, "Introduction to *Adhunik Kavi* 'From My Point of View,'" 97–8.
106 Varma, "Introduction to *Adhunik Kavi* 'From My Point of View,'" 113.
107 Varma, "Introduction to *Adhunik Kavi* 'From My Point of View,'" 113.
108 Varma, "Introduction to *Adhunik Kavi* 'From My Point of View,'" 113.
109 *Jagat* and *jag* have the same meaning.
110 Mahadevi Varma, "Chapter 6," in *Sketches from My Past: Encounters with India's Oppressed*, trans. Neera Kuckreja Sohoni, 67.
111 See Mahadevi Varma, "Merī Sahitya Yātrā: Kavitā Ke Sandarbh Mein," in *Mahadevi Sahitya Samagra*, ed. Nirmala Jain, 3: 409–15.
112 Varma, "Introduction to *Adhunik Kavi* 'From My Point of View,'" 101.
113 See Rubin, *Of Love and War*, xiii.
114 Rubin, *Of Love and War*, xiii.
115 Mahadevi Varma, "Merī Sahitya Yātrā: Gadya Ke Sandarbh Mein," in *Mahadevi Sahitya Samagra*, 3: 416–19.
116 For more on this, see in the same volume: Varma, "Merī Sahitya Yātrā: Kavitā Ke Sandarbh Mein."
117 Varma, "Merī Sahitya Yātrā: Kavitā Ke Sandarbh Mein," 412.
118 Varma, "Introduction to *Adhunik Kavi* 'From My Point of View,'" 109.
119 Varma, "Introduction to *Adhunik Kavi* 'From My Point of View,'" 98.
120 See Nirala, "Garībon Kī Pukār," in *Nirala Rachanavali*, Vol. 1, 51. The poem was first published in 1923 in *Matvālā*, a literary magazine. It includes many words that have Persian and Arabic roots.
121 Nirala, "Vidhvā," *Nirala Rachanavali*, Vol. 1, 60. Also published first in 1923 in *Matvālā*.
122 Nirala, "Bhikshuk," in *Nirala Rachanavali*, Vol. 1, 64. Published in 1923 in *Matvālā*.
123 Sumitranandan Pant, "Vah Letī Hai Tarū Chāyā Mein," in *Yugānt*, https://www.hindi-kavita.com/HindiYugaantPant.php#Yugaant24. Original lines are: "वह जागी है अथवा सोई?/मूर्च्छित या स्वप्न-मूढ़ कोई?/नारी कि अप्सरा या माया?/अथवा केवल तरु कि छाया?"
124 For original, see Varma, "Mein Aur Tū," in *Rashmi*, 56–62.
125 Varma, *Rashmi*, 62. The original lines are "मुझे बाँधने आते हो लघु/सीमा में चुपचाप,/कर पाओगे भिन्न कभी क्या/ज्वाला से उत्ताप?"

126 David Rubin, *The Return of Sarasvati*, 153.
127 Rubin, *The Return of Sarasvati*, 153–4.
128 Singh, *Mahadevi*, 62.
129 Varma, "Uttar," Nihar, 56–7.
130 Original lines are as follows: "इस एक बूँद आँसू में/चाहे साम्राज्य बहा दो / वरदानों की वर्षा से / यह सूनापन बिखरा दो"
131 The original lines are "पर शेष नहीं होगी यह/मेरे प्राणों की क्रीड़ा,/तुमको पीड़ा में ढूँढा/तुम में ढूँढूँगी पीड़ा!"
132 For more, see Aamir Mufti, "Towards a Lyric History of India," in Jackson and Prins, *The Lyric Theory Reader*, 603–17.
133 Mufti, "Towards a Lyric History of India," 606.
134 Mufti, "Towards a Lyric History of India," 606.
135 Varma, *Neerja*, 16–17. For original, see: "चाहता है यह पागल प्यार,/अनोखा एक नया संसार!"
136 Varma, *Neerja*, 16–17.
137 See Varma, "Apnī Baat," in *Rashmi*, 1–4.
138 Varma, "Apnī Baat," 3.
139 Varma, "Apnī Baat," 4.
140 Varma, "Apnī Baat," 1.
141 See Orsini, "Reticent Autobiographer."
142 I am thinking of the excellent work done by Schomer.

Chapter 5

1 Salman Rushdie, *Imaginary Homelands: Essays and Criticism 1981-1991*, 16.
2 Rushdie, *Imaginary Homelands*, 10.
3 Sisir Kumar Das, "The Idea of an Indian Literature," in *The Idea of an Indian Literature: A Book of Readings*, 202–7. See Das, 205.
4 Das, "The Idea of an Indian Literature," 205.
5 Das, "The Idea of an Indian Literature," 202.
6 See T. B. Macaulay, "Minute," accessed February 7, 2020, http://www.columbia.edu/itc/mealac/pritchett/00generallinks/macaulay/txt_minute_education_1835.html.
7 Vinay Dharwardker, "The Historical Formations of Indian-English Literature," in *Literary Cultures in History: Reconstructions from South Asia*, 199–267. See page 204.
8 Dharwardker, "Formations of Indian-English Literature," 205.
9 Dharwardker, "Formations of Indian-English Literature," 205.
10 Dharwardker, "Formations of Indian-English Literature," 205.
11 For more, see Harish Trivedi, "The Hindi Postcolonial—Categories and Configurations," *Comparative Literature Studies*, 400–7.

12 See Homi Bhabha, *The Location of Culture*.
13 See Raja Rao, "Foreword," in *Kanthapura*.
14 Published in 1889. For more on the influence of this novel on Malayalam novels and Indian literature in general, see Ayyappa Paniker, *A Perspective of Malayalam Literature*. See also K. M. Tharakan, *A Brief Survey of Malayalam Literature*.
15 Thakazhi Sivasankara Pillai, "The Story of My *Chemmeen*," in *Chemmeen*, trans. Anita Nair. The piece is not paginated.
16 See Nagarjun, *Varun Ke Bete*.
17 "Long live the revolution!" (Hindi/Urdu phrase).
18 See Nagarjun, *Varun Ke Bete*.
19 Pillai, "The Story of My *Chemmeen*."
20 See a translation of the address here: Munshi Premchand, "The Nature and Purpose of Literature," *Social Scientist*, 82–6. Translator's name is not given.
21 Thakazhi Sivasankara Pillai, "*Chemmeen* that Gifted Me Both Good Fortune and Sorrow," in Pillai, *Chemmeen*, trans. Nair. The piece is not paginated.
22 Pillai, "*Chemmeen* that Gifted Me."
23 Pillai, "*Chemmeen* that Gifted Me."
24 Pillai, "*Chemmeen* that Gifted Me."
25 See "About Sahitya Akademi," Sahitya Akademi, accessed February 9, 2020, http://sahitya-akademi.gov.in/aboutus/about.jsp.
26 Pillai, "The Story of My *Chemmeen*."
27 I will be referencing the following edition: T. S. Pillai, *Chemmeen*, trans. Narayana Menon, introduction by Santha Rama Rau.
28 UNESCO, "Historical Collection," accessed February 9, 2020, http://www.unesco.org/culture/lit/rep/index.php.
29 See Sarah Brouillette, *UNESCO and the Fate of the Literary*. The book presents, among other things, a cogent argument on UNESCO's role in funding cultural and literary institutions, and how that is connected with policy-making and globalization.
30 Edouard J. Maunick, "A Library of World Classics," *UNESCO The Courier*, 5–8.
31 J. C. Aggarwal and S. Agrawal, *Documentation Encyclopedia of UNESCO and Education Part II*, 649.
32 UNESCO, "Historical Collection," http://www.unesco.org/culture/lit/rep/index.php.
33 Various book jacket covers of *Chemmeen* can be found on this blog: *La estanteria*, April 2014, accessed February 9, 2020, http://laestanteriablog.blogspot.com/2014/04/muralla-de-redes-thakazhi-sivasankara.html.
34 Roughly translated as: An Indian love or love story: Novel. Thakazhi Sivasankara Pillai, *Un Amour Indien: Roman*, trans. Nicole Balbir. The translation is from the English translation of *Chemmeen* by Narayana Menon.
35 Thakazhi Sivasankara Pillai, *Chemmeen: Un Amour Indien*.

36 Rough translation: barrier made of net. See Thakazhi Sivasankara Pillai, *Muralla de redes*, trans. Juan Fonseca. The Spanish translation is also from Menon's English version.
37 Thakazhi Sivasankara Pillai, *Machuare*, trans. Bharati Vidyarthi.
38 Thakazhi Sivasankara Pillai, *Chingri*, trans. Bommana Viswanatham and Nilina Abraham. The Bengali version of the novel includes an introduction by Narayana Menon, not by Santha Rama Rau. The Bengali version is most likely a translation from the English translation, rather than from Malayalam.
39 See previous note.
40 Thakazhi Sivasankara Pillai, R. Surendran, and K. Balakrishnan, "Thakazhi in Conversation with R. Surendran," *Indian Literature*, 162–71.
41 Surendran and Balakrishnan, "Thakazhi in Conversation with R. Surendran."
42 Thakazhi Sivasankara Pillai, "Society as Hero," in *Authors Speak*, 291–304.
43 Meenakshi Mukherjee, *The Perishable Empire: Essays on Indian Writing in English*, 191.
44 Mukherjee, *The Perishable Empire*, 191.
45 Raji Narasimhan, "*Chemmeen*: Its Passage through Three Languages," in *Translation as a Touchstone*, 2.
46 Narasimhan, "*Chemmeen*: Its Passage," 3.
47 Mukherjee, *The Perishable Empire*, 189.
48 Mukherjee, *The Perishable Empire*, 189.
49 Mukherjee, *The Perishable Empire*, 189.
50 Narasimhan, "*Chemmeen*: Its Passage," 18.
51 Narasimhan, "*Chemmeen*: Its Passage," 7.
52 Narasimhan, "*Chemmeen*: Its Passage," 7.
53 Narasimhan, "*Chemmeen*: Its Passage," 8.
54 Narasimhan, "*Chemmeen*: Its Passage," 17.
55 Narasimhan, "*Chemmeen*: Its Passage," 18.
56 Pillai, *Chemmeen*, trans. Anita Nair, 233–4.
57 Pillai, *Chemmeen*, trans. Narayana Menon, 215–6.
58 Pillai, *Machuare*, 163. The original is as follows:

"परी के बढ़ाए हुए हाथों के बीच से वह उसकी छाती से जा लगी । दोनों के अधर मिल गए । परी ने उसके कान में कहा, 'मेरी करुत्तम्मा !'

'हूँ !'

परी करुतम्मा की पीठ पर हाथ फेरने लगा । परी ने फिर पुकारा, 'करुत्तम्मा !'

'ऊँ !'—अर्धचेतनावस्था में करुत्तम्मा ने फिर जवाब दिया ।

मैं तेरा कौन हूँ ?

परी के कपोलों को अपने दोनों हाथों से पकड़ती हुई और अर्धनिमिलित नेत्रों से उसे देखती हुई करुतम्मा ने कहा, 'कौन ?' 'मेरे रतनभंडार !'

दोनों फिर एक हो गए । उस अनंदानुभूति में वह परी के कान में कुछ-कुछ कहती रही ।

उस गाढ़े आलिंगन से अलग होने की शक्ति उसमें नहीं थी ।"

59 Sanju Thomas, "Toward a Monolingual World," in *Redefining Translation and Interpretation in Cultural Evolution*, 20–41. See page 34.
60 Unless Parliament decided otherwise, the use of English for official purposes was to cease fifteen years after the constitution came into effect, that is on January 26, 1965. This, of course, did not happen. See https://www.mea.gov.in/Images/pdf1/Part17.pdf.
61 M. T. Ansari, *Islam and Nationalism in India: South Indian Contexts*, 162.
62 Ansari, *Islam and Nationalism*, 162.
63 Meena Pillai, "On Adapting *Chemmeen*: Myth as Melodrama," in Pillai, *Chemmeen*, trans. Anita Nair. Paginations are not given in Nair's translation of the novel, where interviews, insights, and articles are collated.
64 See Ansari, *Islam and Nationalism*.
65 Pillai, *Chemmeen*, trans. Anita Nair, 39.
66 Pillai, *Chemmeen*, trans. Anita Nair, 40.
67 See Ansari, *Islam and Nationalism*.
68 Meena Pillai, "On Adapting *Chemmeen*."
69 Anita Nair, "Translator's Notes," in Pillai, *Chemmeen*.
70 Arundhati Roy, *The God of Small Things*, 43.
71 Roy, *The God of Small Things*, 43.
72 Roy, *The God of Small Things*, 43.
73 Roy, *The God of Small Things*, 43.
74 Roy, *The God of Small Things*, 43.
75 Roy, *The God of Small Things*, 43.
76 Roy, *The God of Small Things*, 43.
77 Roy, *The God of Small Things*, 43.
78 Roy, *The God of Small Things*, 43.
79 Roy, *The God of Small Things*, 208–9.
80 Roy, *The God of Small Things*, 208–9.
81 Roy, *The God of Small Things*, 209.
82 Roy, *The God of Small Things*, 44.
83 Mullaney, *Arundhati Roy's The God of Small Things: A Reader's Guide*, 68–9.
84 Mullaney, *A Reader's Guide*, 69.
85 Mullaney, *A Reader's Guide*, 69.
86 Mullaney, *A Reader's Guide*, 69.
87 S. P. Swain, "Erotic Pornography and Sexuality: A Study of *The God of Small Things*," in *Arundhati Roy: The Novelist Extraordinary*, 144–9. See page 149.
88 Swain, "Erotic Pornography," 149.
89 Roy, *God of Small Things*, 51.

90 Leila Neti, "'The Love Laws': Section 377 and the Politics of Queerness in Arundhati Roy's *The God of Small Things*," 223–46. See page 229.
91 Neti, "The Love Laws," 229.
92 Neti, "The Love Laws," 229.
93 "Like Sculpting Smoke: Arundhati Roy on Fame, Writing and India," *Kyoto Journal: Insights from Asia*, November 5, 2011, https://kyotojournal.org/conversations/arundhati-roy-on-fame-writing-and-india/.
94 "Like Sculpting Smoke."
95 "Like Sculpting Smoke."
96 "Like Sculpting Smoke."
97 Arundhati Roy, "What Is the Morally Appropriate Language in Which to Think and Write?" (lecture, W. G. Sebald Lecture on Literary Translation, British Library, London, on June 5, 2018), https://lithub.com/what-is-the-morally-appropriate-language-in-which-to-think-and-write/.
98 Roy, "Morally Appropriate Language."
99 Roy, "Morally Appropriate Language."
100 Roy, "Morally Appropriate Language."
101 Roy, "Morally Appropriate Language."
102 Roy, "Morally Appropriate Language."
103 Roy, "Morally Appropriate Language."
104 Roy, "Morally Appropriate Language."
105 Geetha Ganapathy-Doré, *The Postcolonial Indian Novel in English*, 150.
106 Ganapathy-Doré, *The Postcolonial Indian Novel*, 150.
107 Ganapathy-Doré, *The Postcolonial Indian Novel*, 150.
108 Ganapathy-Doré, *The Postcolonial Indian Novel*, 150.
109 Pillai, "Society as Hero," 301–2.
110 Meenakshi Mukherjee, "Indian Novels in Translation," *Indian Literature*, 57–65.
111 Mukherjee, "Indian Novels in Translation," 61.
112 Mukherjee, "Indian Novels in Translation," 62.
113 Mukherjee, "Indian Novels in Translation," 62.
114 Pillai, *Chemmeen*, trans. Narayana Menon, 4.
115 Pillai, "The Story of my *Chemmeen*."
116 Pillai, *Chemmeen*, trans. Menon, 3.
117 Pillai, *Machuare*, 5. Original is "बप्पा नाव और जाल ख़रीदने जा रहें है."
118 Raji Narasimhan, "*The God of Small Things*: A Wrong Book to Translate," in *Translation as a Touchstone*, 141.
119 Arundhati Roy, *Māmūlī Cīzoṃ Kā Devatā: Upanyāsa*, trans. Nilabh.
120 K. P. M. Basheer, "Estha, Rahel Now Speak Malayalam," *The Hindu*, October 4, 2016, https://www.thehindu.com/news/cities/Kochi/Estha-Rahel-now-speak-Malayalam/article13352071.ece.

121 Basheer, "Estha, Rahel Now Speak Malayalam."
122 Sanju Thomas, "Towards a Monolingual World," 24.
123 Santha Rama Rau, Introduction of Pillai, *Chemmeen*, trans. Narayana Menon, vi.
124 Rau, introduction of *Pillai*, trans. Menon, vi.
125 Thakazhi Sivasankara Pillai, "Indianness in Indian Literature," 65–70.
126 Pillai, "Indianness," 67.
127 Pillai, "Indianness," 67.
128 Pillai, "Indianness," 67.
129 Pillai, "Indianness," 68.

Conclusion

1 See Buddhadeva Bose, "Comparative Literature in India," *Yearbook of Comparative and General Literature*, 1–10. See also Vinayak Krishna Gokak, *The Unity of World Literature and Indian Literature*, 14. Gokak writes that comparative literature focuses on a particular work.
2 See *The Idea of an Indian Literature: A Book of Readings*. See also Gokak, *The Unity of World Literature and Indian Literature*. Gokak writes that through translation, modern Indian languages can develop world literatures—say, for instance, in Kannada, or African literature in Kannada (16–18). Gokak's idea of what might constitute a regional literature resembles Rashmi Sadana's suggestion that the regional is arbitrary in India; see Sadana, *English Heart, Hindi Heartland: The Political Life of Literature in India*, 103. See also Swapan Majumdar, *Comparative Literature: Indian Dimensions*. Majumdar points out that understanding Indian literature as a compendium of several regional literatures could not be further from the truth. Literatures that get qualified as "regional" literature have individual cultural and literary histories. More than two decades ago, A. K. Ramanujan grappled with the equally head-spinning cultural and philosophical quandary of defining an Indian way of thinking. He writes that the answer to the question, which is also the title of his essay—"Is there an Indian way of thinking?"—will depend on the nature of the emphasis placed on the individual elements of the question. See Ramanujan, "Is There an Indian Way of Thinking? An Informal Essay," *Contributions to Indian Sociology* 23, no. 1 (1989): 41–58. See also E. V. Ramakrishnan's "Is There an Indian Way of Thinking about Comparative Literature?," Cornell University Global South Project, accessed February 7, 2020, http://www.globalsouthproject.cornell.edu/is-there-an-indian-way-of-thinking-about-comparative-literature.html.
3 Ipsita Chanda, "'World Literature': A View from Outside the Window," in *Contextualizing World Literature*, 29–40. See, 31.

4 Chanda, "A View from Outside the Window," 38.
5 Bose, "Comparative Literature in India," 7.
6 Helgesson and Vermeulen, "Introduction: World Literature in the Making," 1.
7 Bhattacharya, *Postcolonial Writing in the Era of World Literature*, 9.
8 Bhattacharya, *Postcolonial Writing in the Era of World Literature*, 9.
9 Bhattacharya, *Postcolonial Writing in the Era of World Literature*, 15.
10 Bhattacharya, *Postcolonial Writing in the Era of World Literature*, 9.
11 Chanda, "A View from Outside the Window," 34–5.
12 Bhattacharya, *Postcolonial Writing*, 2.
13 Cheah, *What Is a World?*, 11.
14 Cheah, *What Is a World?*, 11–12.
15 André Lefevere, "Translation and Comparative Literature: The Search for the Center," 129–44. See, 133.
16 Lefevere, "Translation and Comparative Literature," 141.
17 Lefevere, "Translation and Comparative Literature," 141.
18 Lefevere, "Translation and Comparative Literature," 141–2.
19 Lawrence Venuti, *The Translator's Invisibility*.
20 Apter, *Against World Literature*, 4.
21 Apter, *Against World Literature*, 31.
22 Apter, *Against World Literature*, 8.
23 Apter, *Against World Literature*, 335.
24 Apter, *Against World Literature*, 342.
25 Susan Bassnett, *Translation and World Literature*, 4–5.
26 Lawrence Venuti, "Hijacking Translations: How Comp Lit Continues to Suppress Translated Texts," *Boundary*, 179–204. See, 202.
27 Venuti, "Hijacking Translations."
28 J. Hillis Miller, "Thoughts That Do Lie Too Deep for Tears: Comparative Literature Versus World Literature," *The Canadian Review of Comparative Literature*, 378–96. See, 378.
29 Miller, "Thoughts That Do Lie Too Deep for Tears," 379.
30 Miller, "Thoughts That Do Lie Too Deep for Tears," 389.
31 Miller, "Thoughts That Do Lie Too Deep for Tears," 389.
32 Miller, "Thoughts That Do Lie Too Deep for Tears," 389.
33 Miller, "Thoughts That Do Lie Too Deep for Tears," 389.
34 Miller, "Thoughts That Do Lie Too Deep for Tears," 389.
35 Kadir, "To World, To Globalize," 2.
36 See Trivedi, "Translation and World Literature."
37 Kadir, "To World, To Globalize," 7.
38 Kadir, "To Compare, To World," 6.

39 Revati Krishnaswamy, "Toward World Literary Knowledges: Theory in the Age of Globalization," *Comparative Literature*, 399–419.
40 Sarah Lawall, "Introduction," in *Reading World Literature: Theory, History, and Practice*. In her "Introduction" to *Reading World Literature: Theory, History, and Practice*, Lawall writes that the essays collected in the book show world literature as an invitation to read the world and as an academic practice that falls short—when it does—only by failing to read as fully as possible.
41 Mariano Siskind, *Cosmopolitan Desires: Global Modernity and World Literature in Latin America*.

Bibliography

"Adhunik Hindi Kavitā." *Sarasvati* 6 (June 1916).
Aggarwal, J. C. and Suren Agrawal. *Documentation Encyclopaedia of UNESCO and Education Part II*. New Delhi: Concept, 1991.
Anantharam, Anita, ed. *Mahadevi Varma: Political Essays on Women, Culture, and Nation*. Amherst: Cambria Press, 2010.
Ansari, M. T. *Islam and Nationalism in India: South Indian Contexts*. Oxon: Routledge, 2016.
Apter, Emily. *Against World Literature: On the Politics of Untranslatability*. London: Verso, 2013.
Arnold, Matthew. "On the Modern Element in Literature." In *Essays by Matthew Arnold*, 453–72. London: Oxford University Press, 1914.
Bakshi, Padumalal-Punnalal. *Vishva Sahitya*. Lucknow: Ganga-Granthagaar, 1924.
Banerjee, Hiranmay. *The Humanism of Tagore: Special Lectures*. Mysore: University of Mysore, 1968.
Basheer, K. P. M. "Estha, Rahel Now Speak Malayalam." *The Hindu*, October 4, 2016. https://www.thehindu.com/news/cities/Kochi/Estha-Rahel-now-speak-Malayalam/article13352071.ece.
Bassnett, Susan, ed. *Translation and World Literature*. New York: Routledge, 2019.
Bassnett, Susan. "Introduction: The Rocky Relationship Between Translation Studies and World Literature." In Bassnett, *Translation and World Literature*, 1–14.
Bassnett, Susan, and Harish Trivedi. "Introduction." In *Post-colonial Translation: Theory and Practice*, edited by Susan Bassnett and Harish Trivedi, 1–18. Oxon: Routledge, 1999.
Behl, Aditya, and David Nicholls. "Introduction." In *The Penguin New Writings in India*, edited by Aditya Behl and David Nicholls, ix–xi. New York: Penguin Books, 1994.
Bhabha, Homi. *The Location of Culture*. London: Routledge, 1994.
Bhattacharya, Baidik. *Postcolonial Writing in the Era of World Literature: Texts, Territories, Globalizations*. Oxon: Routledge, 2018.
Bhattacharya, Sabyasachi. *Rabindranath Tagore: An Interpretation*. New Delhi: Penguin, 2011.
Biswas, A. R. *Critique of Poetics*. New Delhi: Atlantic Publishers & Distributors, 2005.
Block de Behar, Lisa, Paola Mildonian, Jean-Michel Djian, Alfons Knauth, Dolores Romero Lopez, and Marcio S. Silva, eds. *Comparative Literature: Sharing Knowledges for Preserving Cultural Diversity*. Oxford: EOLSS Publishers, 2009.

Bose, Buddhadeva. "Comparative Literature in India." *Yearbook of Comparative and General Literature* 8 (1959): 1–10.

Bose, Buddhadeva. "Tagore in Translation." *Yearbook of Comparative and General Literature* 12 (1963): 15–25.

Brouillette, Sarah. *UNESCO and the Fate of the Literary*. Stanford: Stanford University Press, 2019.

Burney, Fatima. "Locating the World in Metaphysical Poetry." *Journal of World Literature* 4, no. 2 (2019): 149–68.

Casanova, Pascale. *The World Republic of Letters*. Translated by M. B. DeBevoise. Cambridge: Harvard University Press, 2007.

Castillo, Debra A. "Gender and Sexuality in World Literature." In *The Routledge Companion to World Literature*, edited by Theo D'haen, David Damrosch and Djelal Kadir, 404–12. Abingdon: Routledge, 2012.

Chanda, Ipsita. "'World Literature': A View from Outside the Window." In *Contextualizing World Literature*, edited by Jean Bessière and Gerald Gillespie, 29–40. Brussels: Peter Lang, 2015.

Chatterjee, Partha. *Lineages of Political Society: Studies in Postcolonial Democracy*. New York: Columbia University Press, 2011.

Chaturvedi, Nareshchandra. *Chānd Fānsī Aṅk*. New Delhi: Radhakrishna Prakashan, 1997.

Chaudhuri, Rosinka. "The World Turn'd Upside Down." *Interventions* 22, no. 2 (2020): 145–71.

Chaudhuri, Supriya. "Singular Universals: Rabindranath Tagore on World Literature and Literature in the World." In *Tagore: The World as His Nest*, edited by Sangeeta Datta and Subhoranjan Dasgupta, 74–88. Kolkata: Jadavpur University Press, 2016.

Cheah, Pheng. *What Is a World?: On Postcolonial Literature as World Literature*. Durham: Duke University Press, 2016.

Collins, Michael. *Empire, Nationalism, and the Postcolonial World*. Oxon: Routledge, 2012.

Dalmia, Vasudha. *The Nationalization of Hindu Traditions: Bharatendu Harischandra and Nineteenth Century Banaras*. New Delhi: Oxford University Press, 1997.

Damrosch, David. "World Literature in a Postcanonical, Hypercanonical Age." In *Comparative Literature in the Age of Globalization*, edited by Haun Saussy, 43–53. Baltimore: The Johns Hopkins University Press, 2006.

Damrosch, David. *What Is World Literature?* Princeton: Princeton University Press, 2003.

Das, Sisir Kumar. "The Idea of an Indian Literature." In *The Idea of an Indian Literature: A Book of Readings*, edited by Sujit Mukherjee, 202–7. Mysore: Central Institute of Indian Languages, 1981.

Das, Sisir Kumar. "Introduction." In Vol. 1 of *The English Writings of Rabindranath Tagore*. New Delhi: Sahitya Academy, 1994.

Das, Sisir Kumar, and Sukanta Chaudhuri, eds. *Rabindranath Tagore: Selected Writings on Literature and Language.* New Delhi: Oxford University Press, 2001.

Das, Sisir Kumar. "Introduction." In Das and Chaudhuri, *Rabindranath Tagore: Selected Writings on Literature and Language*, 1–21.

Das, Sisir Kumar, and Sukanta Chaudhuri. "Notes." In Das and Chaudhuri, *Rabindranath Tagore: Selected Writings*, 376–413.

Dasgupta, Sayantan, and Chandra Mohan. "About CLAI." Comparative Literature Association of India. Accessed February 9, 2020. http://www.clai.in/index.html.

Dasgupta, Subhas. "Tagore's Concept of Translation: A Critical Study." *Indian Literature* 56, no. 3 (2012): 132–44.

Dasgupta, Subha Chakraborty. "Texts on Translation and Translational Norms in Bengal." *Translation Today* 3, no. 1/2 (2006): 162–75.

Datta, Roby. *Echoes from East and West.* Cambridge: Galloway and Porter, 1909.

Dev, Amiya. "Comparative Indian Literature." *Yearbook of Comparative and General Literature* no. 34 (1985): 114–17.

Dev, Amiya. "Comparative Literature in India." *CLCWeb: Comparative Literature and Culture* 2, no. 4 (2000): 1–8.

Dev, Amiya. *The Idea of Comparative Literature in India.* Calcutta: Papyrus, 1984.

Devi, Indira. "Genesis of English *Gitanjali.*" *Indian Literature* 11, no. 2 (1958): 3–4.

Devraj, N. K. *Chhayavaad Kā Patan.* Chapara: Vina Mandir Press, 1948.

Dharwardker, Vinay. "The Historical Formations of Indian-English Literature." In *Literary Cultures in History: Reconstructions from South Asia*, edited by Sheldon Pollock, 199–267. New Delhi: Oxford University Press, 2003.

Dhawan, R. K., ed. *Arundhati Roy: The Novelist Extraordinary.* New Delhi: Prestige Publication, 1999.

Dutta, Krishna and Andrew Robinson, eds. *Rabindranath Tagore: An Anthology.* New York: St. Martin's Griffin, 1999.

Dvivedi, Mahavir Prasad. *Svādhīnta.* Nagpur: Deshsevak Press, 1907.

Dyson, Ketaki Kushari. *In Your Blossoming Flower-garden: Rabindranath Tagore and Victoria Ocampo.* New Delhi: Sahitya Akademi, 1988.

Figueira, Dorothy. "Comparative Literature: Can This Marriage Be Saved?" *Canadian Review of Comparative Literature / Revue Canadienne de Littérature Comparée* 44, no. 3 (2017): 420–35.

Frost, Robert. *Conversations on the Craft of Poetry.* New York: Holt, Rinehart, and Winston, 1961.

Gaeffke, Hans Theodor. *Hindi Literature in the Twentieth Century.* Wiesbaden: O. Harrassowitz, 1978.

Ganapathy-Doré, Geetha. *The Postcolonial Indian Novel in English.* Newcastle: Cambridge Scholars Publishers, 2011.

Ganguly, Debjani. *This Thing Called the World: The Contemporary Novel as Global Form.* Durham: Duke University Press, 2016.

Ghosh, Ranjan. "The Ethics of Reading Sahitya." In *Thinking Literature Across Continents*, edited by Ranjan Ghosh and J. Hillis Miller, 207–31. Durham: Duke University Press, 2016.

Gilbert, Sandra M., and Susan Gubar. "Gender, Creativity, and the Woman Poet." In Yopie and Prins, *The Lyric Theory Reader*, 522–7.

Goethe, Johann Wolfgang. *Conversation with Eckermann*. Translated by John Oxenford. New York: University of New York, 1901.

Gokak, Vinayak K. *The Concept of Indian Literature*. New Delhi: Munshiram Manoharlal Publishers, 1979.

Gokak, Vinayak K. *The Unity of World Literature and Indian Literature*. Bangalore: Bangalore University, 1976.

Guha, Naresh. "Discovery of a Modern Indian Poet." *Mahfil* 3, no. 1 (1966): 58–73.

Heine, Elizabeth. "W. B. Yeats: Poet and Astrologer." *Culture and Cosmos* 1, no. 2 (1997): 60–75.

Helgesson, Stefan, and Pieter Vermeulen. "Introduction: World Literature in the Making." In *Institutions of World Literature*, edited by Stefan Helgesson and Pieter Vermeulen, 1–20. New York: Routledge, 2016.

"Hindustan Kī Rāshtra Bhāshā Aur Hindi." *Sarasvati* 3 (March 1916).

Iyer, N. E. Vishwanatha. *Anuvād: Bhashayai Samasyaāi*. New Delhi: Gyan Ganga, 2007.

Jackson, Virginia, and Yopie Prins, eds. *The Lyric Theory Reader: A Critical Anthology*. Baltimore: Johns Hopkins University Press, 2014.

Jackson, Virginia, and Yopie Prins. "General Introduction." In Jackson and Prins, *The Lyric Theory Reader*, 1–9.

Kabir. *Songs of Kabir*. Translated by Rabindranath Tagore. New York: The Macmillan Company, 1915.

Kadir, Djelal. "To Compare, To World Two Verbs, One Discipline." *The Comparatist* 34, no. May (2010): 4–11.

Kadir, Djelal. "To World, To Globalize: Comparative Literature's Crossroads." *Comparative Literature Studies* 41, no. 1 (2004): 1–9.

Kalidas. *Sacontalá*. Translated and preface by Sir William Jones. London: Edwards, 1790. http://www.columbia.edu/itc/mealac/pritchett/00litlinks/shakuntala_jones/.

Kopf, David. *The Brahmo Samaj and the Shaping of the Modern Indian Mind*. Princeton: Princeton University Press, 1979.

Krishnamoorthy, K. "The Meaning of 'Sahitya': A Study in Semantics." *Indian Literature* 28, no. 1 (1985): 65–70.

Krishnaswamy, N., and Lalitha Krishnaswamy. *The Story of English in India*. New Delhi: Foundations Books, 2006.

Krishnaswamy, Revati. "Toward World Literary Knowledges: Theory in the Age of Globalization." *Comparative Literature* 62, no. 4 (2010): 399–419.

Lawall, Sarah. "Introduction: Reading World Literature." In *Reading World Literature: Theory, History, and Practice*, edited by Sarah Lawall, 1–64. Austin: University of Texas, 2010.

Lefevere, André. "Translation and Comparative Literature: The Search for the Center." *TR: Traduction, Terminologie, Redaction* 4, no. 1 (1992): 129–44.

Lefevere, André. *Translation, Rewriting, and the Manipulation of Literary Fame*. London: Routledge, 2016.

"Like Sculpting Smoke: Arundhati Roy on Fame, Writing and India." *Kyoto Journal: Insights from Asia*, November 5, 2011. https://kyotojournal.org/conversations/arundhati-roy-on-fame-writing-and-india/.

Mandal, Somdatta. "From Periphery to the Mainstream: The Making, Marketing and Media Response to Arundhati Roy." In Dhawan, *Arundhati Roy: The Novelist Extraordinary*, 23–37.

Mandal, Sujit Kumar. "Translation as Reception." PhD diss., Jadavpur University, 2013.

Maunick, Edouard J. "A Library of World Classics." *UNESCO The Courier*, 39 (January 1986): 5–8.

Meireles, Cecilia. "Tagore in Brazil." In *Rabindranath Tagore: A Centenary Volume*, 334–7. New Delhi: Sahitya Akademi, 1961.

Meisami, Julie. *Structure and Meaning in Medieval Arabic and Persian Lyric Poetry*. London: Routledge, 2003.

Miller, J. Hillis. "Thoughts That Do Lie Too Deep for Tears: Comparative Literature Versus World Literature." *The Canadian Review of Comparative Literature* 44, no. 3 (2017): 378–96.

Mishra, Vijay C. "Two Truths are Told: Tagore's Kabir." *South Asia: Journal of South Asian Studies* 1, no. 2 (1978): 80–90.

Mishra, Jyotiprasad "Nirmal." "Vaktavya." In *Stri-Kavi-Kaumudi*, edited by Jyotiprasad "Nirmal" Mishra, 11–18. Allahabad: Gandhi Hindi Pustak Bhandar, 1931.

Mody, Sujata S. *The Making of Modern Hindi: Literary Authority in Colonial North India*. New Delhi: Oxford University Press, 2018.

Mohan, Kamlesh. "Image of Women in *Stree Darpan* (1909–1928)." *Proceedings of the Indian History Congress* 52 (1991): 762–70.

Mufti, Aamir. *Forget English! Orientalisms and World Literatures*. Cambridge: Harvard University Press, 2016.

Mufti, Aamir. "Towards a Lyric History of India." In Jackson and Prins, *The Lyric Theory Reader*, 603–31.

Mukherjee, Meenakshi. "Indian Novels in Translation." *Indian Literature* 15, no. 3 (1972): 57–65.

Mukherjee, Meenakshi. *The Perishable Empire: Essays on Indian Writing in English*. New Delhi: Oxford University Press.

Mukherjee, Sujit. *Toward a Literary History of India*. Shimla: Indian Institute of Advanced Studies, 1975.

Mukherjee, Sujit. *Translation as Discovery: And Other Essays on Indian Literature in English Translation*. New Delhi: Allied Publishers, 1981.
Mukherjee, Sujit. *Translation as Recovery*. New Delhi: Pencraft International, 2004.
Mullaney, Julie. *Arundhati Roy's The God of Small Things: A Reader's Guide*. New York: Continuum, 2002.
Nagarjun. *Varun Ke Bete*. Allahabad: Kitab Mahal, 1957.
Narasimhan, Raji. *Translation as a Touchstone*. New Delhi: Sage Publications, 2013.
Narasimhan, Raji. "*Chemmeen*: Its Passage through Three Languages." In Narasimhan, *Translation as a Touchstone*, 1–18.
Narasimhan, Raji. "The God of Small Things: A Wrong Book to Translate." In Narasimhan, *Translation as a Touchstone*, 141–58.
Neti, Leila. "'The Love Laws': Section 377 and the Politics of Queerness in Arundhati Roy's *The God of Small Things*." *Law & Literature* 29, no. 2 (2016): 223–46.
Nirala, Suryakant. *Nirala Rachanavali*. New Delhi: Rajkamal Prakashan, 1983.
Nirala, Surayakant. "Adhivās." In *Nirala Rachanavali*, Vol. 1., edited by Naval Kishor, 35–6. New Delhi: Rajkamal Prakashan, 1983.
Nirala, Suryakant. "Jūhī Kī Kalī." In *Nirala Rachanavali*, Vol. 1, edited by Naval Kishor 31. New Delhi: Rajkamal Prakashan, 1983.
Nirala, Suryakant. "Toṟatī Pathar." In *Nirala Rachanavali*, Vol. 1, edited by Naval Kishor, 323–4. New Delhi: Rajkamal Prakashan, 1983.
Nirala, Suryakant. "Khaṟī Bolī Ke Kavi Aur Kavitā." In *Nirala Rachanavali*, Vol. 5, edited by Naval Kishor, 300–11. New Delhi: Rajkamal Prakashan, 1983.
Nirala, Suryakant. *Parimal*. Lucknow: Parimal Prakashan, 1921. Available at: https://www.hindi-kavita.com/HindiParimalSuryakantTripathiNirala.php.
Nirala, Surayakant. "Pantji Aur Pallav." In *Nirala Rachanavali*, Vol. 5, edited by Naval Kishor, 164–208. New Delhi: Rajkamal Prakashan, 1983.
Ocampo, Victoria. "Tagore on the Banks of the River Plate: West Meets East." In *Rabindranath Tagore: A Centenary Volume*, 27–47. New Delhi: Sahitya Akademi, 1961.
Orsini, Francesca. *The Hindi Public Sphere*. Oxford: Oxford University Press, 2002.
Orsini, Francesca. "The Reticent Autobiographer: Mahadevi Varma's Writings." In *Telling Lives in India: Biography, Autobiography, and Life History*, edited by David Arnold and Stuart Blackburn, 54–82. Indianapolis: Indiana University Press, 2004.
Orsini, Francesca, and Laetitia Zecchini. "The Locations of (World) Literature: Perspectives from Africa and South Asia." *Journal of World Literature* 4, no. 1 (2019): 1–12.
Owen, Stephen. "The Anxiety of Global Influence: What is World Poetry?" *The New Republic*, November 19, 1990.
Painker, Ayyappa, "The Impact of Tagore and his Works on Kerala Life and Literature." In *Rabindranath Tagore in Perspective*, 181–6. Calcutta: Visva-Bharati, 1989.

Paniker, Ayyappa. *A Perspective of Malayalam Literature*. Madras: Anu Chithra Publications, 1990.
Pant, Sumitranandan. *Chhayavaad: Punarmūlyāṅkan*. Allahabad: Lokabharati Prakashan, 1965.
Pant, Sumitranandan. *Gunjan*. Allahabad: Bharati Bhandar, 1932. Available at: https://www.hindi-kavita.com/HindiGunjanPant.php.
Pant, Sumitranandan. *Kalā Aur Būḍhaā Chānd*. Allahabad: Bharati Bhandar, 1958. Available at: https://www.hindi-kavita.com/HindiKalaAurBoorhaChandPant.php#Chand13.
Pant, Sumitranandan. *Pallav*. Allahabad: Indian Press Limited, 1926.
Pant, Sumitranandan. *Yugānt*. Allahabad: Lokabharati Prakashan, 1936. Available at: https://www.hindi-kavita.com/HindiYugaantPant.php.
Paz, Octavio. "The Manuscript of Tagore." Lecture presented at Delhi University, 1967.
Paz, Octavio. "Los manuscritos de Rabindranath Tagore." In *El signo y el garabato*, 146–9. México: J. Moritz, 1973.
Pillai, Thakazhi Sivasankara. *Cheemeen*. Translated by Narayana Menon. Introduction by Santha Rama Rau. New York: Harper & Brother, 1962.
Pillai, Thakazhi Sivasankara. *Chemmeen*. Translated by Anita Nair. New Delhi: HarperCollins, 2011.
Pillai, Thakazhi Sivasankara. *Chemmeen: Un Amour Indien*. Translated by Nicole Balbir. Pondicherry: Kailash éditions, 1999.
Pillai, Thakazhi Sivasankara. *Chingri*. Translated by Bommana Viswanatham and Nilina Abraham. New Delhi: Sahitya Akademi, 1965.
Pillai, Thakazhi Sivasankara. "Indianness in Indian Literature." *Indian Literature* 29, no. 1 (1986): 65–70.
Pillai, Thakazhi Sivasankara. *Machuare*. Translated by Bharati Vidyarthi. New Delhi: Sahitya Akademi, 1959.
Pillai, Thakazhi Sivasankara. *Muralla de redes*. Translated by Juan Fonseca. Barcelona: Círculo de Lectores, 1965.
Pillai, Thakazhi Sivasankara. "Society as Hero." In *Authors Speak*, edited by K. Satchidanandan, 291–304. New Delhi: Sahitya Akademi, 2006.
Pillai, Thakazhi Sivasankara. *Un Amour Indien: Roman*. Translated by Nicole Balbir. Paris: Mercure de France, 1965.
Pillai, Thakazhi, R. Surendran, and K. Balakrishnan. "Thakazhi in Conversation with R. Surendran." *Indian Literature* 43, no. 3 (1999): 162–71.
Pizer, John. *The Idea of World Literature*. Baton Rouge: Louisiana State University Press, 2006.
Pound, Ezra. "Rabindranath Tagore." *Fortnightly Review* 99 (1913). https://fortnightlyreview.co.uk/2013/04/rabindranath-tagore/
Pound, Ezra. *The Selected Letters of Ezra Pound*. Edited by D. D. Paige. New York: New Directions Publishing.

Pound, Ezra. "Tagore's Poems." *Poetry Magazine* 1, no. 3 (December 1912): 92–4.
Prasad, Jaishankar. *Lahar*. Allahabad: Bharati Bhandar, 1934. Available at: https://www.hindi-kavita.com/HindiLeharJaishankarPrasad.php.
Premchand, Munshi. "The Nature and Purpose of Literature." *Social Scientist* 39, no. 11/12 (2011): 82–6.
Puchner, Martin, Suzanne Conklin Akbari, Wiebke Denecke, Barbara Fuchs, Caroline Levine, Pericles Lewis, and Emily R. Wilson, eds. *The Norton Anthology of World Literature, Volume E*. New York: Norton, 2018.
Rai, Alok. *Hindi Nationalism*. New Delhi: Orient Longman, 2001.
Ramazani, Jahan. *The Hybrid Muse: Postcolonial Poetry in English*. Chicago: University of Chicago Press, 2000.
Ramazani, Jahan. *A Transnational Poetics*. Chicago: The University of Chicago Press, 2009.
Rao, Raja. *Kanthapura*. Delhi: Oxford University Press, 1938.
Roy, Arundhati. *The God of Small Things*. New York: Random House, 1997.
Roy, Arundhati. *Māmūlī Cīzoṃ Kā Devatā: Upanyāsa*. Translated by Nilabh. New Delhi: Rajkamal Prakashan, 2004.
Roy, Arundhati. "What is the Morally Appropriate Language in Which to Think and Write?" Lecture given at the W. G. Sebald Lecture on Literary Translation, British Library, London, June 5, 2018. https://lithub.com/what-is-the-morally-appropriate-language-in-which-to-think-and-write/.
Roy, Raja Ram Mohun. *Translations of Several Principal Books, Passages and Texts of the Vedas, and Some Controversial Works on Brahmunical Theology: With an Introductory Memoir*. Calcutta: Elysium Press, 1903.
Rubin, David. *Of Love and War: A Chayavad Anthology*. New Delhi: Oxford University Press, 2005.
Rubin, David. *The Return of Sarasvati*. New Delhi: Oxford University Press, 2002.
Rushdie, Salman. *Imaginary Homelands: Essays and Criticism 1981–1991*. London: Penguin Books, 1992.
Sadana, Rashmi. *English Heart, Hindi Heartland: The Political Life of Literature in India*. Berkeley: University of California Press, 2012.
Sahitya Akademi. "About Sahitya Akademi." Accessed February 9, 2020. http://sahitya-akademi.gov.in/aboutus/about.jsp.
Said, Edward. *The World, the Text, and the Critic*. Cambridge: Harvard University Press, 1983.
Sarkar, Shymal Kumar. "Tagore on Translation." *The Visvabharati Quarterly* 43, no 1/2 (1978): 66–85.
Schomer, Karine. *Mahadevi Varma and the Chhayavad Age of Modern Hindi Poetry*. Berkeley: University of California Press, 1983.
Sen, Nabaneeta Dev. "The Reception of Rabindranath Tagore in England, France, Germany, and The United States." PhD diss., Indiana University, 1964.

Sengupta, Debjani. "The Relevance of Rabindranath Tagore's Politics on His 158th Birth Anniversary." *The Wire*, May 7, 2019. https://thewire.in/history/rabindranath-tagore-politics.
Shankar, Subramanian. "Literatures of the World: An Inquiry." *PMLA* 131, no. 5 (2016): 1405-13.
Sharma, Ramvilas. *Bhārat Kī Bhāshā Samasyan*. New Delhi: Rajkamal Prakashan, 1978.
Sharma, Ramvilas. *Mahavir Prasad Dvivedi Aur Hindi Navjagaran*. New Delhi: Rajkamal Prakashan, 1977.
Sharp, H., ed. "Minute, dated the 2nd February 1835, by T. B. Macaulay." In *Selections from Educational Records Part I 1781-1839*, 107-17. Delhi: National Archives of India, 1965.
Shukla, Ramchandra. *Hindi Sahitya Kā Itihās*. Banaras: Nagari Pracharini Sabha, 1929.
Silberstein, Thomas. "Tagore and Germany." *Indian Literature* 4, no. 1/2 (1960): 90-2.
Singh, Dudhanath. *Mahadevi*. New Delhi: Rajkamal Prakashan, 2009.
Singh, Gurbhagat. *Differential Multilogue: Comparative Literature and National Literatures*. New Delhi: Ajanta Publications, 1991.
Singh, Namvar. *Chhayavaad*. New Delhi: Rajkamal Prakashan, 1955.
Siskind, Mariano. *Cosmopolitan Desires: Global Modernity and World Literature in Latin America*. Evanston: Northwestern University Press, 2014.
Snell, Rupert. *The Hindi Classical Tradition: A Braj Bhāṣā Reader*. London: School of Oriental and African Studies, 1991.
Spivak, Gayatri. "Resident Alien." In *Relocating Postcolonialism*, edited by David Theo Goldberg and Ato Quayson, 46-65. Oxford: Blackwell, 2002.
Spivak, Gayatri Chakravorty. *Outside in the Teaching Machine*. New York: Routledge, 1993.
Srinivasachariar, M. *History of Classical Sanskrit Literature*. New Delhi: Motilal Banarsidass, 1937.
Swain, S. P. "Erotic Pornography and Sexuality: A Study of *The God of Small Things*." In Dhawan, *Arundhati Roy: The Novelist Extraordinary*, 144-9.
Tagore, Rabindranath. *Dear Mr. Tagore: Ninety-five Letters Written to Rabindranath Tagore from Europe and America, 1912-1941*. Edited by A Aronson. Calcutta: Visva-Bharati, 2000.
Tagore, Rabindranath. "Bengali National Literature." In Das and Chaudhuri, *Rabindranath Tagore: Selected Writings on Literature and Language*, 179-94.
Tagore, Rabindranath. *Anubād-Charcha*. Kolkata: Vishva Bharati, 1917.
Tagore, Rabindranath. "East to West." *The Atlantic Monthly* 139 (June 1927): 732.
Tagore, Rabindranath. *Gitanjali*. India, 1910. Available at: http://www.tagoreweb.in/.
Tagore, Rabindranath. *Gitimalya*. India, 1914. http://www.tagoreweb.in/.
Tagore, Rabindranath. *Gitanjali*. Translated by William Radice. New Delhi: Penguin India, 2011.

Tagore, Rabindranath. *Gitanjalí: poemas místicos*. Translated by Pedro Requena Legarreta. Mexico: S.N., 1918.

Tagore, Rabindranath. *Gitanjali: Song Offerings*. With introduction by W. B. Yeats. London: The Indian Society, 1912.

Tagore, Rabindranath. *Gora*. Translated by W. Pearson. London: Macmillan, 1924.

Tagore, Rabindranath. *The Home and the World*. London: Macmillan and Company, 1916.

Tagore, Rabindranath. "Introduction to the Bengali Language." In Das and Chaudhuri, *Rabindranath Tagore: Selected Writings on Literature and Language*, 335–45.

Tagore, Rabindranath. *Letters from Abroad*. Madras: S. Ganesan, 1924.

Tagore, Rabindranath. "Literary Creation." In Das and Chaudhuri, *Rabindranath Tagore: Selected Writings on Literature and Language*, 151–63.

Tagore, Rabindranath. *My Reminiscences*. New York: Macmillan and Company, 1917.

Tagore, Rabindranath. *Nationalism*. London: Macmillan, 1917.

Tagore, Rabindranath. "The Nobel Prize Acceptance Speech." In Vol. 5 of *The English Writings of Rabindranath Tagore*. New Delhi: Atlantic Publishers, 2007.

Tagore, Rabindranath. *Ofrenda lírica, gitanjali, poemas*. Translated by Juan Ramón Jiménez and Zenobia Camprubí de Jiménez. Madrid: Imprenta Clásica Española, 1915.

Tagore, Rabindranath. "Poems." *Poetry Magazine* 1, no. 3 (December 1912): 84–6.

Tagore, Rabindranath. "The Prose Poem." In Das and Chaudhuri, *Rabindranath Tagore: Selected Writings on Literature and Language*, 331–4.

Tagore, Rabindranath. "Sakuntala." In *Rabindra Rachanabali*, Vol. 3. Kolkata: Vishva Bharati, 1941.

Tagore, Rabindranath. "Sakuntala: Its Inner Meaning." Translated by Jadunath Sarkar. In *Sakuntala*, xiii–xxix. London: Macmillan and Co., 1920.

Tagore, Rabindranath. *Selected Letters of Rabindranath Tagore*. Edited by Krishna Dutta and Andrew Robinson. Cambridge: University of Cambridge, 1997.

Tagore, Rabindranath. *Rabindranath Tagore: An Anthology*. Edited by Krishna Dutta and Andrew Robinson. New York: St. Martin's Griffin, 1999.

Tagore, Rabindranath. *The Essential Tagore*. Edited by Fakrul Alam and Radha Chakravarty. Cambridge: The Belknap Press of Harvard University Press, 2011.

Tagore, Rabindranath. "Universal Literature." In *Angel of Surplus*, edited by Sisirkumar Ghosh, 94–104. Calcutta: Visva Bharati, 1978.

Tagore, Rabindranath. "Visva Sahitya." In *Rabindranath Tagore in the 21st Century*, edited by Debashish Banerji, 277–88. Translated by Rijula Das and Makarand Paranjape. New Delhi: Springer India, 2015.

Tagore, Rabindranath. "Vishva Sahitya." 1907. https://tagoreweb.in/Essays/sahityo-51/bishwasahityo-1942.

Tagore, Rabindranath. "Vishva Sahitya." In *Sahitya*. Translated Vanshidhar Vidyalankar. Bombay: Hindi Granth Ratanakar, 1929.

Tagore, Rabindranath. "World Literature." In Das and Chaudhuri, *Rabindranath Tagore: Selected Writings on Literature and Language*, 138–50.

Thakazhi, R. Surendran, and K. Balakrishnan. "Thakazhi in Conversation with R. Surendran." *Indian Literature* 43, no. 3 (1999): 162–71.

Tharakan, K. M. *A Brief Survey of Malayalam Literature*. Kottayam: Ashram Press, 1990.

Tharu, Susie J., and Ke Lalita, eds. *Women Writing in India*. New York: Feminist Press at the City University of New York, 1991.

Thomas, Sanju. "Toward a Monolingual World: Indian English Fiction and Translations in India." In *Redefining Translation and Interpretation in Cultural Evolution*, edited by Olaf Immanuel Seel, 20–41. Hershey: IGA Global, 2017.

Tihanov, Galin. "The Location of World Literature." *Canadian Review of Comparative Literature* 44, no. 3 (September 2017): 468–81.

Trivedi, Harish. "The Hindi Postcolonial—Categories and Configurations." *Comparative Literature Studies* 53, no. 2 (2016): 400–7.

Trivedi, Harish. "Translation and World Literature: The Indian Context." In Bassnett, *Translation and World Literature*, 15–28.

UNESCO. "Historical Collection." Accessed February 9, 2020. http://www.unesco.org/culture/lit/rep/index.php.

Varma, Mahadevi. *Agnirekha*. New Delhi: Rajkamal Prakashan. 1990. Available at: https://www.hindi-kavita.com/HindiAgnirekhaMahadeviVerma.php.

Varma, Mahadevi. "The Art of Living." Translated by Chandra Agarwal. In Behl and Nicholls, *The Penguin New Writings in India*, 96–100.

Varma, Mahadevi. *Deepshikha*. Allahabad: Bharati Bhandar, 1942. Available at: https://www.hindi-kavita.com/HindiDeepshikhaMahadeviVerma.php.

Varma, Mahadevi. "Introduction to *Adhunik Kavi* 'From My Point of View.'" Translated by Francesca Orsini. In Anantharam, *Mahadevi Varma: Political Essays*, 89–116.

Varma, Mahadevi. *Shrāṅkhalā Kī Kaṛiyāṅ*. Allahabad: Hindi Sahitya Press, 1942.

Varma, Mahadevi. "The Links in Our Chain." Translated by Shobna Nijhawan. In Anantharam, *Mahadevi Varma: Political Essays*, 71–88.

Varma, Mahadevi. *Links in the Chain*. Edited and translated by Neerja Sohini. New Delhi: Katha, 2003.

Varma, Mahadevi. "Merī Sahitya Yātrā: Gadya Ke Sandarbh Meiṅ." In Vol. 3 of Nirmala Jain, *Mahadevi Sahitya Samagra*, 416–19. New Delhi: Vani Prakashan, 2000.

Varma, Mahadevi. "Merī Sahitya Yātrā: Kavitā Ke Sandarbh Meiṅ." In Vol. 3 of Nirmala Jain, *Mahadevi Sahitya Samagra*, New Delhi: Vani Prakashan, 2000, 409–15.

Varma, Mahadevi. *Adhunik Kavi*. Allahabad: Hindi Sahitya Sammelan, 1940.

Varma, Mahadevi. "My Childhood Days." Translated by Anita Anantharam. In Anantharam, *Mahadevi Varma: Political Essays*, 37–42.

Varma, Mahadevi. *Neerja*. Allahabad: Bharati Bhandar, 1934. Available at: https://www.hindi-kavita.com/HindiNirjaMahadeviVerma.php.

Varma, Mahadevi. *Nihar*. Allahabad: Sahitya Bhavan, 1930. Available at: https://www.hindi-kavita.com/HindiNeeharMahadeviVerma.php.

Varma, Mahadevi. *Path Ke Sāthī*. Allahabad: Bharati Bhandar, 1956.

Varma, Mahadevi. *A Pilgrimage to the Himalayas, and Other Silhouettes from Memory*. Translated by Radhika Prasad Srivastava and Margaret B. Lillian. London: Peter Owen, 1975.

Varma, Mahadevi. *Pratham Āyām*. Allahabad: Bharati Bhandar, 1952. Available at: https://www.hindi-kavita.com/HindiPrathamAayamMahadeviVerma.php.

Varma, Mahadevi. *Rashmi*. Allahabad: Sahitya Bhavan, 1932. Available at: https://www.hindi-kavita.com/HindiRashmiMahadeviVerma.php.

Varma, Mahadevi. "Sahitya, Sanskriti Aur Shāsan." In *Mere Priya Sambhāshaṇa*, 42–6. New Delhi: National Publishing House, 1983.

Varma, Mahadevi. *Selected Poems*. Translated and preface by L. S. Sinha. Calcutta: Writers Workshop, 1987.

Varma, Mahadevi. *Sketches from My Past: Encounters with India's Oppressed*. Translated by Neera Kuckreja Sohoni. Boston: Northeastern University Press, 1994.

Varma, Mahadevi, *Mahadevi Sahitya Samagra, Vol. 3*. New Delhi: Vani Prakashan, 2000.

Varma, Mahadevi. "Who Are You in My Heart?" Translated by Sarah Houston Green. In Anantharam, *Mahadevi Varma: Political Essays*, 27–8.

Venuti, Lawrence. "Hijacking Translations: How Comp Lit Continues to Suppress Translated Texts." *Boundary 2* 43, no. 2 (May 2016): 179–204.

Venuti, Lawrence. *The Translator's Invisibility*. Oxon: Routledge, 1995.

Visva-Bharati. "Educational Ideas." Accessed February 9, 2020. http://www.visvabharati.ac.in/EDUCATIONAL_IDEAS.html

"Wall of Networks—Thakazhi Sivasankara Pillai." *La Estanteria*, April 2014. Accessed February 9, 2020. http://laestanteriablog.blogspot.com/2014/04/muralla-de-redes-thakazhi-sivasankara.html.

Young, Howard. "The Invention of an Andalusian Tagore." *Comparative Literature* 47, no. 1 (1995): 42–52.

Index

Anantharam, Anita 97
Andrews, Charles Freer 33
Ansari, M. T. 129
Apter, Emily 5, 147–8
Arlyn Sokol, Kathy 135
Arnold, Matthew 13–15, 145
A. S., Priya 139

Bakshi, Padumalal-Punnalal 84–5, 89
Banerjee, Hiranmay 47
Benjamin, Walter 147
Bhabha, Homi 117, 146
Bharavi 14
Bhattacharya, Baidik 4, 146
Bihari 85, 89
Blavatsky, Madame 40
Bose, Buddhadeva 52, 143–6
Brahmo Samaj 10–13, 21, 24–5, 29, 49

Camprubí de Jiménez, Zenobia 58–9
Casanova, Pascal 5, 150
Chakori, Rameshvari Devi 104
Chakravarty, Ajit 39, 49, 55
Chakravorty, Amiya 39
Chanda, Ipsita 144–6, 149
Chandra, Naveen 84
Chatterjee, Partha 17
Chatterji, Ramananda 30
Chatterji, Saratchandra 124
Chaucer 43–4
Chaudhuri, Sukanta 13
Chauhan, Subhadra Kumari 80
Cheah, Pheng 4, 146
Comparative Literature Association of India 32
Coomaraswamy, Ananda 30, 49
Culler, Jonathan 73

Damrosch, David 144
Dandi 14
Das, Sisir Kumar 13, 116

Datta, Roby 49
Dev, Amiya 33
Devi, Indira 39
Devraj, N. K. 79, 81
Dey, Manna 129
Dharwadker, Vinay 116
Dularelal, Sri 84–5
Dutta, Satyendranath 32
Dvivedi, Mahavir Prasad 75, 93

Eliot, T.S. 54, 63

Faiz, Ahmad Faiz 113, 141, 145

Ganapathy-Doré, Geetha 136
Gandhi 94–5, 120
Goethe 14, 27–9, 32, 54, 57, 85
Gokak, V. K. 33
Gorkhy 89

Harioudh 92–3
Helgesson, Stefan 5
Henderson, Alice Corbin 41
Homer 84, 89
Houston, Sarah Green 97

Jackson, Virginia 73
Jadavpur University 32–3, 143–4
Jones, William 43–5
Joyce, James 86

Kabir 46–7
Kadir, Djelal 149
Kalidas 14–15, 44, 54, 63, 72, 89, 144
Kariat, Ramu 129
Keats, John 148
Kipling 17–18, 23, 33, 35, 55, 85, 89
Kopf, David 25
Krishnaswamy, Revathi 149

Lawall, Sarah 149
Lefevere, André 146–7

Macaulay, T. B.   10, 116
Magh   14
Mahadevi   170 n.5
Mahila Vidyapith College   103
Matiram   85, 89
Meireles, Cecilia   61
Meltzl, Hugó   15
Menon, Narayan   121–3, 126–8, 130, 138, 140
Meyer-Franck, Helen   30
Miller, J. Hillis   148
Mira   83, 89–92, 94–8, 100, 106, 114
Mishrabandhu   93
Mistral, Gabriela   57
Monroe, Harriet   41
Moretti, Franco   5, 150
Mufti, Aamir   5, 113, 146
Mukherjee, Hrishikesh   129
Mukherjee, Meenakshi   124–5, 137–8
Mukherjee, Sujit   33, 52
Mullaney, Julie   133

Nabhadas   95
Nagarjun   119, 123
Nair, Anita   123, 126, 128, 131, 138, 140
Narasimhan, Raji   125–6, 139
National Council of Education   9
NCE   9–10, 12, 17, 23, 31–2
Nehru, Rameshwari   102
Neruda, Pablo   57
Neti, Leila   134
Niccodermi, Dario   58
Nilabh   139
Nirala, Suryakant Tripathi   4, 63, 66, 71–3, 75, 77–80, 83, 86, 89, 111

Ocampo, Victoria   57–8, 61
Orsini, Francesca   107, 114

Pandey, Mukutdhar   74–5
Pant, Sumitranandan   4, 63, 66–8, 70–1, 73–4, 76–80, 100–1, 110–11, 146, 151
Paz, Octavio   57
Petrarch   41
Pillai, T.S.   2, 7, 118–21, 124, 128, 133, 137–8, 140–1, 145–6, 150–1

Pound, Ezra   40–2, 48, 50, 63, 86, 145
Prasad, Jaishankar   63, 66, 71, 73, 76–80, 110–11
Premchand, Munshi   76, 120
Prins, Yopie   73
Priyadas   95

Radice, William   38
Rama Rau, Santha   140
Ramaswamy, Sundara   121, 125
Ramón Jiménez, Juan   58, 59
Rao, Raja   117
Reed, John   41
Requena Legarreta, Pedro   59–60
Rivas, Joaquín Méndez   59–60
Rothenstein, William   37–40, 43, 45, 48–9, 52, 54
Roy, Arundhati   2, 7, 117–18, 121, 131, 133–6, 138–40, 146, 150–1
Roy, Raja Ram Mohan   10, 29
Rubin, David   97, 99–100, 110, 112
Rushdie, Salman   116–17, 126, 133

Said, Edward   37
Saroj, Shivsingh   93
Schomer, Karine   76, 78, 94, 100
Sen, Kshiti Mohan   52
Shakespeare   14–15, 89
Sharma, Ramendra Kumar   83
Sharma, Ramvilas   94
Shukla, Ramchandra   77, 112
Shukla, Ramshankar   94
Singh, Dudhanath   100, 112
Singh, Gurbhagat   33
Singh, Namvar   74
Sinha, L. S.   97–8, 100
Siskind, Mariano   150
Sister Nivedita   49
Sobti, Krishna   139
Srivastav, Manoharlal   83–4
Sterling, George   41

Tagore, Rabindranath   2–4, 7, 9–61, 63, 65, 67, 74–9, 84–6, 89, 98, 105, 115, 124, 140, 143, 145, 146, 151
Tennyson   17–18, 23, 33, 35, 55, 63, 85, 89
Thomas, Sanju   128, 139

Tolstoy 57, 89, 145
Trivedi, Harish 117, 126
Tulsidas 14, 75, 84–5, 89

UNESCO 121–2

Valmiki 83–4, 89
Varma, Mahadevi 2, 4, 7, 63, 66–73, 77–83, 89–114, 139, 146, 151
Varma, Nirmal 139
Vasconcelos, José 57
Venuti, Lawrence 147–8
Vermeulen, Pieter 5

Vidyalankar, Vanshidhar 16
Vidyapati 19, 21, 33, 63, 89
Vidyarthi, Bharati 121–2
Vijaya 58
Visva Bharati 12, 29, 34

Wells, H. G. 40
Weltliteratur 27–8, 33

Yeats, W. B. 38, 40–6, 48, 52–4, 61, 63, 145
Yesudas 129
Young, Howard 57–8

www.ingramcontent.com/pod-product-compliance
Lightning Source LLC
Chambersburg PA
CBHW061830300426
44115CB00013B/2317